BIRMINGHAM CANAL NAVIGATIONS
A HISTORY

Portrait of my bike with ghosts in Galton Cutting by Catharine Kingcome, oil on canvas.

BIRMINGHAM CANAL NAVIGATIONS
A HISTORY

PHIL CLAYTON

THE CROWOOD PRESS

First published in 2022 by
The Crowood Press Ltd
Ramsbury, Marlborough
Wiltshire SN8 2HR

enquiries@crowood.com

www.crowood.com

© Phil Clayton 2022

All rights reserved. No part of this publication may be reproduced or transmitted in any form or by any means, electronic or mechanical, including photocopy, recording, or any information storage and retrieval system, without permission in writing from the publishers.

British Library Cataloguing-in-Publication Data
A catalogue record for this book is available from the British Library.

ISBN 978 0 7198 4019 7

Frontispiece: 'This is a painting of my bike in Galton Cutting, Smethwick, a place that grew on me as I began to appreciate its undeniable, albeit sombre, beauty and grandeur. I became fascinated by its history, and felt it must be full of ghosts. It was so busy in its heyday, but now is eerily empty and quiet, apart from announcements drifting down from Galton Bridge Station above. So, as well as my bike, I've painted the ghosts of a navvy, a boatwoman leading a horse towing a boat, and a motorboat and boatman. The inspiration for the navvy, horse and boat came from old photos while the motorboat and boatman were inspired by photographer Kev Maslin's photo of contemporary working boatman Reuben Carter and his boat. The boatwoman is completely imaginary. I deliberately painted the boats monochrome because, in this composition, they are ghosts from the past, contrasting with the present day scene. My purpose was not to create a composition set in the past, but one portraying how the cutting looks now, and how I feel when I am there alone with an almost overpowering sense of history.'

Catharine Kingcome, 2021

Typeset by Simon and Sons

Cover design by Blue Sunflower Creative

Printed and bound in India by Parksons Graphics

Contents

Dedication		6
Acknowledgements		6
Introduction		7
Chapter 1:	'The Cut of all Cuts'	11
Chapter 2:	The System Grows	26
Chapter 3:	Improving the BCN	40
Chapter 4:	Water Supply	59
Chapter 5:	Traffic	73
Chapter 6:	Working the BCN	89
Chapter 7:	The Railway Connection	111
Chapter 8:	Trials and Tribulations	124
Chapter 9:	Decline	138
Chapter 10:	Into a New Canal Age	154
Bibliography and References		172
Index		174

Dedication

To the BCN Society, which founded, fostered and maintains my interest in the wonderful web of waterways that we call the Birmingham Canal Navigations.

Acknowledgements

Many people, over many years, have contributed to this book. First, and foremost, two great friends of the BCN, Martin O'Keeffe, BCN Society President, and Ray Shill, Historian. During the research period, Ray and Martin have been unfailingly generous in sharing resources and knowledge.

Thanks are due to several archivists: Phil Wild (BCN Society), Mike Skidmore (Dudley Canal & Tunnel Trust), Phil Hughes (Monmouthshire, Brecon & Abergavenny Canals Trust), Ian Gray (Sandwell) and Elaine Nicholson (Dudley).

Other folk have willingly shared information, images and time: Steve Bingham, Mary Bodfish, Bob Bowden, David Brown, Nigel Chapman, Ruth Collins, Carole Cooper, Ron Element, Tony Gregory, Keith Hodgkins, Bob Howells, Cathy Kingcome, Tony Kulik, Andy Lowe, Roy Martin, Barry McGowan, the late Dave Necklen, Sue Necklen, Maria Nicholson, Pamela Paget-Tomlinson, Hugh Potter, Colin Sidaway, the late Vic Smallshire, Sue Swain, Andy Tidy, Joanna Turska, David Walker, Brenda Ward, the late John Whitehouse, Wolverhampton Arts & Heritage, and the Committee of Wolverhampton Boat Club. My apologies to anyone I have missed.

Thanks also to The Crowood Press for advice and encouragement and, as ever, to my wife Dot, for her patience and support. Uncredited images are from the author's collection. Any errors in this work are entirely the author's.

Image Credits

Unless otherwise specified, photographs are from the author's collection.

BCNS, pages 12, 15, 16, 21 (top), 35, 50, 51 (top), 58, 63 (top), 69, 73, 76, 80, 83, 84, 91, 97, 99, 100 (bottom), 101, 104, 109 (top), 118 (right), 126, 132, 136 (bottom), 149, 153, 156 (left and right), 159 (top), 160, 162, 164; Mary Bodfish, page 60; British Waterways, pages 119, 148; David Brown, page 108; Nigel Chapman Collection, page 79; Conurbation, page 155; Carol Cooper, page 146; Dunlop House Magazine, page 86; Ron Element, page 127; A.W. Gregory Collection, pages 122 (photo taken by R Wyndham Shaw), 147; Fred Heritage Collection, page 141; Keith Hodgkins, page 94; Phil Hughes, page 49 (top); T.W. King Collection, Dudley Archives, page 130; Tony Kulik, page 96; Andy Lowe, pages 9, 51 (bottom), 55, 62, 98; RD McMillan Collection, page 81; Roy Martin, page 151; Dave Necklen Collection, pages 56 (bottom), 57, 100 (top), 103 (bottom), 128, 129; Maria Nicholson, page 173; Martin O'Keeffe, pages 20, 45 (top), 48, 77, 87, 103 (top); Pam Paget-Tomlinson, page 121 (top); Hugh Potter, pages 82, 95, 107, 152; Sandwell Archives, page 71; Ray Shill, pages 13, 21 (bottom), 25, 28 (top), 38, 39 (top), 47 (top); Colin Sidaway, pages 109 (bottom), 110; Staffordshire Record Office, page 114; Sue Swain, page 158; Brenda Ward, page 165; Phil Wild, pages 8, 17, 111; Wolverhampton Arts & Heritage, page 102; Wolverhampton Boat Club, page 121 (bottom).

Introduction

A glance at a map shows the Birmingham Canal Navigations to be an extensive complexity of cuts. The original length, between coal pits at Wednesbury and the town of Birmingham, opened in 1769 and through the course of time, by expansion and acquisition, the network grew until almost 160 miles (258km) of narrow canal cobwebbed an area of less than 20 miles (32km) from both north to south and east to west – the greatest concentration of cuts in the country. The canal-building era in the district lasted for just under a century, from the construction of the original Birmingham Canal to the opening of the Cannock Extension Canal to Hednesford, the BCN's most northerly point, in 1863. When Henry Rodolph de Salis, a director of the premier inland waterways carrying firm of Fellows, Morton and Clayton, produced his guide, *Bradshaw's Canals and Navigable Rivers of England and Wales*, in 1904, he was able to say of the BCN that, 'The system is a very complicated one, owing to many improvements and fresh canals which have been added to it from time to time.' One or two smaller arms and branches were put in after the Cannock Extension; indeed, the Dudley Canal Trust opened a completely new tunnel as recently as 1989, but to all intents and purposes these dates bracket the era of canal building in the region.

In the middle of the eighteenth century, Birmingham and the area west of the town, the district later to be called the Black Country, were on the cusp of great changes that would turn them into one of the world's first great industrial regions. Birmingham became the city of a thousand trades and the Black Country's convulsive industrialization turned it black by day and red by night. Birmingham had long been developing as a manufacturing focus for the surrounding area; poll tax returns from 1379 mention several smiths. Tudor antiquarian John Leland passed through around 1538 on one of his 'itineraries', approaching from the south. He came first to outlying Deritend, 'through a pretty Street .... as I remember, is called *Dirtey*. In it dwell Smithes and Cutlers ....' Birmingham itself he described as 'a good Markett Towne' stretching for a quarter mile 'up a meane Hill'. Although he saw only one parish church, he noted, 'many Smithes in the Towne that use to make Knives and all mannour of cutting Tooles, and many Loriners that make Bittes, and a great many Naylors. Soe that a great part of the Towne is maintained by Smithes who have theire Iron and Sea-Cole out of *Stafford-shire*.' Birmingham and the neighbouring mineral-producing area were therefore intimately and inextricably linked, but, and it is one of the biggest buts in the West Midlands, never

INTRODUCTION

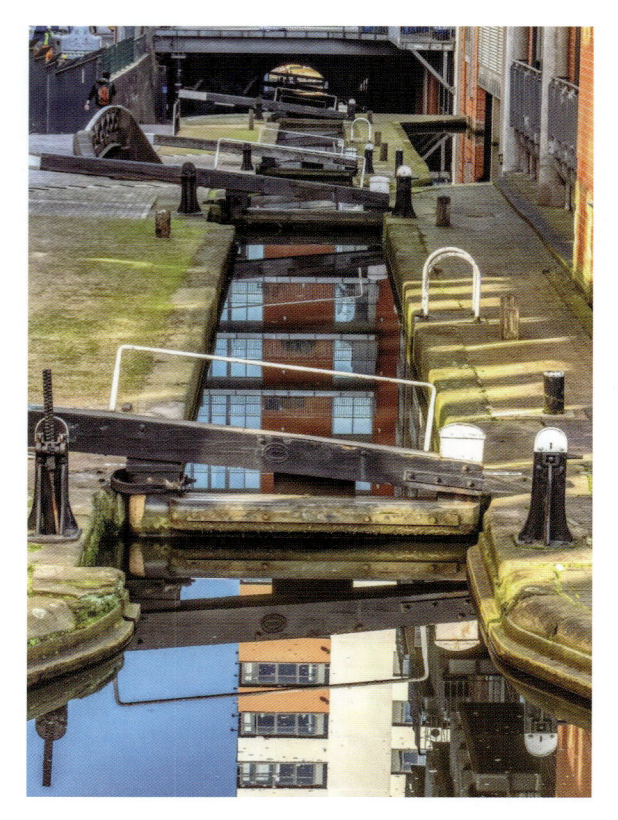

The climb to Birmingham. A section of Farmer's Bridge Locks, the 'Old Thirteen'. This is the steepest part of the thirty-eight lock ascent from Fazeley.

confuse a Brummie with a Black Countryman, or wench!

By the 1750s, Birmingham's range of industries had expanded. Guns and brassware were prominent, as was the production of 'toys'. A word of uncertain etymology, and sometimes used disparagingly as in 'Brummagem Toys', a reference to counterfeit coins, it covered a wide range of small items made from iron, steel, brass and other materials and included goods such as buckles, snuff boxes, trinkets, tweezers, hinges, toothpick cases, watch chains, corkscrews, buttons, tortoiseshell boxes and filigree work. Working practices were developing; specialization was being introduced and local entrepreneurs were there at the beginnings of what would become mass production.

Mere miles to the west, men had delved beneath the area that was to become the Black Country for centuries before it acquired the name and developed into one of the most bizarre landscapes in the United Kingdom. In some places a conjoining of coal seams had led to the formation of the Thick Coal, a 30ft (9m) layer outcropping on the surface or lying shallowly beneath it. This had long been picked at for domestic fuel together with iron ore, which, smelted using charcoal, could be hammered into shape by hand, and later by using water-powered tilt hammers on the many headwaters of Rivers Stour and Tame. Clay and limestone, metaphorically as well as literally the Black Country's building blocks, were also abundant and readily accessible.

Towards the end of the 1750s, the great Ironmaster John Wilkinson had set up a new ironworks at Bradley near Bilston in what would be the heart of the Black Country, applying Abraham Darby's development of the use of coke for smelting ore rather than the charcoal that had so denuded the region's woodlands. By 1766, Matthew Boulton had opened his great new Manufactory at Soho, a mile and a half north of Birmingham, just over the Staffordshire border from the town, and James Watt had visited in March 1767. Late the following summer, he stayed at Soho for a fortnight. The entrepreneur and the inventor struck up an immediate liking for each other. Early in 1769, Watt was in London, taking out the patent on his separate condenser, an invention that would increase the efficiency of the steam engine to a point where it would become industry's driving force. Eventually Boulton, the extrovert entrepreneur who would soon sell the power that all the world desired to have, persuaded Watt, the introvert engineer described by Samuel Smiles as 'timid, desponding, painfully anxious and easily cast down by failure', to move to Birmingham. The Soho Manufactory, where the Brummie pioneered mass production, and the later Foundry where the Scotsman's engines were developed, became world leaders, as well as, for a while, tourist attractions for the wealthy. Iron making in the Black Country and iron using in Birmingham were both developing quickly, and the stage was set for a tremendous spurt in growth.

The brake to development was transport. No navigable rivers flowed through the area, the nearest being the Trent and Severn, and although attempts were made in the latter part of the seventeenth century to develop the Severn-bound Stour for navigation, these, through floods and local opposition, eventually came to nothing. As in the rest of the country, contemporary roads were not up to the task of transporting heavy, bulky loads. Nearly a century before, naturalist and antiquarian Robert Plot had commented in his *Natural History of Staffordshire* that although the county's roads were generally good, those around Wednesbury, Sedgley and Dudley were 'uncessantly worn with the carriage of coale'. In 1726, John Ward, of the Dudley family, whose future fortunes were to be closely linked with canals, was called before a Parliamentary Committee to describe the state of the 10-mile (16km) stretch of road between Birmingham and Wolverhampton. It was, he said:

in the Winter Season, in a very ruinous condition, and in some places almost impassable, and this very great decay of the Road has been by the great number of Carriages constantly passing, laden with Iron and Iron wares from Wolverhampton and thereabouts … and by carrying great quantities of Coal for the use of the Town of Birmingham.

As a result of this and similar petitions, improvements had been made to the local road system, with the establishment of Turnpike Trusts, and Birmingham was linked with Wolverhampton via West Bromwich and Wednesbury in 1727. By 1760, an alternative route between the two towns through Smethwick and Dudley had been turnpiked, but the roads were still not strong enough to withstand the sheer weight and pressure of the heavy traffic using them. A fresh solution was needed, and local merchants and manufacturers turned their thoughts northwards towards Manchester where work on the Duke of Bridgewater's canal was already progressing in the first years of the decade.

A fossil canal. Izons Old Turn, a bend on the original Birmingham Canal, was cut off in the 1820s and abandoned in 1954. Its long-infilled course can still be conjectured curving between Pudding Green Junction and the distant bend.

INTRODUCTION

More than any other traveller, the boater gains an early and very physical understanding of the region's topography. To reach Birmingham and the Black Country involves climbing locks; this is not the Midland Plain. To reach the centre of Wolverhampton from my home alongside the Staffordshire & Worcestershire Canal takes about twenty minutes by bus. If I take my boat, it is usually between three and four hours, climbing through twenty-one locks. The same applies whichever way you approach the area by water. From Fazeley on the Coventry Canal, 15 miles (24km) to the north, there are thirty-eight locks. The Stratford-upon-Avon Canal climbs through fifty-four locks on its approach from the river in Stratford to its junction with the Worcester & Birmingham Canal at Kings Norton, 5 miles (8km) south of the city centre, while the latter cut has fifty-eight between its termini. From Stourbridge to the south-west, there are twenty-five. As well as the sheer number of locks, the variety of different approaches to the BCN is a tribute to its centrality and importance.

Geography had another part to play. Although it stands astride the Severn–Trent watershed, no large rivers flow through the region. Maintaining an adequate water supply for the canals was a constant problem. The multiplicity of headstreams of Tame and Stour had been utilized for centuries by millers who were naturally jealous of their water and loath to lose it to a canal. Reservoirs were the early answer, but soon necessity and technology came into play and steam pumping engines were introduced, supplied by Boulton and Watt. Thus began the industrial symbiosis that would characterize the canal, as raw materials from the Black Country were transformed by Birmingham industry. The town was already growing, but, used as we are to seeing the canal in an urban setting, we should remember that when opened, it terminated on the very edge of Birmingham, in an area still largely of fields and orchards. The Black Country, yet to earn its name, was also still mainly countryside, with hamlets, villages and market towns such as Dudley scattered across an agriculturally poor landscape populated by craftsman-farmers who might have worked a nail shop alongside a smallholding. Local placenames – Cradley Heath, Withymoor, Woodside, Primrose Hill, Windmill End – paint a pre-industrial picture.

The Birmingham Canal Navigations developed into a large and prosperous concern, secure in its traffic and trade throughout the nineteenth century. Unlike many canal companies, the BCN, through its close relationship with the London and North Western Railway, suffered less from rail competition and its decline rather mirrored that of the railways themselves. Some stretches closed early, being lost to subsidence triggered by the very mining that had encouraged their spread in the first place. The mid-twentieth century saw most losses, when the canals had largely lost their reason for existence and were generally perceived by many as little more than linear rubbish dumps or death traps for children. From the early 1960s, a growing awareness of local canals and their place in the area's heritage led to the formation and growth of voluntary groups with a common aim of preserving what was being lost, often in the face of hostility from the authorities in charge of the very waterways they were attempting to save. The famous 'Battle of Stourbridge', just off the BCN, when preservationists flew in the face of the powers that be to reopen a stretch of canal, and the saving of the Dudley Tunnel were two key early events in what has been called the new canal age.

I have boated and walked all the towpaths of the 100 miles (160km) of still extant Birmingham Canal Navigations and have searched for the remains of lost waterways, the other 60 miles (97km) of routes that are no longer in existence. In some cases, these have been completely obliterated, but in other places their remains are still to be found, dried up echoes in the landscape. Several Black Country towns still display inexplicable humps in the road; inexplicable, that is, to passing motorists, but not to anyone who knows something of the history of the place.

CHAPTER I

'The Cut of all Cuts'

The later eighteenth century was a time of unprecedented technical advancement in Britain and 1769 was a significant year in that period of spectacular industrial growth. On its fifth day, James Watt had patented his separate condenser: 'a new method of lessening the consumption of steam and fuel in fire-engines' and arguably the most important invention in the development of efficient steam power. Later that year, on 3 July, Richard Arkwright had also taken out a patent for his water-powered Spinning Frame, a machine that would lead to a transformation in the production of textiles and the growth of the factory system. Josiah Wedgwood had already perfected his 'black basaltes', a clay body or mixture, ideal for the classical-style vases that he was to make so fashionable, and in June the potter opened his works at Etruria beside the course of the developing Trent & Mersey Canal.

'This Day for our New Navigation'

Later that year, on Monday, 6 November, Birmingham celebrated. Streamers played in the air and bonfires blazed while people danced around them. Hammers and files, the workaday tools of the town, were laid aside while the local lads and lasses made their way to the wharf where three boats had arrived laden with coal from the Wednesbury pits. This was the day when the canal opened to the town. The *Leeds Intelligencer* reported the event a fortnight later, as did papers in places as far apart as Oxford, Kent and Salisbury:

> We learn from Birmingham that on Monday the 6th Inst. the Inland Navigation to that Place was so far completed as to admit Boats coming up to the Town, for the first Time, laden with Coals. On this Occasion the Bells rung, and the Banks of the Canal were crouded with Company from Morning till Evening. As a result, the price of coals had fallen from nine pence to four pence halfpenny per hundred; a circumstance of utmost importance to that great manufacturing town, in which consumption of coals is prodigious.

A neat summary of the original canal was published, stating that work had begun on 11 April 1768 and had been carried on with 'such spirit and dispatch' that 16 miles (26km) had been cut, twelve locks and thirty-two bridges built as well as several stop gates, while fifteen 'barges' had been finished 'on the company's account', besides many other private boats.

John Freeth, Birmingham publican, coffee house proprietor and political ballad writer, had been composing odes and ditties for thirty years and was

BIRMINGHAM LADS BY JOHN FREETH

This day for our new navigation
We banish all cares and vexation;
The sight of the barges each honest heart glads
And the merriest of mortals are Birmingham lads.
Birmingham lads, jovial blades,
And the merriest of mortals are Birmingham lads.

Not Europe can match us for traffic,
America, Asia and Afric;
Of what we invent each partakes of a share,
For the best of wrought metals is Birmingham ware
Birmingham ware, none so rare
For the best of wrought metals is Birmingham ware.

Since by the canal navigation,
Of coals we've the best in the nation;
Around the gay circle your bumpers then put,
For the cut of all cuts is a Birmingham cut,
Birmingham cut, fairly wrought,
For the cut of all cuts is a Birmingham cut.

hardly likely to let this opportunity slip. His *Inland Navigation* prophesied that the place would become 'The grand Mechanic Warehouse of the World' and that its goods would spread 'from the Tagus to the Ganges', while another work, *Birmingham Lads*, boasted 'of coals we've the best in the nation' and 'the best of wrought metal is Birmingham ware'. The first three of innumerable coal boats arriving in Birmingham with Black Country coal over the next two centuries were unloaded at the canal's first, temporary, terminus near the Dudley Turnpike. As befits a place that is constantly reinventing and rebuilding itself, this is now not far from Brindley Place, where the city's lads and lasses can still be found disporting themselves.

Beginnings

The first mention of Birmingham in relation to a canal scheme had been as the terminus of a branch from a proposed waterway between Wilden Ferry on the Trent to the Weaver at Frodsham Bridge, an idea first mooted in 1758 and which subsequently developed into the Grand Trunk, or Trent & Mersey Canal. Although Matthew Boulton became a subscriber, it seems that few others in the town were as keen, for the branch to Birmingham had been dropped before the Trent and Mersey Bill was passed by Parliament in May 1766. Other schemes were in the air; waterways to link Shugborough (now known, in canal terms, as Haywood) with the Severn, and to strike out from Fradley, near Lichfield, to Coventry and then on to Oxford and, by way of the Thames, to the capital. Birmingham, on its plateau, was to be islanded by these proposals. This could not be allowed to happen by the forward-thinking men of a town of over 30,000 inhabitants and the spark was a short piece published in the local paper.

Aris's Birmingham Gazette,
Monday, 26 January 1767.

This called for a meeting to discuss 'The Utility of a Navigable Cut from the Wolverhampton Canal, through the Coal Works, to this Town'. The 'Wolverhampton Canal' was to become the Staffordshire & Worcestershire, whose seed had been sown a year earlier and which had already been started. An earlier letter in the *Gazette* had pointed out the benefits that a canal would bring to Birmingham by cutting the price of coal, while the local social conscience was stirred by the fact that the Navigation would also be advantageous to the poor. Gentlemen and inhabitants were invited to discuss the matter and, if the scheme should be approved, appoint a 'proper person' to make a survey and prepare an estimate for the works involved. The results were written up in *A Journal of the Meetings and Proceedings respecting the Navigation*, the Birmingham Canal's first Minute Book. As well as reiterating the advantages listed earlier, mention was made of the savings to be brought about by reducing the numbers of horses employed on the carriage of coals and other commodities.

Three dozen gentlemen attended and agreed to subscribe towards the expenses, contributing a guinea apiece, except for one Thomas Blockley who pledged 10s 6d. The list was headed by Henry Carver Esq., followed by Dr John Ash. Appropriately enough perhaps, in view of the main cargo the canal was to carry, Francis Coals and Robert Coals also signed up. They were soon followed by a further 130 subscribers, including many of the great men of commerce and industry in contemporary Birmingham: manufacturers Matthew Boulton, Samuel Galton, Samuel Garbett and John Ryland; men of letters such as John Baskerville, Pearson & Aris, Freeth & Sons and historian William Hutton; and Lloyd & Son of the banking family.

Enter James Brindley

On the strength of the interest shown and the money subscribed, James Brindley was appointed to produce a plan and estimates for two different routes. Following his success on the Duke of Bridgewater's Navigation joining Manchester to his coal mines 7 miles (11km) out of the town at Worsley, the engineer was already in great demand among the burgeoning canal proprietors of the nation.

BIRMINGHAM NAVIGATION

SWAN INN JUNE 4TH 1767

AT A NUMEROUS MEETING HELD THIS DAY, MR BRINDLEY PRODUCED A PLAN AND ESTIMATE OF MAKING A NAVIGABLE CANAL FROM THIS TOWN TO THE STAFFORDSHIRE & WORCESTERSHIRE CANAL, THRO' THE PRINCIPAL COAL WORKS, BY TWO DIFFERENT TRACKS, AND GAVE IT AS HIS OPINION, THAT THE BEST WAY WAS FROM NEAR NEW HALL, OVER BIRMINGHAM HEATH, TO OR NEAR THE FOLLOWING PLACES (VIZ) SMETHWICK, OLDBURY, TIPTON GREEN, BILSTON, AND FROM THENCE TO THE STAFFORDSHIRE & WORCESTERSHIRE CANAL, WITH BRANCHES TO DIFFERENT COAL WORKS BETWEEN THE RESPECTIVE PLACES.

The Swan Inn.

James Brindley. Former pub sign, Birmingham.

PATRONAGE

By the time of the meeting on 10 July, £35,400 had been subscribed and Bentley and Holloway were making good progress with the landowners; all thirty approached so far had either signed their consent, or, at the least, were not openly opposed to the canal. Along with John Meredith, they had further approached such local luminaries as the Earls of Denbigh, Dartmouth and Warwick, Lord Craven and Sir Roger Newdigate for their patronage in the undertaking and had met with promises of attention and support.

By 14 August's meeting, William Bentley and George Holloway had solicited the support and promises of assistance from Lord Gower, Lord Grey, Sir Walter Bagott, Mr Anson and Mr Gilbert. The first was particularly significant as a member of the Leveson-Gower family, major Staffordshire landowners. He was a skilled parliamentarian and already a supporter of Brindley's Grand Trunk Canal, which would pass through his estate at Trentham. Thomas Anson of Shugborough, hard by the later junction of the Trent & Mersey and the Staffordshire & Worcestershire Canals at Haywood, was another parliamentarian, who in 1762 had inherited the vast fortune amassed by his brother, Admiral George Anson. William Legge, second Earl of Dartmouth, whose Sandwell estate was on the line of the canal, became a particular advocate for the Company in parliamentary matters. All three families later had branch canals of the BCN named after them.

A further meeting was held at the Swan Inn in early June where Brindley presented his survey and estimates. The engineer pronounced the scheme to be 'very practicable' and that the 'Upper Way, or Course' was the most 'Eligible'. On the strength of this meeting the newspaper advertisement on the previous page was inserted.

A further meeting was quickly called to open a subscription to raise funds towards the cost of obtaining an Act of Parliament, necessary to enable the promoters to purchase the land required and for completing the work. It was deemed that £50,000 would be sufficient for the entire undertaking, including all expenses. Brindley's plan, estimate and opinion, together with some calculations of the amount of coal likely to be carried, were open for inspection at the offices of Mr Meredith, Attorney at Law. A Committee of Thirty-Nine Gentlemen was appointed and Samuel Garbett, William Bentley, John Kettle and Matthew Boulton were to receive payment for their canal work. William Bentley and George Holloway were to 'wait upon the respective Land Owners' and obtain permission to make the canal across their land. Garbett was an astute businessman with wide-ranging interests in the town and further afield. An early supporter, he would, before long, become a fly in the ointment as far as the Company was concerned.

Perhaps realizing that the original Committee of thirty-nine was unwieldy, a General Meeting of the Proprietors on 30 November appointed a Select Committee of nine, of whom five would be accounted a quorum. They could spend any sum up to £1,000 without reference to the full Committee. Drs John Ash and William Small, Henry Carver Esq., Samuel Garbett Esq., John Kettle, William Bentley, Matthew Boulton, Joseph Wilkinson and William Welch were duly appointed. James Brindley was to be approached to fix a day to meet the coal owners and masters and it was stressed that the 'Primary and Principal Object of this Undertaking was and is to Obtain a Navigation from the Collieries to this Town'.

First Act of Parliament

The Birmingham Canal Act received Royal Assent on 24 February 1768. When printed, it stretched to fifty pages and included ninety-nine clauses covering such areas as finance, constitution, water supply and mining. After setting out the advantages of the scheme, the Proprietors were listed and given the formal name of 'The Company of Proprietors of the Birmingham Canal Navigation'. One important clause empowered the Staffordshire & Worcestershire Navigation to complete the canal if the Birmingham Company failed to carry out the work within six months of it being opened to the town and to be reimbursed for its costs.

> **WHAT'S IN A NAME?**
>
> Assistant Engineer Samuel Simcock is nearly always referred to in the Company Minute Book as 'Simcox', while Ryders Green is often Riders and Lapal Tunnel is Lappal, but this is nothing compared to the confusion over the name of the western terminus of the canal. This stems from the first paragraph of the Act where two names are listed: 'Autherley otherwise Aldersley, in the Parish of Tettenhall, near Wolverhampton'. The first name came from the farm on whose land it was sited, but later, with the opening of the Birmingham & Liverpool Junction Canal in 1835, half a mile (680m) north along the Staffs & Worcs, the name was transferred to the new junction. Aldersley later became the accepted name for the Birmingham Canal junction, but exactly when the official renaming came about is difficult to ascertain. It is 'Autherley Junction' in the Company's early twentieth-century Distance Tables and the location of the canal house at the foot of Wolverhampton Locks was still recorded as at 'Autherley Jct.' in the BCN rent journal of 1921. However, a pencil note on the large-scale BCN Deed Plan, where the name AUTHERLEY is scored out and replaced by ALDERSLEY, is dated 'Nov 1925' and perhaps records the official change.

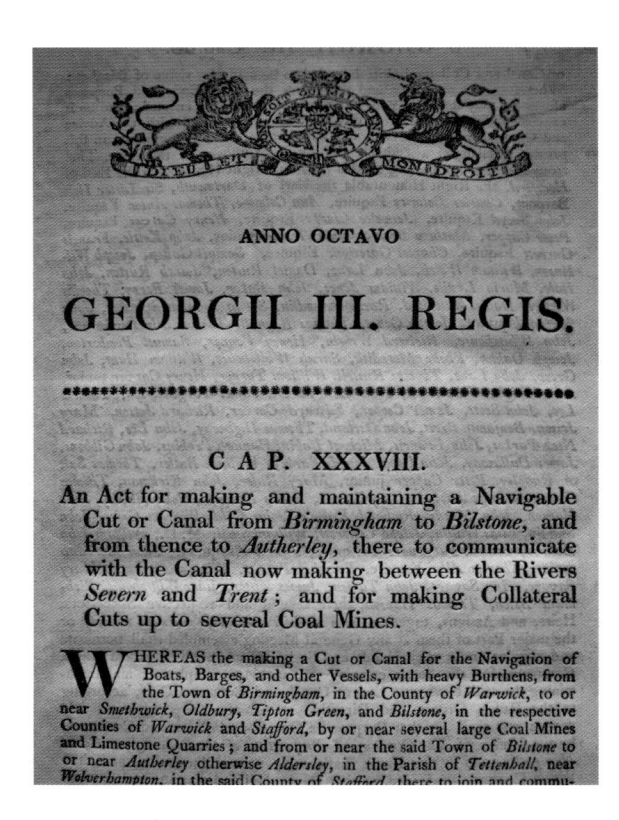

Birmingham Canal Act Introduction.

First General Assembly

A meeting with James Brindley was fixed for 2 March. Busy with several concurrent schemes, he advised the Committee that a Superintendent or Head Clerk be appointed to conduct the works, together with a deputy or Under-Clerk, and recommended that they attend 'some one of the Navigations now compleating to acquaint themselves of the Nature of Navigation Business, the better to Qualify themselves for the respective Offices'. The first General Assembly of Proprietors of the Birmingham Canal Navigation met on 25 March 1768. Holding between one and ten shares each, sixty-four attended in person, while a further sixteen were represented by proxy. John Meredith, who had kept the Minutes from the beginning, was appointed Clerk, with John Kettle as Treasurer. Brindley was to be Engineer and Surveyor, along with George Holloway as Clerk of the Works. Brindley was to be paid £120 for the attendance and expenses of himself and his Clerk, Robert Whitworth, in London, while a further £80 was to be laid out for purchasing two pieces of plate

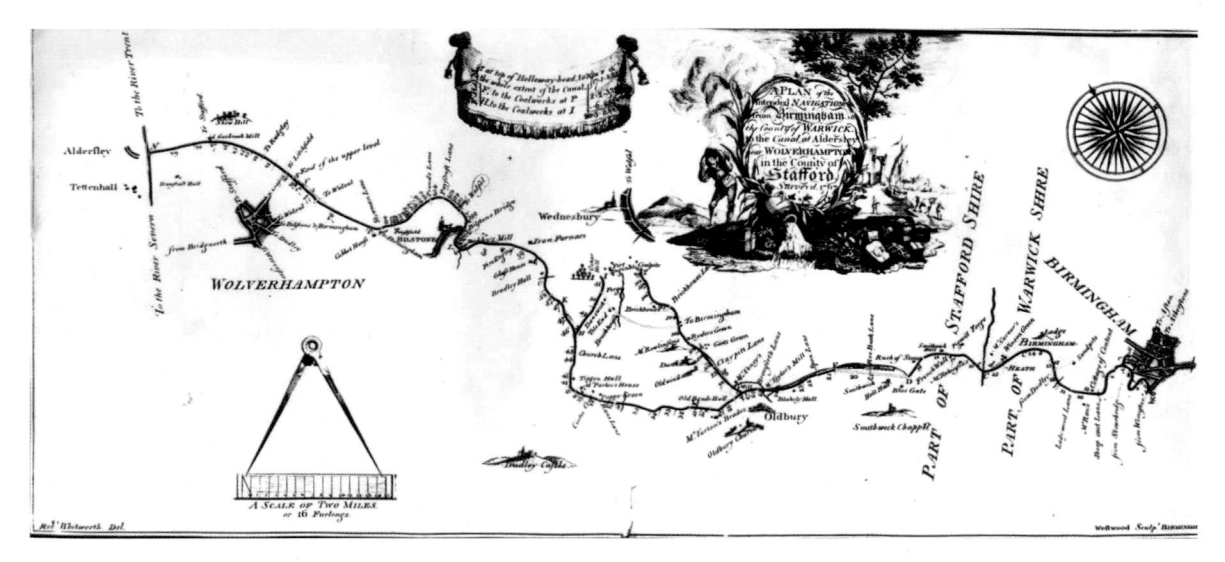

Robert Whitworth's plan of the proposed Birmingham Canal, 1767.

to be presented to William Bentley and Joseph Wilkinson in gratitude for their work in furthering the Act.

It was also resolved that before any part of the work on the Navigation be started, the land should be agreed for and the money paid, or a tender made. A call of 10 per cent on shareholders was made to cover these outlays and a Committee, according to the directions of the Act, was elected. Almost hidden away in the middle of all these resolutions was perhaps the most germane of them all: 'That the Navigation be immediately begun, and that the Committee pursue Mr Brindley's Instructions to execute the same and provide the necessary Materials for that purpose.'

Committee Matters

The Committee met for the first time on 30 March, then around another sixty times before the opening of the canal. Some members, such as John Lane and Joseph Wilkinson, barely missed a meeting, while Matthew Boulton, busily engaged on his other enterprises, only managed to attend a quarter of them. The new Committee set to work with a will, their first meeting looking to procure windlasses and gins for work on the tunnel proposed at Smethwick, as well as measuring and laying out land along the proposed line. An advertisement was to be placed in the *Birmingham Gazette* for 'proper persons to undertake the execution of the Canal', stipulating that they should be free of any other engagements. In early April, under the Chairmanship of William Bentley, they were contracting for 'twenty hundred thousand bricks' and ordering deals (planks made of fir or pine and used for construction). In early June, a special messenger was sent to require Mr Brindley to meet the Committee 'with all possible expedition'. The reason was not immediately spelt out, but related to some 'special matters relative to this undertaking'.

Under or Over?

These 'special matters' were problems along the course of the Smethwick Tunnel, where excavations had revealed 'running sand and other bad materials'. We can imagine the engineer, closely followed by Committee members, as he 'examined and surveyed the course of the intended Tunnel, and maturely weighed and considered the consequences attendant upon proceeding thereupon'. His conclusion was to abandon tunnelling and to 'carry the Canal over the Hill by Locks and Fire Engines'. Having retired to the Bull's Head at West

Bromwich, the Committee, swayed by Brindley's assurance that it would be 'less expensive and equally beneficial ... and will not be attended with more delay than Tunnelling', not surprisingly supported their engineer's plan, ordering that the Clerk of the Works should follow Brindley's instructions.

This change of plan led to problems, most immediately that of the provision of water for the locks. Samuel Simcock, Brindley's brother-in-law, who, together with Robert Whitworth was one of the engineer's assistants supervising the work, was dispatched to survey the land around the summit for likely brooks, springs and other supplies. He was to report back to the next meeting with the quantities that each source would provide. Simcock appears to have measured the width and depth of seven streams, multiplying his measurements together to arrive at a total for each source. Having added them all up, he presented his findings: '200¾ inch'. This baffled the Committee members, who simply wanted to know how many boats a day the canal would be able to carry through the locks and a letter was sent off to Brindley to find an explanation. A fortnight later, on 5 August, a dozen Committee members returned to the Bull's Head to visit and examine the works and found that they were being 'conducted and carried on with regularity'. Stonemasons were sought to work on the locks, with advertisements being inserted in the Gloucester, York and Manchester papers.

The Second General Assembly of the Proprietors, held on 30 September 1768, ordered that an engraved seal, produced at the meeting and attached to the resolutions and orders of the day, should be adopted as the Common Seal of the Company.

Having held almost all their meetings, from the initial one of 28 January 1767, at the Swan Inn, the Committee was ordered to acquire a house or office that would be suitable for the Book-keeping Clerk to conduct his business, as a secure place to hold the company's books, and for the Committee to hold its meetings. It was to be distinguished by the 'Public mark of "Navigation Offices"'. In view of the continuing progress of the canal – *Aris's Birmingham Gazette* had reported in the middle of October that nearly 5 miles (8km) had been completed and that it was expected to be open fully

Birmingham Canal Seal adopted by the successor BCN.

within a year – a call of 10 per cent was made on all Proprietors, to be paid on 3 December. Compared with many other canal completions, the *Gazette*'s prediction was only slightly optimistic.

Changes

The original plan for a tunnel at Smethwick having been abandoned, there were now to be six locks raising the canal above its level course from Birmingham, followed by a summit pound of about 1 mile (1.6km) and then six locks down to regain the level to the Wednesbury Mines, the Committee's priority being to ensure a supply of coal into the town. Brindley's earlier plan had been to take the line to Wolverhampton on the same level as the bulk of the Navigation, but a fresh proposal was now aired, suggesting that by branching off at the third lock on the western side, the canal would have a better water supply and would pass through a greater tract of coal mines. Not only that, the deviation would bring greater benefits for the public, would avoid passing 'thro' a deal of dangerous and uncertain land' and would save money. Brindley's opinion was again sought, a messenger being dispatched to find the peripatetic engineer.

His reply was considered 'too concise' in a 'Matter of such Consequence', and the Committee waived proceedings until he could give a more explicit account, giving his reasons, an estimate of costs and explanation of the likely benefits.

Another Act

In December 1768, it was found necessary to apply for a second Act of Parliament as a 'misapprehension' had occurred in the original Act. The first sentence of that Bill had listed the various places the Navigation would pass through in the 'respective Counties of Warwick and Stafford', but no mention was made of 'Salop' (Shropshire). This oversight had to be corrected and the Committee further wished to discover whether any part of the canal would pass through Worcestershire. Having discovered this one mistake, the Committee resolved to ensure that no further ones occurred by ordering a plan to be drawn up of the canal and its branches 'so far as they are already set out' and that the name of each landowner and the extent of his land to be cut through should be given. It was to be kept up to date each month by 'some of the surveying Clerks'. At the same time, the Committee decided to employ a number of 'Inferior Clerks or walking Surveyors' to make a daily check on the numbers of men working in each gang and take particular notice of whether they were there for the whole day, or only a part of it. A copy of the Petition to the House of Commons was presented to the Committee on 1 February 1769 and to a Special General Meeting two days later. Besides correcting the county omission, it also sought to extend the powers for making reservoirs, necessitated by the change of plan at Smethwick. The Bill became law in April.

Where Will it End?

A Proprietors' meeting was called in May to determine on the 'proper place or places for the Termination of the Canal near Birmingham'. This was to become a most contentious issue. Three 'Tracts from Sheepcote Lane' had been suggested and the Proprietors almost unanimously decided to proceed on the course into Charles Colmore's land as far as Friday Street where a temporary wharf was to be established. Deciding on the further continuation or termination of the cut was to be deferred until the next General Assembly. In the meantime, plans were to be drawn up, under the inspection of Mr Brindley, showing the land suitable for wharves and warehouses between the Dudley Road and Colmore's Newhall Ring, and at land in and near the Brickiln Piece owned by Sir Thomas Gooch.

As the first stage of the construction of the Navigation entered its conclusive phase, there was a need for more finance. At the end of June, following Holloway's report that a considerable sum of money, 'not less than £3,000', would be needed over the next three months and Treasurer Kettle's reply that only £2,100 was available, it was resolved that the Committee would borrow the sum of £3,000 at 5 per cent interest for six months and in July a further call of 10 per cent on the Proprietors was made. The Committee also expressed concern about its engineer for, 'observing that Mr Brindley hath frequently pass'd by and sometimes come into Town without giving them an opportunity to confer with him upon the progress of this undertaking', they expressed their dissatisfaction at not being able to see him and asked that, in future, he would give them notice so that they might have the opportunity to consult him on matters 'respecting the execution of the works that may appear to them necessary'.

As well as works at the Birmingham end, cutting was also progressing on the line towards Wolverhampton, the Committee noting that the bridge at Tividale was awaiting stone for its completion. The last day of July and the first one of August saw two Committee meetings, 'by particular appointment', as Brindley was in attendance. He had resurveyed the proposed terminations of the canal in Birmingham and the routes to access them and, having calculated the respective costs 'which had not been before minutely done by Mr Simcock', he made his recommendation. This was to end the canal at Brickiln Piece rather than Newhall Ring as stated in the Act. It was to prove rather more difficult than that.

The same meetings discussed less weighty but no less important matters as the design of a cart for delivering coal around town and the acquisition of a weighing machine for use at the 'Temporary Wharfs'. The fourth General Assembly, held in late September, ordered that the Committee, augmented by seventeen other Proprietors, should prepare a list of rules and bye-laws for the Company. By the middle of October, the Company was looking for a 'proper person to be advertised for to superintend and conduct the Wharf at the termination of the Canal near Birmingham' and Mr Bentley was to look out for 'proper persons to attend at the Locks'. Notices from the Navigation Office were seeking carts and horses for the delivery of coals, warning felons of the dire consequences of damaging or destroying 'Banks or other Works' – transportation for seven years – and, the first of many such, complaining about people trespassing on their land and causing problems by taking dogs with them and 'throwing Sticks and other Things into the Canal'.

A report of 'considerable Damage' by some 'malicious Person or Persons' induced the Committee to further action, offering a reward of twenty guineas for their discovery. A special Committee meeting about this 'accident to the canal at the temporary wharf' was called on 1 November when Bentley was able to report that despite the misfortune 'it will be possible to navigate near the Town in a few days' and was therefore requested to give the 'necessary directions that Coals may be brought near the Town as early as possible. Two days later the Committee was ordering six 'Centry Boxes, sufficient to contain One Man each' as well as a 'capacious one … for the use of Mr Brookes', and was then adjourned for a fortnight, until after the canal's opening.

On to Wolverhampton

Meanwhile the line towards Wolverhampton and the descent to join the Staffordshire & Worcestershire Canal was being progressed and Brindley, worrying that there would not be enough water beyond Bilston, suggested that it would be insufficient for a flight of 6ft (1.8m) locks. He determined to build all the locks, except the bottom one at the junction, to a 3ft (0.9m) depth, with only the last one being 6ft (1.8m) deep. This could have resulted in a flight of over forty locks. He recommended that the reservoir being built at Smethwick be increased in size and that Simcock should look for land for further reservoirs. The engineer, perhaps in view of his recent experience at Smethwick, also expressed his 'entire disapprobation of carrying the Canal through the Hill at Oldbury', instead recommending a wide detour around it.

With the first arm of the Navigation open for business and the next under construction, it was time for some mutual congratulation and the sixth General Assembly, on 1 December, resolved that William Bentley should be presented with a gold medal of the value of fifty guineas and suitably inscribed 'with a proper devise', and that Treasurer John Kettle and the gentlemen who had organized the running of the temporary wharf should be thanked for their attention and assistance. Bentley was still awaiting his medal sixteen months later, but in the meantime a dispute aired at the Assembly had developed into a very public row. One of the stated aims of the Navigation had been to provide cheap coal for the poor of the town, but some prominent citizens, led by Samuel Garbett, felt that the Company was failing in its public duty. He resigned from the Committee and drew up a petition which led to a flurry of press correspondence and accusations on both sides.

Opposition

Soon after its opening, the Company was being accused of adopting a monopolistic and overbearing approach and even of lengthening the course of the canal 'by turning so as to increase the Tonnage to the Proprietors'. Brindley and Simcock had later to attend a Special General Meeting, declaring that they had never varied the route 'for any purpose whatsoever except where the nature of the ground required it & to give accommodations to Owners of Coal Mines, who otherwise could not have access to the Canal'. Indeed, they had 'set out its present Line, as was incumbent upon them so to do as Engineers without any instructions whatever or without any intention to benefit the Company at the Expence of the Public'. This did not stop one wag from suggesting that Samuel Simcock was aiming for immortality by incorporating his initials in the canal route!

At the beginning of 1770, having decided that Brickiln Piece would be the most suitable site for the Company's Wharf, it was, perhaps conveniently, discovered that the temporary wharf at Friday Street was losing water and the land beyond it was thought to be 'exceeding bad'. Progressing in that direction on to Mr Farmer's land might be 'attended with disagreeable consequences' and Farmer was advised to avoid any unnecessary expense in making permanent wharves. There is a hint, at the end of January, that Committee meetings may have become a little less than businesslike as members needed reminding to address the Chair, that the first business of the meeting should be to examine the accounts, that matters for discussion should be proposed at a previous meeting and that Minutes of the last meeting should be approved. There were problems with the extension as the clause requiring the completion of the works within six months of opening to Birmingham had not been met and the Staffs & Worcs Company, concerned to link up with the coal fields as soon as possible, had written to the Birmingham Navigation in January 1770 to ask when the work would be finished. Although Brindley asserted in August that progress 'appeared to me Satisfactory', it was slow, and a suggestion to September's General Assembly that 'there appear'd a great deal of money expended for the quantity of work done' in the past twelve months resulted in a select committee of three being established to 'examine minutely' the accounts over that period.

Terminal Arguments

The question of the Birmingham terminus rumbled on. Charles Colmore, who was in a 'state of suspense' over the issue, protested that the new deviation to Brickiln Piece injured his interests, insisting that the original plan be followed and the canal end on his land at Newhall Ring. He had gone so far as having an Act of Parliament passed, forcing the Company to finish the canal to Newhall Ring. Nevertheless, the Proprietors determined, by a vote of 333 to 46 at a Special General Assembly in May 1771, that Brickiln Piece should be the site for the Company's wharves and so both branches were eventually built. The canal to Newhall Ring crossed the Dudley Turnpike on an aqueduct and, after arguments over the price of land, the Newhall Branch was completed in March the following year. In June 1771, Brindley had been asked to 'as soon as possible to set out and determine the course of the Canal into Brickiln Piece and the best method for executing the same', and the go-ahead was given the following month. In December, Brindley informed the Committee that coals 'would in a short time be brought to the Brick kiln piece Wharf' and in April 1772 the cutting, the replacement for the tunnel originally conceived, was nearly finished, for a resolution was passed prohibiting boats to pass 'till all the loose soil from the sides of the Cut on the towing path is removed'.

In May, six boatloads of sand from the 'Deep Cutting' were to be laid on the wharf and paving and building work was being started there. It was being used in an unfinished state by August, as 'all Persons who have any Coals, Slack or other materials upon the Wharf between the two Canals … to

Deep Cutting, 1960s. Although the natural contours have long since been altered, the buildings on the bridge give a clue to the original surface level.

remove the same entirely by Saturday night'. This was to allow the paving of the wharf, but it seems that the wish of the Company to finish it in a fine manner ran against the desires of the boatmen for somewhere to unload their coal, for, in October, the stop gate to the wharf had been broken open, many boats 'forced their passage into it & several works for the compleation of the wharf were pull'd down and Destroyed'. Mr Hobson, a Clerk, was instructed to tell the boat owners to remove them immediately till the wharf was 'sufficiently completed for Business, of which time due notice would be given them'. A temporary warehouse, 'about 48 feet by 18 feet', was ordered to be built in November, followed the next year by the fine range of offices on Paradise Street. The Newhall Ring Wharf was mainly used for stone,

The Company Offices, 1895.

Newhall Ring and Brickiln Piece. From Thomas Hanson's Plan of Birmingham, 1778.

timber and merchandise, while the Brickiln Piece or Paradise Street Wharf concentrated on coal.

New Proposals

While this parochial business had been going on, events were taking shape that would affect the Company away from the line of the original canal. A meeting in August 1770 instructing Simcock 'immediately to set out the course of the Canal from Bilston to the first lock towards Autherley', also considered correspondence from the Clerk of the Coventry Navigation. This was requesting a meeting between deputations from the two companies some days before a proposed meeting, in Lichfield, about building a canal from the 'Staffordshire Trunk through Lichfield and Walsall to the Birmingham Canal at Wednesbury', was due to be held.

While such high-level discussions were being carried out, the day to day work of planning and construction continued. There was further debate about the size of the Wolverhampton Locks. The depth, 3ft (0.9m) or 6ft (1.8m), needed to be decided so that orders for the proper-sized timber could be made. Brindley, attending three days later, wished to postpone the decision until he had made certain of the available water supply. The land the canal passed over was already industrialized in places, as reference to part of the route between Bilston and Autherley passing over 'old Coal Work' indicates. Much of the ground, though, was still agricultural and there was a constant demand for posts and rails to fence off the canal and towpath, 'not only to secure peoples' Lands from trespass but also to secure the quick from being destroyed by the Horses hauling the Boats & people walking along the towpath'. The posts and rails would eventually rot away, but the 'quick' – hawthorn – could be laid into virtually impenetrable hedges. This was a skilled job: in October, 1770, the Company was looking for 'proper persons to set Quick along the Canal from Oldbury to Bilston immediately'. They must have found them and they must have been efficient, for a month later the Committee was ordering that no more quick be set along the canal until double posts and rails were provided for protecting the new hedges.

Bricks and More Bricks

Bricks were also required in vast quantities and were made as near to the locations of locks and bridges as possible. As early as February 1768, William Bentley was detailed to look for a good bed of clay in the vicinity of the intended canal and obtain leave of the landowners to 'bore in their respective Lands for that purpose, and to employ proper Persons not only for the discovery of such Delphs of Clay, but to get and throw up a sufficient quantity to make Bricks for the use of the Navigation'. In April 1770, James Brindley recommended that 600,000 bricks should be provided for use on the locks at Aldersley and the following month a Mr Tomkys told the Committee that he would make as many as four million bricks. Trials for clay were to be made at different places near the locks at Autherley.

There was a further demand for bricks as a recommendation was made in early July, at a special meeting of the Committee called by Brindley, that brick bridges should be constructed rather than swivel ones, as the latter were often out of order, 'causing delays on the course of the Canal'. To help with this, bricklayers were to be brought from Autherley to work between Tipton and Bilston. By April 1771, with Brindley being called on to set out the course of the canal from Wolverhampton to the junction, land being acquired and contracted for, and 'Cutters' being readied, there was a need for yet more bricks and 'proper persons' were being sought to produce three million 'this season'. They were certainly needed, as on 10 May it was ordered that 100,000 be immediately sent from Tomkys' to Birmingham for the construction of the aqueduct crossing Dudley Road and a month later he was being contracted for a further million. A more durable material was required for the parapets of bridges and quoins of locks. Stone was quarried at Fownes and Aston's Quarry in Tipton, while a mine at Gornal provided the hollow posts for the locks, the shaped quoins where the rounded heel post of the lock gates turned.

BRICKS

Brickmaking, using the abundant clays of the Black Country, had been carried on for centuries and was very much stimulated by the demand of the canals and developing industries until it became one of the predominant local trades. By the mid-nineteenth century, there were seventy firms firing bricks, five of which produced over a million a year. Many were established by canals and their products are to be found along towpaths and in bridge abutments and copings today. Hamblet's Blue Brick Co., established in 1851 next to the canal at Albion by Pudding Green, covered 135 acres (54h) by 1898, had twenty-six kilns and ran a fleet of forty narrowboats.

Towpath, Old Main Line, Tipton.

Towpath, Windmill End.

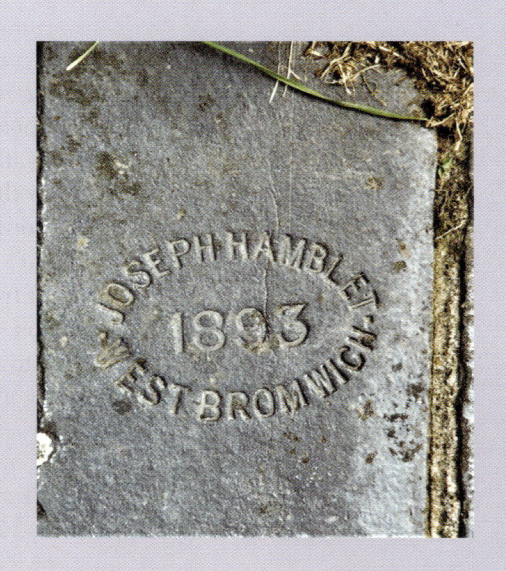

Towpath, Worcester & Birmingham Canal.

Argument and Compromise

Progress at the western end was still too slow for the Staffordshire & Worcestershire concern and a short newspaper spat between the companies in December 1770 was followed by a petition to Parliament for a Bill to allow the older company to complete the works on its own, as allowed for in the Birmingham Company's Act. In the spring of 1771, the Earl of Dartmouth acted as arbiter between the two companies and a letter was written to his lordship thanking him for the 'great Trouble & he has had in adjusting the Company's affairs with the Wolverhampton Company'. A 'Deed of Compromise' was drawn up between the two

Houses by Wolverhampton Top Lock, 2018. Only the middle part of the block would have been built originally.

Completion

Agreement was reached between the two companies to open the communication before 14 September, but the Birmingham Committee had decided, ten days earlier, to defer this as the towing path and bridges were not finished. The junction was opened on 21 September 1772, nearly two and a half years after the time proposed in the Act and only a few days before James Brindley died, at midday on the 27th. The *Leeds Intelligencer* reported the death of 'the celebrated Engineer, at Turnhurst, in Staffordshire after a long illness which gradually wore him away, and which was brought upon him by too intense an application of mind to accomplish the great works in which he was engaged'. The Birmingham Canal was one of his great works and, ironically, on the day of his death, its General Assembly had resolved to settle his account, adding that 'they shall always be desirous of his Advice upon the Company's affairs when they may require the Assistance of an Engineer'. Although there were soon to be exceptions, the Company was generally able to find further experts, both from among the burgeoning ranks of nationally recognized civil engineers and from within its own workforce.

companies, with the Birmingham concern paying the Parliamentary expenses.

On 9 August 1771, the Committee resolved that water should be let into the canal between Bilston and Wolverhampton as soon as it was ready to receive it, but by the end of the month it was being let out to facilitate 'several repairs and Alterations' and a wholesale inspection of the route was ordered. By the following May, flaws in the works due to the haste to complete to Aldersley were becoming apparent, notably in the woodwork and ironwork for the locks. At the same time, a boat loaded with sand was to be sent to stem leaks in the Wolverhampton summit and water was to be turned in, much of it from mine drainage engines. Houses for lock-keepers were to be built in four places down the flight, namely 'on the spoil' at Little's Lane near the first lock; by the fifth near Cannock Road; by the tenth at Spaw Well Lane; and near the fifteenth at Stafford Road. Land was also required for erecting a warehouse and lock house at Autherley and for making a reservoir 'between the 17th & 19th Locks for supplying the large Lock at the junction', though the reservoir was never made and the bottom lock caused problems for over a decade.

Bridges at Aldersley. Looking from the site of the Birmingham Canal house across the junction bridge to the Staffordshire & Worcestershire's Aldersley Bridge, 2021. The BC's bridge was narrow, leading only to the house.

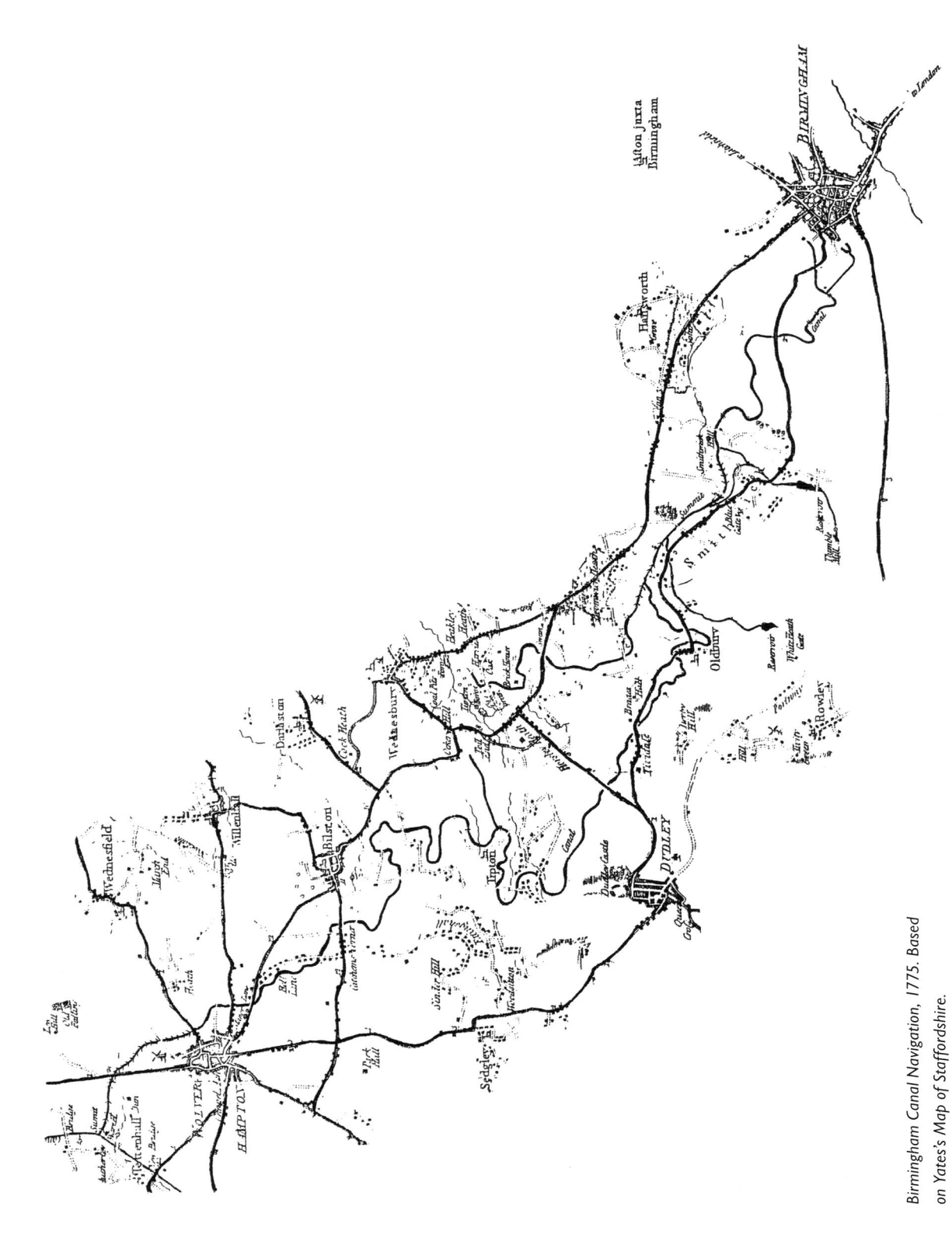

Birmingham Canal Navigation, 1775. Based on Yates's Map of Staffordshire.

CHAPTER 2

The System Grows

The Birmingham Canal first crossed the watershed by Horseley Fields, then still living up to its bucolic name, just over half a mile (680m) from the top lock at Wolverhampton. It is noticeable that streams on the western side of the watershed, leading to the Stour and the Severn, are generally much steeper than those flowing north and eastwards to join the Tame and Trent. When the Birmingham cut opened fully, there were twenty locks in under 2½ miles (4km) from Aldersley to the watershed, to contrast with the nine at Smethwick in the other 20 miles (32km) to the eastern termini. The Smethwick Locks carried the canal up and down over a minor hill, so the height difference between the canal in Wolverhampton and Birmingham was only 20ft (6m), while between the top and bottom of Wolverhampton Locks it was 132ft (40m). Over the next couple of decades, the Birmingham Company would be greatly involved with, but often in opposition to, schemes to develop canals on either side of the watershed.

North to Fazeley

The original canal into Birmingham, from Wednesbury, left untouched a great area of coal-bearing land further north around Walsall, and it was with a view to exploiting this that a meeting, in which Samuel Garbett was involved, was called at Lichfield in August 1770, 'for the Consideration of the Utility of making a Cut or Canal from the Staffordshire Trunk through Litchfield and Walsall to join the Birmingham Canal at or about Wednesbury'. A trio of Birmingham Committee men was dispatched to find out about this potentially dangerous development and the result was a rather haughty letter sent to the Clerks to the Committee of the proposed canal. Pointing out that no line or plan had yet been produced for the course of the intended scheme, 'they are utterly incapable to form any judgement of it'. There was also much opposition from landowners, the canal passing through a largely agricultural district where any benefits might seem less immediate and, in January 1771, the plan was abandoned.

It was August 1781 before the proposal was raised again, at a meeting held in Warwick concerning:

> a Navigable Canal from Bilston, Sedgley and Wednesbury, in the County of Stafford, to Faseley, in the County of Warwick, there to join the Coventry Canal intended forthwith to be carried on from Atherstone to that Place, together with a Branch from Salford-Bridge to Deritend, near the lower part of the Town of Birmingham.

This scheme, with the direct intention of breaking the Birmingham Canal's monopoly of the carriage of coal from the Wednesbury pits, was a plain threat to the Company, which responded with its own plans, minuted in December, for a canal from the Wednesbury branch 'through the Coal Lands upon the lower Level'. Competition was bitter, with little thought given to working together.

> **A UNION CANAL?**
>
> A letter to the *Oxford Journal* in November 1781 proposed that the Grand Trunk, Birmingham, Coventry and Oxford Companies should unite to form a new company, the Union Canal, 'or any other fit and descriptive Title', to make a navigation from the east side of the Birmingham Canal, as near as possible to the town to Fazeley, and from there to divide in order to join the Grand Trunk at Fradley and the Coventry at Atherstone. There was no cooperation from the Birmingham concern.

'Envy, like a dark shadow, follows closely the footsteps of prosperity' William Hutton

A petition presented to Parliament at the end of January 1782 from coal mine and landowners in support of the proposed canal was counteracted by one the following month pointing out that the Proprietors of the Birmingham Canal had completed their navigation at a cost of upwards of £120,000 and that it 'answered very effectually all the purposes for which it was intended to the great Benefit of the neighbourhood of its Track and of the Publick'. The rival canal, they said, would be virtually parallel to theirs and would bring no benefits to the public or the town. Bills for both schemes were introduced in March and cancelled each other out.

In June, the promoters of what became known as the Birmingham and Fazeley Canal Company reached agreement with the Grand Trunk, Coventry and Oxford companies and gave notice that they had raised enough subscriptions to build the canal. By an agreement reached at Coleshill, the Oxford Company was to complete its route to the Thames, while the Coventry would extend from Atherstone to Fazeley. The Fazeley concern itself undertook to finish the Coventry's route as planned between that place and Whittington, as the latter company could not raise the finance for the whole length. The Grand Trunk was to complete the canal to a junction at Fradley.

In response, the 'old company', as William Hutton, the town's historian and contemporary commentator, described the Birmingham concern, decided to build an extension of the canal from New Hall to Digbeth, effectively cutting off any approach by their rival from Fazeley. They also reintroduced the plan to build to the lower level, extending the canal from Ryders Green at Wednesbury to Broadwaters, 3½ miles (5.6km) nearer to Walsall, with six collateral cuts to coal mines. There was also to be a 'Navigable Canal from or near the Town of Birmingham to join the Coventry Canal at or near Fazeley'.

Parliamentary Manoeuvres

This was followed by a great flurry of Parliamentary activity, with the Birmingham Company introducing its own Bill and establishing a permanent Subcommittee in London, lobbying Members and Peers, and preparing petitions written in the most compelling language. A proposal by Warwickshire coal owners to alter tonnage rates would 'entirely cut up and destroy the whole meaning and intention of the last application to Parliament of the Birmingham Navigation Company', and would amount to a 'prohibition upon the exportation of Staffordshire Coals into the Counties of Warwick, Northampton and Oxford'. There were postponements and delays, including one brought about by a proposal to make the Rivers Tame, Anker and Trent navigable to avoid having to build the canal altogether, but the Birmingham Company's Bill became law in June 1784.

The Act was for the building of the canal to Fazeley as well as the Broadwaters extension, together with half a dozen collateral cuts and the line to the lower part of Birmingham. Soon, most of the subscribers to the rival concern had reached an agreement with the Birmingham Company, by which their shares were bought at cost and this

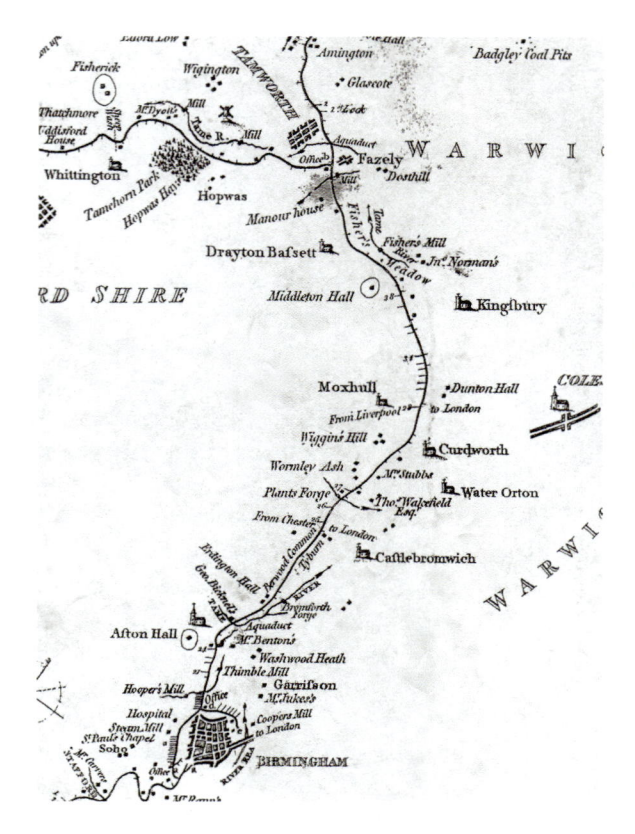

Birmingham & Fazeley Canal. Extract from William Wright's 1791 plan showing the B&F and the extension to Whittington. The Birmingham Company's length stretched as far as Sheep Wash on the plan. Also shown is the Digbeth Branch descending through six locks into the Rea valley.

A CHANGING LANDSCAPE

The routes of the various canals, as delineated in the Act, portray a landscape during its transition from an agricultural past to an industrial future. The Broadwaters extension, for instance, was to start on the south side of Ryders Green, continue over the Green to cross the land of Dunkirk Farm and then the 'Waste of West Bromwich'. It would pass several pools and cross over brooks that still flowed open to the sky. Of the collateral cuts, one was to end in Brooke's Meadow and a further two in Wednesbury Open Field. This was a time when 'The Brick House' was enough of a local landmark to be named in the Act, when Butcher's Forge Pool spoke of an established iron trade and when there was already 'an old Engine' belonging to Lord Dudley, at Broadwaters.

was followed shortly by a further Act consolidating the two companies under the descriptive but ungainly title of 'the Company of Proprietors of the Birmingham and Birmingham and Fazeley Canal Navigations'. A date for completion was set at 24 June 1787 and in order that the works 'shall be begun and carried on with as much Expedition as may be', the cut was to be started simultaneously from Birmingham and Fazeley.

Eighteenth-Century NIMBYism

On the line to Fazeley the influence of local land-owners was shown in a clause stipulating that the

Fisher's Mill Bridge, near Middleton Hall.

canal could not pass within 500yd (457m) of Pipe Hall, belonging to the Reverend Walter Bagot, or Middleton Hall, the home of the Dowager Lady Middleton. Additionally, in Middleton parish the towpath was to be on the east side of the canal, away from the village and hall, and 'a good and commodious Bridge, for Horses, Carts and other Carriages, shall be made … and be ever maintained' by the Canal Company along with a further bridge. Both halls have survived, and the towpath follows the east side for the entire 13½ miles (22km) between Fazeley and Aston Junction, though this would anyway have been the case as it is usual to find towpaths built on the 'downhill' side of valleys.

Down to Digbeth

In May 1782, the Birmingham Company turned its attention towards the canal to Digbeth, with a General Assembly agreeing to proceed in June. In November 1785, James Watt suggested several alterations to plans for the extension from Farmer's Bridge to 'the lower part of the Town' and these were lodged at the Company's offices so that 'any Person desirous of undertaking … the same' could inspect them and submit estimates before 19 December. The existing Birmingham Canal, open now for sixteen years, was already playing its part in the continued growth of the town and the bridges over the Digbeth extension were ordered to be built 'the full width of the respective streets'. A few decades later, in 1828, the town's giddy growth had prompted James Dobbs to write a song, *Brummagem I Can't Find*, lamenting the loss of well-known sights and streets. In one verse he harked back to one of the town's staple trades:

> I remember one John Growse, who buckles made in Brummagem.
> He built himself a country house to be out of the smoke of Brummagem.
> But though John's country house stands still, the town has walked right up the hill.
> He lives beside a smoky mill, in the middle of the streets of Brummagem.

In the meantime, the Committee was eager to settle with the landowners along the 'Works from Ryders Green to Broad Waters'. Samuel Bull, who had been taken on by the Company in December 1771, was to mark out the course and provide Mr Meredith with a list of landowners, measurements and information.

Enter John Pinkerton

Seeking an engineer to take overall responsibility for the works, the Committee had contacted John Smeaton, who expressed his approval of what 'the Company's Surveyors have done', suggesting that his attendance would be unnecessary, but that 'if the Committee persist in their requisition for His attendance He will make it convenient some time on this side Christmas'. The work on the ground was let out in several contracts. John Pinkerton took the one for the Broadwaters extension, having submitted his estimates to the Committee in January 1784. However, in April, the contractor was 'representing to the Committee' that he was unable to complete several bridges, aqueducts and culverts through the lack of 315,000 bricks and was unable to complete and fill the cut 'and thereby secure the banks'.

By October 1785, a 'proper House' was ordered to be built for the lock-keeper at Ryders Green and the canal there was to be opened 'so soon as the Banks … are completely Water tight'. At the end of the month, Pinkerton was reporting that he was preparing to complete the works below Ryders Green within the next ten days, but that the canal was anyway ready as far as the coal mines. However, it seems that all was not well for, on the last day of the year, Company Superintendent James Bough was receiving instructions to examine the state of the locks, bridges, culverts, aqueducts, towing paths, fences and banks on the canal below Ryders Green, 'as soon as the Weather permits'. It was May before a report, prepared by Bough and Bull, was 'taken into consideration' and a copy was sent to Pinkerton, who was 'desired to see immediately to the Repairs reported to be wanting'. A fortnight later, the contractor 'had given directions that the defects complain'd of should be speedily & effectually repaired', but in July, a further report stated that Pinkerton's works 'upon the lower level are left very incompleat' and another letter was sent 'desiring that the necessary reparations may be done'. Not till then would his account be settled. This set the tone for future works.

Fazeley to Whittington Brook

Pinkerton and Thomas Dadford had both submitted estimates to the Grand Trunk Company for the canal, to be built under the terms of the agreement reached at Coleshill, between Fazeley and Fradley. Pinkerton had been considered 'the most proper Person of the two to undertake the execution of the Canal', but there had been a proviso to seek the opinion of a 'Skilfull Engineer as to the Estimates delivered in before they entered into any decisive Contract'. By February 1784, Pinkerton was working on the section between Fradley and Dennis Brook by Fulfen, near to the present Huddlesford Junction. As this short length was nearly finished, it was agreed in October to allow Dadford, the Trent & Mersey's engineer, to complete it, while Pinkerton should execute the remainder of the stretch to Fazeley. He was to finish the work by Christmas 1786 for £8,716, keeping back £500 to maintain it for a further three years.

A month after the letter to Pinkerton about the defects on the Broadwaters canal, the Birmingham Committee was once more putting pen to paper concerning the contractor, following a report by Bough and Beswick. The letter, on 30 August, to the Grand Trunk Committee, noted that the works 'upon the Line of the intended Canal from Wittington Brook to Hoppas are very imperfectly executed', going on to state that 'the defects complained of are so various and of such magnitude, as seem to call for the serious attention of both Committees, that the Undertakers may forthwith amend the imperfections of their past Works and avoid similar errors in their future proceedings'.

Four Birmingham Committee members went to Lichfield in early October expecting to meet a deputation from the Trent & Mersey, but in the event only their agent and engineer attended. Accompanied by Bull and Beswick, who further reported that a near 2-mile (3.2km) length nearest Fazeley was as yet uncut, they went to view the length, between Whittington Bridge and Fazeley, belonging to the Birmingham Company. They found that the part 'under execution by Mr Pinkerton was very incompleat, injudiciously laid out and in many places very defectively executed' and in a follow-up letter to the Trent & Mersey Committee added that 'the Canal which instead of being made strait as in many places it might have been, is curved in a very improper manner, the puddling benching and many other particulars ... seem to have been met with equal inattention at Least, and in the General the defects are so notorious, as to not require the Eye of an Engineer to discover them.'

The exchange of correspondence may also point out a degree of inter-company friction, as the Birmingham Committee had been 'much surprised at the nonattendance of the Gentlemen delegates of their [Trent & Mersey] Committee', going on the say that 'this [Birmingham] Committee wish in future no Land may be set out for cutting in the remaining line of Canal' without being informed so that James Bough, 'an able Engineer and very capable of directing the execution', 'may attend to the line being properly set out'. They also urged that 'Mr Pinkerton should be called upon to remedy all present defects, and that what remains at present to be executed shall be sett out and proceeded in under the inspection of this Company's Surveyor jointly with your own'. In early November, Pinkerton attended a Birmingham Committee meeting to express his wish that Bough should go with him to adjust the line remaining uncut between Fradley Heath and Fazeley. This relatively short, 10 miles (16km), lock-free length was finally declared open in December 1788.

Boundary Stone at Whittington Brook.

Down to Fazeley

At the beginning of 1786, the Birmingham Canal advertised that plans for the extension to Fazeley would be open for inspection at the beginning of March by prospective contractors and, so as to speed up the works, the Company 'have no objection to let the Works in several Lotts'. Bull and Bough had already begun to survey the ground between Birmingham and Fazeley and Bough produced a profile of the line between Minworth Green and Fazeley early in March when advertisements were to be placed for the work.

There were still problems in settling for the land necessary for the canal, so the Company sent out a letter begging landowners to meet with their deputation and settle terms, but backed up with a threat:

ONGOING EXPENSES: COMMITTEE MINUTES, 10 FEBRUARY 1786

J Houghton apprehends the Company may in the course of the next three Months have demands upon them as under –

The Land taken for the Canal below Riders Green	£2,000
The Dividend due 31st March if £8.8s.p. Share	£4,200
Messrs. Boulton & Watt for Ocker Hill Engine	– near £1,000
Mr Meredith says the Co. owe him	£400 to £500
Mr Sparrow for the Fradley Heath & Fazeley Act near	£500
Mr Sheasby will have occasion for at least	£1,500
The Trent & Mersey Co. on acct. of the Fradley Heath & Fazeley Canal	£1,000
Rents & Salaries due at Lady Day	£500
	£11,200

As you must be sensible so many People as are now employed cannot be stoped in their Work without considerable loss and as every solicitation has been made on the part of the Company, they flatter themselves you will make a point of effecting the settlement proposed and in default thereof they trust you will not think them precipitate in having recourse to the Act of Parliam't as a rule for their Conduct but which it is their earnest wish to avoid.

In April, John Pinkerton was awarded the contract between Minworth and Fazeley, with the stipulation that it be finished by midsummer 1787, while, three months later, Thomas Sheasby was contracted to build the canal between Aston and Minworth by the following midsummer, having proposed 'to execute the same for less than Mr Pinkerton'.

However, there were problems. In August it was proving impossible to value some of the land required until the harvest was brought in and during October they were still settling with some of the landowners and occupiers. A more serious difficulty arose in December when Pinkerton reported that there had been 'a very material mistake made in taking the Levels between Minworth and Fazeley which he wished to be reviewed in the presence of his nephew'. George Pinkerton, together with James Bough, resurveyed the length, with Bough admitting that his level was as much as 4ft 8in (1.4m) out between Minworth and Fazeley, 'including a mistake of five feet and two Inch made by Mr Dadford at the Junction at Fazeley'. As it seemed probable that there were more errors in the levels from Minworth to Birmingham, Samuel Bull was instructed to resurvey the entire length without referring to Bough's calculations or 'Field Books Notes'.

Slow Progress

The Committee, feeling that the work was not progressing well, resolved that Pinkerton should present a weekly report on the number of hands working on cutting, building bridges and locks and all other works on his section. This imposition was no doubt unwelcome, especially as it was to be checked by James Bough, for there was no love lost between contractor and superintendent. The two contractors were also instructed to send in monthly reports of extra work undertaken and were being paid regularly for their work. A Committee Minute of 14 September 1787: 'Resolved that Mr Sheasby be this day paid One Hundred & Sixty pounds & Mr Pinkerton One Hundred Pounds', while a week later they were each to be paid £150 on account. In October, James Bough was marking out the course of the canal through 'the Wheat Lands' and a date, 5 November, was settled with Bough and Sheasby for the completion and filling of the thirteen locks at Farmer's Bridge.

In January 1788, Pinkerton reported that he had 'a greater number of Hands than He expected upon which account He will have occasion for £100 this week and £100 next week'. By the beginning of the following year, when he was taken off the works, a deal of evidence, revealed in later court proceedings, had been put together about the contractor's work. It was stated that 'bricks were laid without mortar and mortar without bricks', and that there was 'such constant failures in the embankment, bridges, locks etc. that it could never be clearly ascertained when the canal was completed'. The Committee inspected the canal on 5 August, and it was open to traffic six days later. The unfortunate collapse of the Coventry Canal's Tame aqueduct, less than half a mile (680m) from Fazeley Junction, meant that southbound trade was stopped for a year and, in December, two locks at Curdworth failed. Such was the remedial work necessary that it would be another thirty-five years before the Birmingham & Fazeley Canal could be said to be in a 'tollerable state of security'.

South to the Severn: the Dudley Canals

The South Staffordshire thick coal outcropped on both sides of the watershed and was first worked, from at least the thirteenth century, within a radius of 3 miles (4.8km) of Dudley Castle. John Ward, the energetic Second Viscount Dudley, owned large estates on the west side of the ridge, an area unserved by canal. In addition to the coal, there were seams of ironstone and fireclay, while the ridge beneath the castle itself, along with the hills stretching away from it, contained extensive outcrops of Silurian limestone. Lord Dudley was keen to exploit his minerals and in February 1775, he introduced a Bill into Parliament petitioning for the right to cut a canal from Stourton on the Staffordshire & Worcestershire Canal to Stourbridge, with two branches across Pensnett Chase, an area he was wishing to enclose. Stourton being nearly 13 miles (21km) closer to the Severn than Aldersley, this was a threat to the Birmingham Canal, as it would make a shorter route to markets in Worcestershire and Gloucestershire. The Committee ordered an investigation of the proximity of the proposed canal to mines, along with the quality and price of coal and the expense of getting it compared with Bilston coal. The Company's allies in Parliament were mobilized and coal masters along the Birmingham Canal in Wolverhampton and Bilston petitioned against the Bill.

Dudley No.1

In its original form, the Bill failed to pass all its stages and was withdrawn, only to be reintroduced in Autumn's new session as two separate ones, for the Stourbridge and the Dudley Canals, on the original line. The Birmingham company once more mounted opposition, but this time Lord Dudley, along with his fellow promoters drawn from the colliery owners, glassmakers and ironmasters west of the watershed, was successful and the Acts were passed in April 1776. The Birmingham Company was keen to protect its water and clauses in the Acts prevented the new canals from approaching within a set distance, a mile (1.6km) in the case of the Dudley, of the older cut. They were also restrained from taking water that could be used to supply the Birmingham Canal and so the Stourbridge Company built a reservoir at Woodside on Pensnett Chase. This still exists and is now a Site of Special Scientific Interest known as Fens Pools.

The Stourbridge and Dudley Canals, although built and owned by different companies, worked

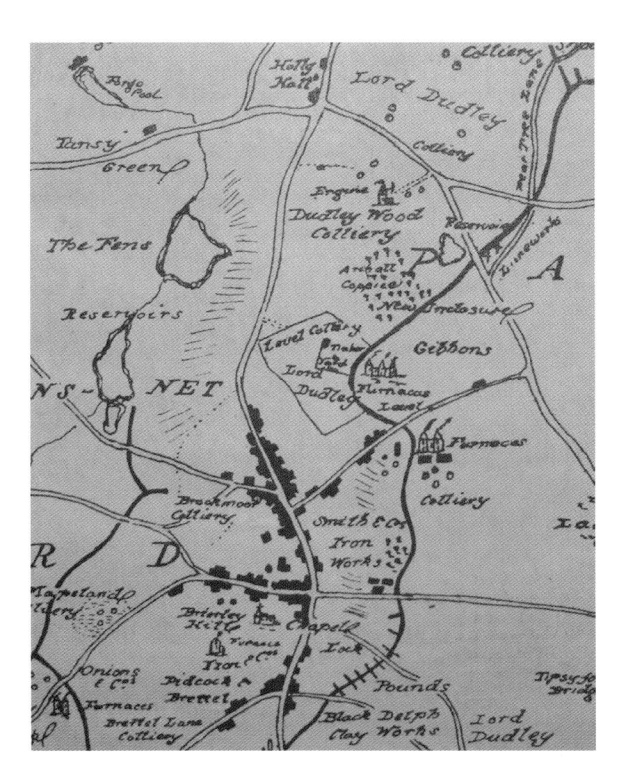

The first Dudley Canal. James Sherriff, 1812.

closely together. Thomas Dadford was surveyor and engineer on the Dudley cut, while his son, another Thomas, occupied the same position on the Stourbridge, the two concerns often sharing Committee members, officers and Clerks. The navigations met at a head-on junction at Black Delph, Brierley Hill, at the foot of a curving flight of nine locks. Above the locks the Dudley then ran on the 'level pond' over Lord Dudley's land to two termini in fields known as Great and Little Ox Leasow, by Woodside. The entire canal was only 2¼ miles (3.6km) long and was completed at a cost of under £10,000. Opened in June 1779, it remained an isolated waterway and probably saw little traffic until the Stourbridge opened on 3 December.

Into the Ridge

In 1775, Lord Dudley, who had been getting limestone from Castle Mill and Wren's Nest, transporting it away expensively by road, began a private canal to link a colliery and limestone mine near

Tipton with the Birmingham Canal. The near half a mile-long (680m) branch, known as Lord Ward's Canal, was finished in 1778, passing through a 226yd (207m) tunnel to end at limestone workings under Castle Hill. The Dudley Canal terminated on one side of the hill, Lord Ward's Canal had entered the other; there was an obvious next step.

Under the Watershed

In December 1783, Messrs Galton and Rickards of the Birmingham Committee met representatives of the Stourbridge and Dudley Canals 'at Lord Dudley's', 'who intimated that there was a plan in agitation for opening a Communication between the Stourbridge and Birmingham Canals'. The plan had become more substantial twelve months later when, at a meeting of the Birmingham Committee attended by Lord Dudley and others, the proposals for making a junction and the advantages this would bring were laid out. The Birmingham Committee was concerned on several points and decided that further consideration was needed. As well as wider concerns about how the proposal might affect the future coal trade on the Fazeley cut and its links with Oxfordshire, the question of water was again raised and the Committee requested a plan of the proposals and an explanation of 'the mode by which the Water to be taken out of this Canal is intended to be returned'. More reservoirs were to be the answer and there was also the expectation that 'A great quantity of Water may be expected to arise in the Tunnel'. To avoid any disputes over water being taken from the respective summit levels, a 'double stop gate or dead Lock' was recommended to be placed in Lord Dudley's Canal, which would hold the right amount of water to balance out any difference in levels.

The Act 'for extending the Dudley Canal to the Birmingham Canal at or near Tipton Green in the County of Stafford' was passed on 4 July 1785. Five locks were to raise the canal from its current end at Woodside to Park Head and from there a tunnel would connect it to Lord Ward's Canal. Nearly a third of the Act was devoted to water issues. The Company was granted the power to take water from fire engines and from mines, particularly from Buffery's Colliery where 'very extensive hollows and Cavities have been formed in and under the same', but was restrained from taking it from the River Tame or any of its tributaries above Wednesbury Forge. The stop lock, of some complexity with 'three or four gates or pairs of gates', was to be built within 400yd (366m) of the Birmingham Canal, had to be controlled by that Company's keeper and was to maintain the Dudley Canal's water 6in (152mm) above the Birmingham's. A fine 'not exceeding Ten Pounds nor less than Forty Shillings' was to be imposed on any boatman misusing the lock, with the threat of jail for any defaulters.

Dudley Tunnel

The 2-mile (3.2km) route of the extension, 1¾ miles (2.8km) of which would be underground, was surveyed by John Snape and checked by Thomas Dadford senior. It was to cost £18,000. The tunnel, 'continued From End to End in a straight Line', would be 9ft 3in (2.8m) wide and 12½ft (3.8m) high with a depth of water of 5½ft (1.7m). The invert, side walls and top arch were to be brick-lined, with 'the Top of the Arch to be clayed four Inches thick, and Brick Ends or other sound Materials laid thereon, so as to conduct the Water in small Streams down the Outside of the Brick Work, thence through small Inlets into the Tunnel'. These weepholes, now thick with accumulated calcite, still perform the task today. John Pinkerton was awarded the contract, possibly his first tunnel work and by the beginning of 1786 was advertising widely for tunnellers. Squeezed between advertisements in the *Derby Mercury* selling pieces of meadowland and a part share in the Trent River Navigation was one from the contractor to 'MINERS, COLLIERS and others, used to the Business, that they may meet with Employment and proper Encouragement by applying to John Pinkerton, the Undertaker …'

Around a dozen shafts were sunk, about 10 chains (200m) apart, until they reached the level of the intended tunnel, from where headings could be driven horizontally until they met and were enlarged to the required dimensions. So much for the theory. In practice, work was slow and by September Pinkerton had spent several thousand pounds to little tangible effect. At the beginning of 1787, with scheduled completion under a year away, the company stopped paying him and demanded he pay back £2,000. In October 1788, John Ward died and was succeeded to the viscountcy by his half-brother William, who showed little of his predecessor's enterprise. Progress on the tunnel slowed and in May 1789 the Committee was told that it 'hath been carried out of the proper line in several parts'. In June the following year, the Company appointed Josiah Clowes, who had spent the previous six years working at Sapperton Tunnel on the Thames and Severn Canal. Clowes completed the tunnel, later installing a stop lock inside it in mid-1793 and building a reservoir at Gad's Green. *Aris's Birmingham Gazette* reported the tunnel open in December 1791, though the official announcement was not made until a shareholders' meeting on 25 June the following year. By then, the Castle Mill Mine had been opened up to become a basin and a new limestone mine begun inside the tunnel. From end to end, and including Lord Ward's Tunnel and the basin, Dudley Tunnel, at 3,172yd (2,900m) was the second longest in England, behind Sapperton, when it opened.

The stop lock inside the tunnel soon proved problematical and it was moved in 1796 to a location nearer the junction with the Birmingham Canal at Tipton. It remained a bone of contention between the two companies and accusations were made about the Birmingham company raising the weirs and thus limiting the headroom inside the tunnel. In May 1794, Birmingham Secretary John Houghton was writing to Thomas Brettle of the Dudley Company regarding complaints made by their stop-lock superintendent of the inconvenience he was suffering 'for want of a Dwelling House upon the Spot' and was requesting that a 'suitable House may be forthwith erected for him'.

Castle Mill Basin in Dudley Tunnel, 1836.

Dudley No.2

The Dudley No.2 Canal, an extension from Park Head to Selly Oak, where it would join the Worcester & Birmingham Canal then under construction, was proposed in August 1792. It was planned to relieve congestion through Dudley Tunnel and to avoid the high tolls charged by the Birmingham Canal. The latter concern had opposed the Worcester scheme, sanctioned the previous year, and went so far as to refuse it a junction in Birmingham, instead ensuring that the canals were separated by a 7ft-wide (2m) piece of land, the Worcester Bar. It opposed the Dudley No.2, raising a petition containing 13,000 signatures against it, but the extension obtained its Act in 1793 and the line was surveyed by John Snape who had worked on the Birmingham & Fazeley. It was to be 10⅞ miles (17km) long, including the 3,795yd (3,470m) Lappal (Lapal) Tunnel and a shorter one of 557yd (509m) under Gorsty (Gosty) Hill. Josiah Clowes was appointed engineer, with William Underhill as resident, and work began early in 1794. Clowes died while the tunnel was under construction and the appropriately named Underhill was given responsibility for its completion. Engineering and financial difficulties hindered progress; Lapal required thirty shafts and three steam pumping engines, while a large 60ft (18m) embankment was built to carry the canal through the landscaped grounds of Leasowes Park, Halesowen. The canal was reported 'now finished, and will be navigable to Birmingham in a few weeks', in January 1798, but it was April before the first two boats unloaded coal at the Worcester & Birmingham's Netherton Wharf in Birmingham.

With the 1802 opening of a junction at Kingswood, linking the Stratford and Grand Junction Canals, and the completion of the Worcester & Birmingham to the Severn in 1815, the Dudley Canal had direct access to the south. By making arrangements over tolls with the Stratford and Worcester concerns, the Dudley

Gosty Hill shaft top, 1992. It is almost possible to imagine the conversation in Dudley Council Planning Office, sometime in the 1950s: 'Look, there's a little black circle on the map here.' 'Oh, ignore it, it'll be nothing to bother about.'

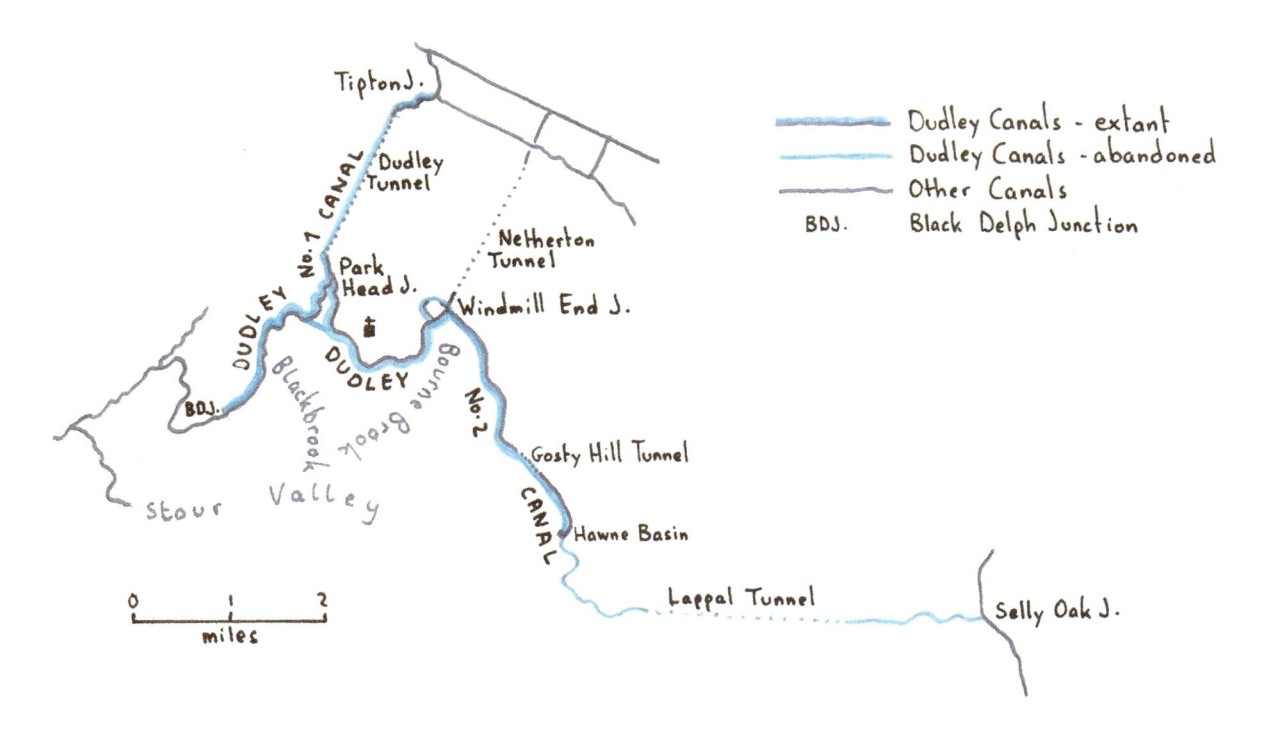

Dudley Canals.

tried to encourage traffic to use its line rather than passing on to the BCN. The removal of the Worcester Bar and replacement with a stop lock in 1815, long opposed by the BCN, concerned as ever over loss of its water, and by the Dudley company, rightly concerned over loss of its trade, led to traffic increasingly using the northerly route through Birmingham rather than the more stoppage-prone Dudley No.2. Thirty years later, with a far more serious problem on the horizon, the Dudley Canal agreed to amalgamate with the BCN, agreement between the companies being reached in October 1845 followed by an Act the following year.

East to the Trent: the Wyrley & Essington Canal

The Wyrley & Essington Canal Act received Royal Assent in 1792 along with half a dozen others, during the period of Canal Mania. It was to run on the level for 6¼ miles (10km) from Horseley Fields to Sneyd near Bloxwich before climbing five locks to Wyrley Bank, with a branch running up a further short flight to a pit at Essington. Another 1¾ miles (2.8km) branch from Sneyd to Birchills north of Walsall would run on the level. As with the

---

YEARS OF MANIA

The financial success of early canals like the Bridgewater, Birmingham and Trent & Mersey, together with the opening of the Thames & Severn Canal in 1789 and the Oxford Canal the following year, thereby completing James Brindley's notion of the Grand Cross linking Mersey, Trent, Severn and Thames, demonstrated the viability and prospects of inland navigation. Coupled with a period of prosperity between the end of the American War of Independence and increasing British involvement in the French Revolutionary Wars, this led to a period of investment and speculation in new waterway schemes, known as 'Canal Mania'. Only one new navigation, the Ipswich & Stowmarket, had obtained its Act of Parliament in 1790; three years later the peak was reached at twenty and by 1797 it was back to one.

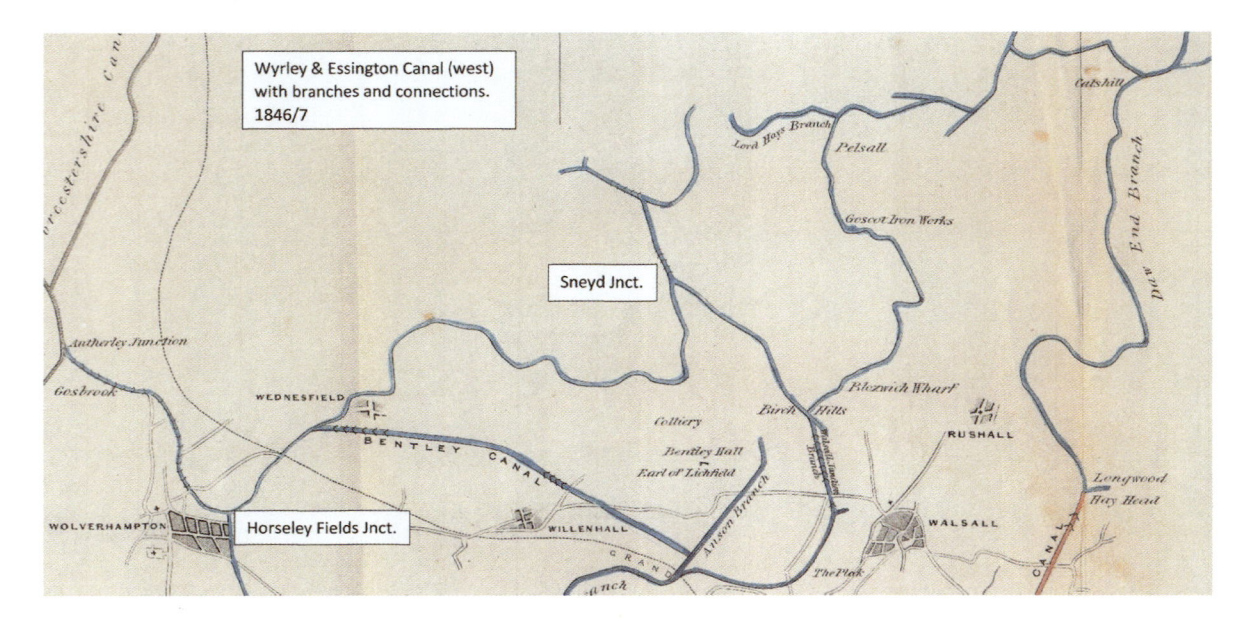

Wyrley & Essington Canal map west.

Birmingham navigation, the canal was built primarily to carry coal, in this case from pits around Essington Wood, Wyrley Bank and the splendidly named New Invention.

Although the Wyrley cut would largely benefit the Birmingham concern by bringing more trade on to it, the usual worries were expressed about water. A clause in the Wyrley Canal Act set its level at 6in (152mm) above the Birmingham Canal's, but upon inspection in September 1794 it was found to be 8in (203mm) below and that the stop lock had only two gates rather than the four that had been required. This led to the Birmingham Canal fastening down stop planks, to stem the flow of water, until the situation was resolved. Although the Wyrley & Essington was opened in November, the situation was still rumbling on two years later, with John Houghton explaining that although it was the 'wish of the Birmingham Canal Committee to give the Wyrley Canal Co. any assistance in their power without detriment to the Birmn Canal', they would lock the gates so that 'no Boats are suffer'd to pass when there is a possibility of any Water escaping out of the Birmingham into the Wyrley Canal'.

On to Huddlesford

At the third half-yearly general meeting in May 1793, the Wyrley Committee were given powers to apply for an Act to extend their canal from Birchills to join the Coventry Canal at Huddlesford, along with a branch from 'Cannock Heath to Hayhead and any other branches, alterations and improvements thought advisable'. The near 15-mile (24km) line was to run from Birchills, passing between Bloxwich and Pelsall to tap the coal-rich land around Brownhills. Near here, at Catshill, a branch ran south for about 5 miles (8km), meandering around Aldridge and Rushall, to limestone workings at Hay Head. Beyond Brownhills, the main line dropped down towards River Tame, falling through thirty locks from Ogley Hay and just skirting Lichfield, to join the Coventry. Work on the Extension began before the original line was completed and the Wyrley & Essington Canal was opened in its full extent, from Horseley Fields to Huddlesford, on 8 May 1797. It was to remain an independent concern for a further forty-three years, but its fortunes remained closely linked with the Birmingham Canal.

THE SYSTEM GROWS

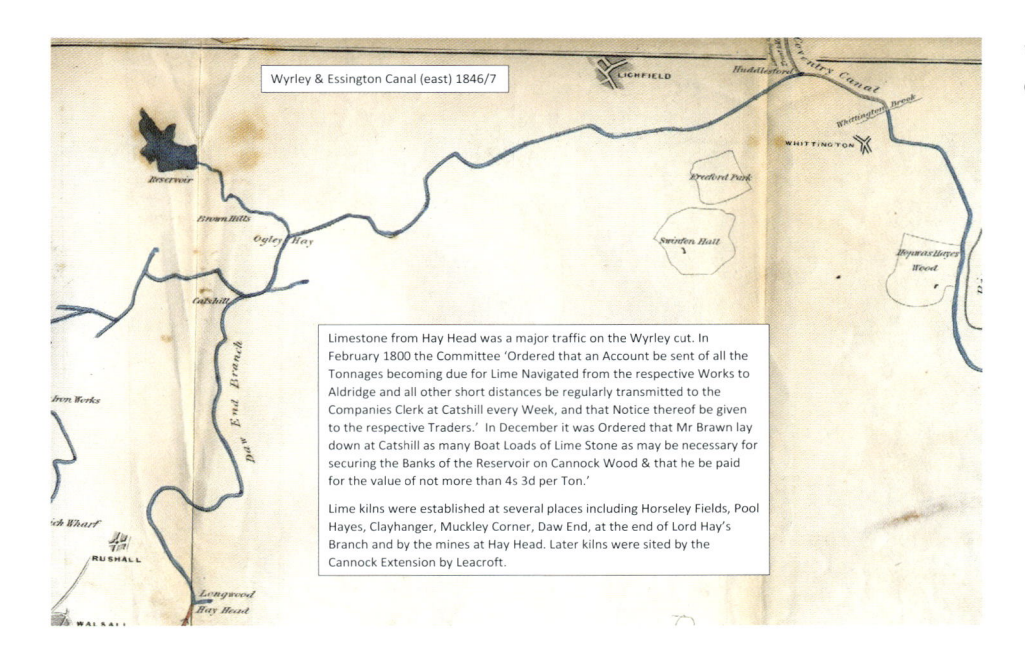

Wyrley & Essington Canal map east.

Limestone from Hay Head was a major traffic on the Wyrley cut. In February 1800 the Committee 'Ordered that an Account be sent of all the Tonnages becoming due for Lime Navigated from the respective Works to Aldridge and all other short distances be regularly transmitted to the Companies Clerk at Catshill every Week, and that Notice thereof be given to the respective Traders.' In December it was Ordered that Mr Brawn lay down at Catshill as many Boat Loads of Lime Stone as may be necessary for securing the Banks of the Reservoir on Cannock Wood & that he be paid for the value of not more than 4s 3d per Ton.'

Lime kilns were established at several places including Horseley Fields, Pool Hayes, Clayhanger, Muckley Corner, Daw End, at the end of Lord Hay's Branch and by the mines at Hay Head. Later kilns were sited by the Cannock Extension by Leacroft.

Hay Head limestone advertisement, Worcester Journal, 28 March 1822.

> *May be had at Mr. Thos. Barnett's, Stourport,*
>
> **B**RINDLEY'S BRITISH CEMENT, prepared from the HAY-HEAD WATER PROOF LIME, and other strongly adhesive substances.
>
> The above truly valuable Composition is sold in Barrels, and sent to any Part of the Kingdom.
>
> J. BRINDLEY warrants the British Cement equal. If not superior, to any hitherto offered to the Public for every description of Stuccoing, &c. &c. and it may be had at a considerably less price than the various Compositions now in use.
>
> The long tried utility of the Hay-Head Lime, and the decided preference it has obtained in the Construction of Aquatic and other Buildings, requiring Strength and Durability, are manifest Proofs of its Superiority. —— On this head, it may, perhaps, be sufficient to observe that the Old Birmingham Canal, and most other Companies, have exclusively used Hay-Head Lime in the Construction of their Works.
>
> J.B. respectfully informs the Public, that his Lime may be had as usual at the Pits, or prepared and sent in Casks, which will be forwarded in the same manner as the British Cement, to any Part of the Kingdom.
>
> Hay-Head is situated near Walsall, Staffordshire

CHAPTER 3

Improving the BCN

Lowering the Summit

The immediate success of the Birmingham Canal soon led to difficulties, with the greatest problems being encountered at Smethwick Locks. Only a week or so after the opening, the Committee resolved that two extra men should be taken on there. More staff could be employed and methods of working the locks more efficiently practised, but none of this could influence the major problem. Nine months later during 'the present Dry season', the summit 'is Daily some Inches under Level' and 'there is great reason to be apprehensive there will not be water sufficient for the more necessary Branches of Commerce'. In August 1771, passage of the locks by carriers was rationed, 'so long as the water continues scarce'. This was pro-rata depending upon the number of boats being owned: the owners of sixteen boats could pass four; those of twelve boats, three; of eight boats, two; and of four and under, one boat.

The locks suffered through time and use and in May 1786, Company Superintendent James Bough was reporting that they were 'much out of repair'. The opening of the Broadwaters extension had brought about more traffic, while the Birmingham & Fazeley would lead to a further increase. In September, 'It having been suggested that the Cutting down the Smethwick Summit to the Level of the Wolverhampton Pond wou'd be attended with great publick utility', the Committee resolved to recommend the proposal to the next General Assembly. At the beginning of the following year, the Committee began to contact landowners along the course of the 'alteration at the Summit', notably the Harborne Church Estate, Mr Gough, Mr Rogers and Mrs Sacheverel.

> **AGREEMENTS BETWEEN THE COMPANY AND LANDOWNERS**
>
> **FROM THE COMMITTEE MINUTES, 21 SEPTEMBER 1787:**
>
> MINUTES OF AN AGREEMENT BETWEEN THOMAS ROGERS ESQUIRE & MESSRS MICHAEL LAKIN & WILLIAM SIMPSON ON BEHALF OF THE PROPRIETORS OF THE BIRMINGHAM & BIRMINGHAM & FAZELEY CANAL NAVIGATIONS. THAT IN CONSIDERATION OF FIVE HUNDRED AND SEVENTY FIVE POUNDS TO BE PAID BY THE SAID COMPANY TO MR ROGERS AT MICHAELMAS NEXT MR ROGERS TO SELL & CONVEY TO THE COMPANY THE TENEMENTS & LAND BELONGING TO MR ROGERS SITUATE AT SMETHWICK IN THE COUNTY OF STAFFORD ON THE NORTH SIDE OF THE OLDBURY TURNPIKE ROAD & IN THE RESPECTIVE OCCUPATIONS OF THOMAS DAVIES & THOMAS HACKETT, ALSO THE LAND HERETOFORE TAKEN

> BY THE COMPANY FOR THE USE OF THE CANAL & FOR WHICH TWO SEVERAL RENTS OF ONE GUINEA AND FIFTEEN SHILLINGS ARE NOW PAID BY THE COMPY.
>
> **FROM THE COMMITTEE MINUTES, 16 NOVEMBER 1787:**
>
> RESOLVED THAT MR HADLEY BE ALLOWED £50 PER ACRE FOR THE LAND WANTED FROM HIS ESTATE FOR THE IMPROVEMENTS OF THE SMETHWICK SUMMIT AND TEN POUNDS P ACRE IN CONSIDERATION OF THE YOUNG TIMBER WHICH IS GROWING THERE BEING DESTROY'D.

Bough and Bull

First Stage

John Smeaton, who was working in an advisory capacity and had produced a report in December 1782 on canal extensions, additions and improvements as well as water supplies is often credited with the work at Smethwick, but it was Birmingham Canal employees James Bough and Samuel Bull who largely planned and carried through the operation. An advertisement was placed in late 1787 referring 'such persons as may be desirous of Undertaking the same to Mr Bull who will explain the methods to be proceeded in & shew the Ground'. These methods were novel and imaginative, involving reducing the summit from its original 491ft (150m) level by 18ft (5.5m) to bring it down to the level of the line to Wolverhampton. The work was moreover to be carried out in two stages. The first stage, 12ft (3.7m) below the existing line, was completed on 2 July, taking out two locks at each end of the original summit. A couple of weeks earlier, *Aris's Birmingham Gazette* had described the scene at Smethwick as the work progressed:

On 26 June, the Committee Minute Book reported that the:

> new Canal … will in a very few days be made navigable, when it is proposed to carry away by the Boats returning to the Collieries a large

> ***ARIS'S BIRMINGHAM GAZETTE, 22 JUNE 1789***
>
> That stupendous work now carrying on … near Smethwick is at this time so far advanced that we understand that water will be let into its new course within a very few days. So vast and seemingly impracticable an undertaking has, we believe, never before been attempted in this kingdom; mountains have been raised and levelled and a canal of a well's depth, has been cut almost under canal, in short it is not easy to convey a just idea of what human art and labour have in this particular instance accomplished. Three hundred labourers employed in the business. Some in digging, some in filling and the greater part in wheeling, in succession up the declivity for a mile in extent, their loaded barrows upon the stages erected for them, presents to the spectator a most pleasing, busy and novel scene and we sincerely hope that the spirited body who could attempt and the engineers who have executed, so great and expensive undertaking, will derive their due advantage from its good success.

> quantity of the Soil necessary to be removed previous to the Navigation's being made still Six feet lower – such Soil to be used in raising and strengthening the Banks of the Canal which have been damaged by the workings of the Coal Mines.

Second Stage

The second lowering, eliminating a further lock at each end, took another nine months and was opened for traffic in April 1790. Within three years, 100 boats a day were crossing the lowered summit compared with the 250 a week accounted by Smeaton during the summer months of 1782. The remaining three locks at Smethwick were duplicated to deal with the increased traffic. This now came up three locks at Spon Lane from the Wednesbury direction, or along the 15-mile (24km) long level from Wolverhampton. Houses at either end of the original summit by locks 6 and 7 had been dismantled and the material recycled to build others at Smethwick Engine and Tipton Green Junction, while Brasshouse Lane and Summit bridges were rebuilt.

Summit Bridge, 1790, now sandwiched between the 1860s railway bridge and mid-1970s Summit Tunnel.

The Smethwick Locks were not the only ones causing concern and in 1784 the deep and wasteful Wolverhampton Bottom Lock was rebuilt and a further one added above it, increasing the flight to twenty-one.

More Plans

Plans for further improvements followed. The Company's Act of 1794, authorizing the extension to Walsall with three collateral branches, to Bradley, Bilston and Willenhall, also approved building a cut between Bloomfield and Deepfields to shorten the original route running around Coseley. Including a tunnel, this was designed to cut about 3 miles (4.8km) off the distance between Wolverhampton and Birmingham. Work started from both ends, with the two arms completed by 1798, but ground to a stop in 1801 when it was decided that completion of the 13/4-mile (2.8km) length was 'not immediately necessary for public accommodation'.

Completion of the project would have to wait for a further thirty-six years, but in the meantime the unconnected arms were able to serve coal and ironstone mines. One branch originally included in the 1783 Act was completed, to Toll End. It came about after a request from several coal owners in the area, opening off the Broadwaters Extension and complete with two locks, in 1801. It was extended by January 1809 to meet the Tipton Green Locks and became the Tipton and Toll End Communication Canal, forming a new link between the Extension and the existing Main Line. The Birmingham Heath Branch, joining Matthew Boulton's Soho Works to the main line, was completed early in 1801 at the time of the enclosure of the Heath.

First Shortenings

In August 1807, following an inspection of the canal, the Committee was looking for further ways of shortening the route by removing some of the original extravagant bends in order to 'make a Cut in a straight line from Bridge to Bridge which would improve the Navigation and leave as much of the present Canal as may appear necessary to contain Boats out of employ & eligible situations for Dockyards which have been found annoyances upon the line of navigation'. This was concerned with improvements in Birmingham that were not immediately forthcoming, but, following the end of the Napoleonic Wars, the Company was able to consider rationalizing the line again and was able to implement improvements in the Oldbury area, between the Brades and Oldbury Brook. The work was let in two sections in May 1820, but hard rock at the Brades resulted in a cost twice the estimate. The great loop around Oldbury, where Brindley had expressed his 'disapprobation' at the idea of

Oldbury Loop cut-off

a tunnel, was cut off at the same time. It was a start, but a far more radical refinement would soon become necessary.

As the economy expanded, more efficient transport was needed. Turnpike mania had peaked just a few decades before its canal counterpart and there was now a whiff of steam in the air. The Birmingham Company, conscious of the growing threats, called in the Colossus of Roads himself in April 1824.

Thomas Telford

As Brindley had been the pre-eminent engineer of his day, so was Thomas Telford a half century later, becoming the first President of the Institution of Civil Engineers from 1820. In 1824, almost Brindley-busy and soon to be engaged in boring a tunnel parallel to the original at Harecastle, Telford was 'employed by the Birmingham Canal Company to plan and direct the several improvements requisite to be made on that canal'. This was the most far-reaching inspection of the Company and its assets since Smeaton's nearly four decades earlier and his report painted an unflattering picture of the BCN:

Upon inspection, I found adjacent to this great and flourishing town a canal little better than a crooked ditch with scarcely the appearance of a haling-path, the horses frequently sliding and staggering in the water, the haling-lines sweeping the gravel into the canal and the entanglement at the meeting of the boats incessant; while at the locks at each end of the short summit crowds of boatmen were always quarrelling, or offering premiums for a preference of passage, and the mine owners, injured by the delay, were loud in their just complaints.

The BCN now controlled over 70 miles (113km) of main line and branches, it had linked up with the Staffordshire & Worcestershire, Coventry, Dudley, Wyrley & Essington, Worcester & Birmingham and Warwick & Birmingham canals and had seen a great increase in traffic, with all the problems that brought to an overcrowded system. Telford's plan was of the man and of its time and was no less than building a new, straight main line, slicing through the loops and bypassing great lengths of the old canal. It was to carve through the hill at Smethwick and carry on,

Lee Bridge.

along the 453ft (183m) level, to ride on embankments above Tame's broad upper valley to join the 473ft (144m) level by way of three locks at Tipton. At the Birmingham end there was to be a large new reservoir at Rotton Park covering 80 acres (32 ha.) and with an average depth of more than 30ft (9m).

First Stage

The work between Birmingham and Smethwick was completed at the start of September 1827, when, as the *Birmingham Journal* reported, it was opened by 'three pleasure boats containing the Committee of the Old Birmingham Canal Company and their friends, accompanied by a band of music, playing cheerful airs'. The banks of the new line, shortening the distance by 1½ miles (2.4km) and the time taken by an hour, were lined with thousands of people. The works were still progressing towards Spon Lane and when finished 'will effect a direct communication between the town … and a considerable coal district without a single lock', while a single horse would be able to bring 'with ease' 50 tons of coal a day. The works were commended for:

> it may be justly stated, that for boldness of design, for skill and ability in the execution, for the extent of the facilities afforded to carriers, they are greatly superior to any other in the kingdom. The despatch and convenience too, afforded by the double towing path, can hardly be sufficiently appreciated.

Two great brick road bridges, Lee and Winson Green, built in 1826, cross the canal on the skew a mile or so from Birmingham. Lee Bridge, named after the prominent canal-supporting family, carried the Dudley Turnpike and, when built, had a 52ft (16m) span with a 66ft (20m) wide roadway and was 50ft (15.3m) askew.

The Mighty Smethwick Ditch

The most difficult section was the 'great excavation' at Smethwick, begun in March 1827 and completed by the end of 1829. This monumental work, precursor of the next generation's great railway cuttings, produced a canal 40ft (12m) wide, edged by large stone blocks and with a wide towpath on each side, lying at the foot of a 70ft (21m) deep cutting. The ground was excavated by men with picks and shovels and removed by others balancing wheelbarrows hauled by horses up planks.

Standing on Brasshouse Bridge, looking down along the cutting and imagining it in terms of hand shovelling, we can gain some idea of the size of the task and, even though vegetation has softened its features, the imagination can capture the impact that the bare gash would have had. Spanning this

Galton Bridge.

STEWARD AQUEDUCT

Telford's line burrowed under Brindley's cut near Spon Lane, where the double brick-arched Steward Aqueduct, named after Committee man Samuel Steward, was built to carry the latter.

Had the Company been in less of a hurry to open this length, the twin of Telford's aqueduct, carrying the Engine Branch over the New Main Line at Smethwick, might have stood here to complete a trio of magnificent cast-iron structures. As it was, to save time, Steward Aqueduct was brick-built. Even so, it is a potent transport location where the Old Main Line crosses the New, the railway runs alongside and the M5 shadows them all – a rare concentration of two centuries of transport history.

Steward Aqueduct.

Telford Aqueduct.

great artificial ditch – it is now known as the Galton Valley, though there was no valley until men came and dug it out – is the elegant cast-iron Galton Bridge. The longest, at 150ft (45.7m), and highest single span anywhere when it was built, the reason for its design was, according to Telford, 'safety combined with economy'. Built over the deepest part of the cutting, if the span had not been so long the abutments would have had to stretch the full depth, leading to 'an immense mass of masonry liable to bulge and be overthrown in rainy seasons' by the pressure of wet ground upon it. This was shown to be a responsible judgment; in November 1829, a landslip in the cutting, caused by the movement of just such wet ground, held up its completion for a month.

The ironwork of the bridge was cast by the Horseley Company, in nearby Tipton, who were also responsible for many of the standard bridges carrying the towpath over the canal and side arms. Although some of its visual power was diminished with the building of the Telford Way link road between Smethwick and the M5 and the covering over of the two canal lines in 1974, most visitors will still agree with its designer that the bridge 'produces variety by its appearance of lightness, which agreeably strikes every spectator of the massive works'.

On 18 December 1829, a convoy of coal boats from the Wednesbury line was able to pass through the great new cutting between the foot of Spon Lane Locks and what had just become Smethwick Junction. When a temporary barrier had been removed, 'a fleet of twenty-six boats loaded with coal immediately entered the line and the whole reached the town in two hours'. This contrasted with the five and a half hours taken originally over the Smethwick Locks, while the distance from the Wednesbury pits had been cut by 2 miles (3.2km) to 7¼ miles (11.7km).

The Island Line and Beyond

Work on the major remaining lengths, the Island Line between Albion and Tipton, and the Bloomfield to Deepfields stretch, were begun but curtailed. The improvements were costing a great deal of money and several other cuts such as the Anson and Ridgacre branches, tapping new reserves of coal, were also under way. It is perhaps not surprising, with so much happening, that the BCN promoted a new Bill to 'consolidate, extend, amend and render more effective' the powers granted by all previous Acts. It also included powers to build seven new cuts, which would allow completion of the Island Line, Factory Locks, the Titford Canal and Coseley Tunnel. The 360yd (330m) tunnel was shorter than the one originally authorized in 1794. It was built, not without difficulty as the ground was broken by old workings, between 1835–7 and was widely reported as being opened on 6 October: 'Considered with reference to its extraordinary dimensions, the difficulties encountered in the execution of it and the important purposes it is calculated to effect, this tunnel may be justly deemed one of the most important public works of the present day.'

Although Telford had died in September 1834, the twin towpath design was his, as well as the imagination that had conjured up a scheme greatly reducing the canal distance between Birmingham and Wolverhampton and finally cutting off the wandering 4¼ miles (6.8km) of what became

---

SUCCESS OF THE TITFORD CANAL: COMMITTEE MINUTES, 23 APRIL 1841

OF THE IMPORTANCE OF THE SERVICE RENDERED BY THE TITFORD CANAL IN KEEPING DOWN THE PRICE OF COAL AT THIS JUNCTURE, IT IS SCARCELY POSSIBLE TO SPEAK IN ADEQUATE TERMS. THOUGH THE TIME ELAPSED SINCE THE OPENING OF THE NEW COMMUNICATION IS LITTLE MORE THAN 3 YEARS, AND THOUGH SCARCELY A PIT WAS SUNK IN THE DISTRICT PRIOR TO COMMENCING THE CANAL, THE ENTERPRISE OF THE MINERS HAS BEEN SUCH, THAT THE QUANTITY LET DOWN BY THE LOCKS IN THE LAST MONTH WAS RATHER MORE THAN 17,000 TONS, EXHIBITING AN INSTANCE OF RAPIDITY IN MINING OPERATIONS ALMOST WITHOUT PARALLEL, AND AFFORDING INCONTESTABLE PROOF OF THE SOUNDNESS OF THE VIEWS ON WHICH THE CANAL WAS UNDERTAKEN.

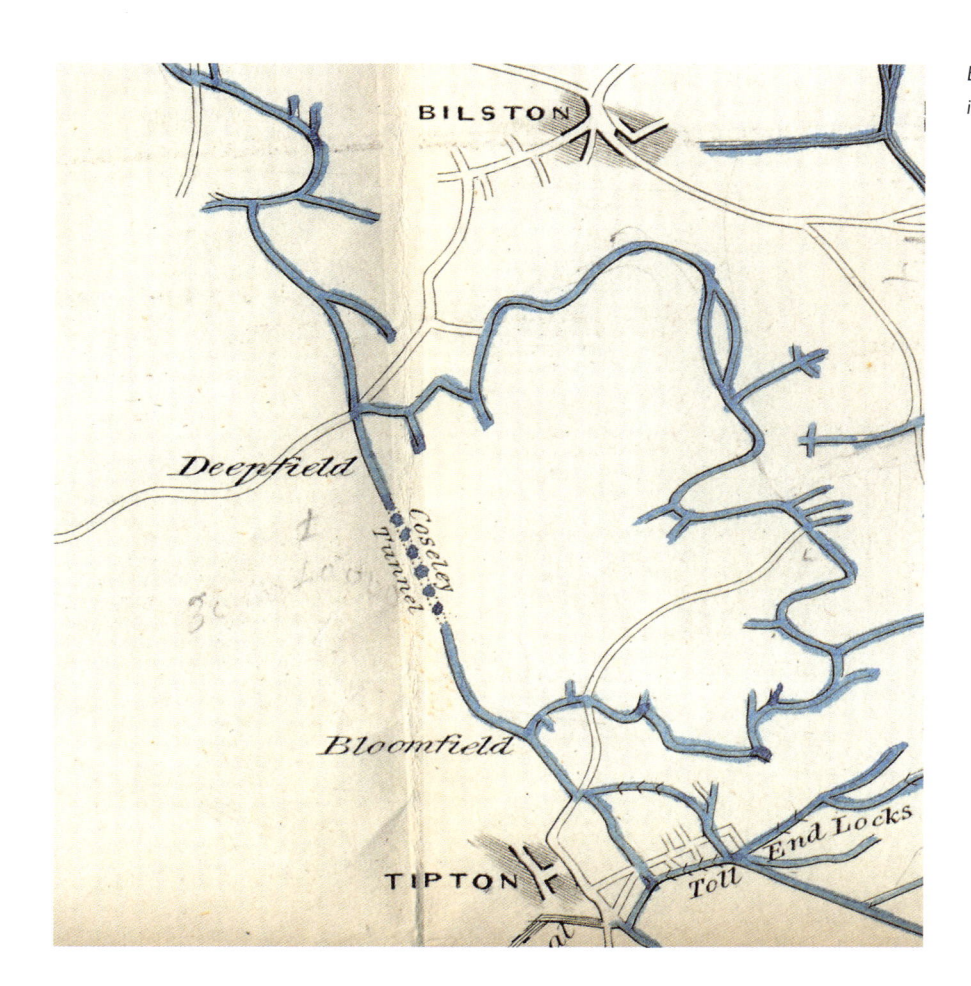

Bloomfield–Deepfields improvements.

Deepfields Junction, 1994. Original Birmingham Canal to left, Coseley Tunnel portal under the white house.

Brades Locks. Thomas Clayton's boat Frome *entering the staircase lock, 1960s.*

the Wednesbury Oak loop. The Titford Canal, climbing six locks later known as 'The Crow', was finished around the same time as the tunnel, opening up large new reserves of coal.

With the Island Line incomplete, traffic from the Wolverhampton side still had to follow the old line and descend Smethwick Locks and mine owners were complaining. The Gower Branch already reached from Albion Junction to within 300yd (274m) of the old line and it was extended, in 1836, to a junction with the old line at Brades Hall. This climbed three locks, the top two forming the only staircase on the BCN.

The Island Line was completed, opening in April 1838, and further works of widening and deepening towards Wolverhampton and Aldersley continued into the next year. The Island Line intersected the Tipton Green and Toll End Communications, giving an additional link between the Birmingham and Walsall levels, while the opening of Bradley Locks in 1841 created a new link between the latter and Wolverhampton levels.

Facts

In August 1838, Company Clerk John Freeth was able to report to the Committee a 'Statement of Fact' about the new works. The canal route between Wolverhampton and Birmingham had been shortened by 7 miles (11.3km), from 20 to 13 miles (32 to 21km), the 'Navigable Route … is now less in length than either the Railway, or the Turnpike Road', the great bulk of trade would no longer need to use the locks at Smethwick, the improvements 'surpass greatly all other Works of the kind in the Kingdom' and the heavy expense incurred by the works had been defrayed by the Company without any increase in tolls. Freeth went on to point out that one effect of the shortening 'has been to subject the Company to a reduction of nearly Six Miles of Tonnage on all Commodities passing between Birmingham & Wolverhampton' and that, to obtain the Act, the BCN was forced to make several permanent reductions of rates, including one of 50 per cent in the Worcester Bar Lock toll on coal. The 'Railway', the Grand Junction, only skirted the Black Country area. but its mention gives an indication of the Company's appreciation of the threat it implied.

Improvements on the Wyrley

Negotiations between the BCN and the Wyrley & Essington Canal, leading to amalgamation in 1840, had been protracted, but building new links between them followed swiftly. The first, shortest and most

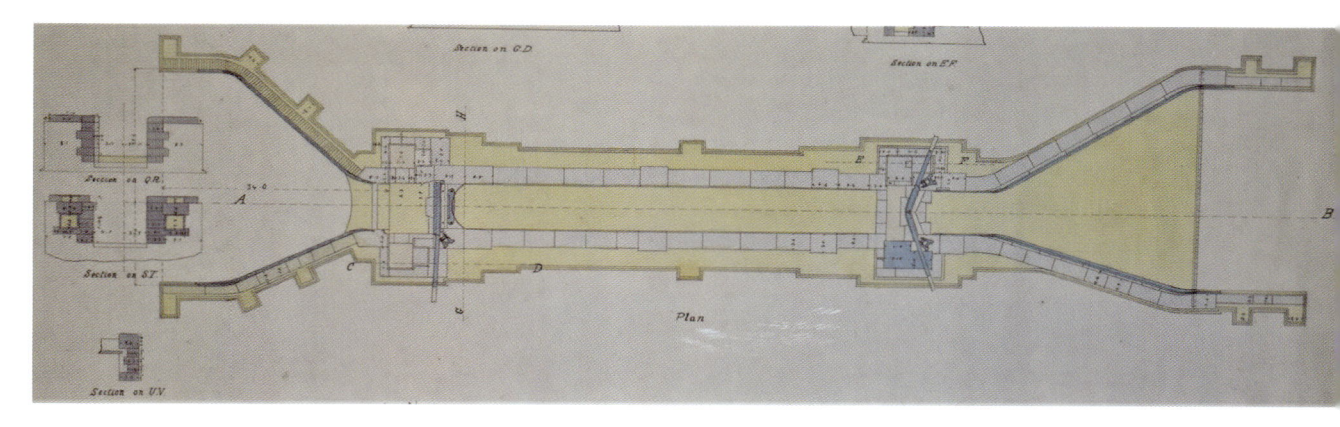

Bentley Canal lock plan.

Fishley Bridge. Remains of original W&E Bridge and BCN replacement.

logical, was the Walsall Junction Canal, opened on 25 March 1841. Its eight locks in five furlongs (1km) joined two points previously 20 miles (32km) apart by canal. With all its advantages – 'The local trader will be relieved, the voyage to Autherley quickened, and the conveyance of heavy commodities from the Walsall level to the Trent much facilitated', along with the fact that it 'has long been wanted by the public' – it is surprising that it was not built earlier.

There were problems with the new lock paddle machinery and, as the Company was also engaged in building flights at Perry Barr and Bentley, they were seeking an explanation. Engineer James Walker knew about the problems, which in part were down to bad workmanship, but was keen to resolve the matter so that 'the locks now building should be free from similar defects and be in every respect adapted to obtain the end in view (the giving of every possible dispatch to the Trade)'. He was having a complete set of paddle gear made in London for a full trial at one of the Bentley Locks 'before proceeding to apply similar machinery at the other locks'.

At the same time, John Freeth was able to report on 'a series of well combined and energetic measures' on the Wyrley Canal. About 20 miles (32km) had been put into good order, with the whole of the main line between Wolverhampton and the top of Ogley Locks being 'well scoured, deepened and widened', so that it was now 'perhaps in a better shape than it ever was before'. Most of the locks were reconstructed, including refacing the walls with blue engineering bricks and replacing the copings. Bridges were also substantially repaired and guarded, culverts strengthened and the towing path improved.

Resultant increases in traffic led to a recirculating pumping station being built at the top of Walsall Locks. The Bentley Canal, climbing through ten locks from the BCN's Anson Branch to the Wyrley & Essington at Wednesfield Junction, opened in 1843. The third connection, the Rushall Canal, had been opened in 1837, following completion of the BCN's next major route.

The Bypass: Tame Valley Canal

With the main-line improvements completed and running smoothly, the Company turned its attention to Birmingham itself. The thirteen Farmer's Bridge Locks caused great congestion, having to pass a vast volume of traffic off the Birmingham Navigations and the Worcester & Birmingham Canal heading for Fazeley and Warwick. *Aris's Birmingham Gazette* on 20 May 1839 reported this.

Rebuilding the canal at Farmer's Bridge with parallel locks would have been difficult and expensive. It had been costed at over £60,000 in 1830 and this had more than doubled by the end of the decade. There had been earlier proposals for a Birmingham bypass cut from the Danks Branch, opened in 1809 from the foot of Ryders Green Locks to Golds Hill colliery and ironworks. This was to run as far as Salford Bridge and join the canal to Fazeley, but through opposition and uncertainty about the mineral potential of the area, the work was not carried out. As far back as 1782, John Smeaton had pointed out that 'to make a navigation from Wednesbury

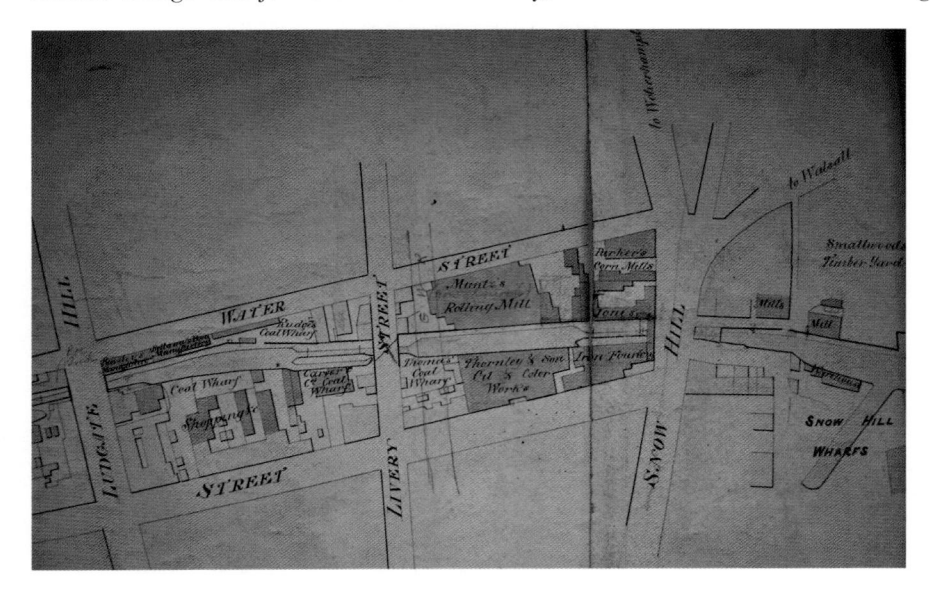

ARIS'S BIRMINGHAM GAZETTE,
20 MAY 1839

The flight of locks at Farmer's Bridge, at the upper part of the town of Birmingham, constitutes the only channel through which iron, coal and minerals are supplied to the lower part, and through which similar products and goods from the upper part of town are conveyed through the Warwick and Coventry Canals to distant markets.

Although these locks are kept open day and night, and also upon Sundays, several branches of trade, to avoid delay at them, have been diverted through other channels; the pressure upon them during the autumnal and winter months is excessive, from twenty to thirty boats being found frequently at the top and as many at the bottom of the locks waiting for a passage.

Nearly seventy steam engines and about 124 wharfs and works are already seated on the banks of the canals between Farmer's Bridge and Bordesley and Aston, and therefore some measure for the relief of the trade passing to the lower part of the town of Birmingham has become indispensably necessary.

The crowded nature of Farmer's Bridge Locks, late 1840s.

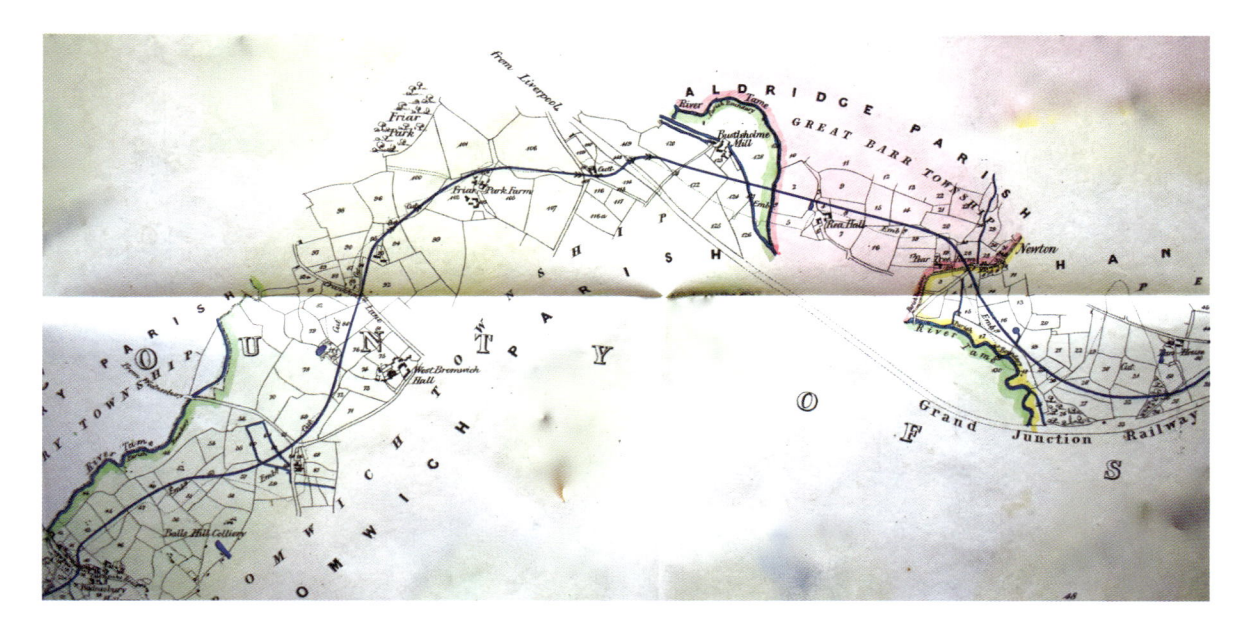

Plan of part of the TVC. The line west of the railway was straightened and 1-mile (1.6km) long, 40ft (12m) high embankment constructed instead of locks.

The cleanly efficient line of the cut would have run through open country when built at Perry Barr Locks.

Taylor Aqueduct.

to Fazly, nothing can be better adapted in point of ground, through so long a course of country, than to pursue the course of the river Tame'. The Act, for a canal from the Danks Branch to Salford Bridge via Perry Barr was passed in 1839 and a further one, altering the line following suggestions from engineers Walker and Burges, the following year.

James Walker was one of the leading engineers of the day, building docks from London to Leith and lighthouses for Trinity House, as well as being involved with numerous railways. Tenders for the Tame Valley Canal and also the Bentley Canal were advertised in November, 'to be delivered in, on or before the 8th day of January 1841'. Striding down the broad valley over a series of high embankments and deep cuttings, the 8½-mile (14km) canal descends 106ft (32m) through Perry Barr Locks, known as the New Thirteen to distinguish them from the Old ones at Farmer's Bridge. Its most intriguing location must surely be Taylor Aqueduct. Here the canal, opened in February 1844, crossed the Grand Junction Railway of 1837, likely the first time a canal crossed an earlier railway.

Apart from a rash of pits and ironworks at its western end, the land crossed by the canal was largely open and agricultural. It cut straight across the Bustleholme Mill pond, so that a culvert had to be provided under the high embankment to supply the mill with water from its shrunken pool. Easy access to transport encouraged the development of sandpits beside the canal and the sinking of Hamstead Colliery, begun in 1875, on the concealed coalfield east of the boundary fault. Loading basins were built, but much of the Tame Valley route retained a semi-rural aspect until the mid-twentieth century spread of housing.

More Links

The Tame Valley Canal directed traffic towards Fazeley rather than passing it through Birmingham on to the Warwick & Birmingham Canal. The latter company proposed and financed the Birmingham & Warwick Junction Canal running for under 3 miles (4.8km) up six locks between Salford and Bordesley Junctions. Although opposed by the BCN on the usual water-supply grounds, this short bypass opened on the same day as the Tame Valley.

The year 1847 saw the opening of the Rushall Canal, joining the Tame Valley with the Daw End Branch of the former Wyrley & Essington by its

Riddian Bridge.

Rushall Canal. The W&E branch to Hay Head on the left.

terminus at Hay Head. There could hardly be a clearer demonstration of the near half-century development in civil engineering than the contrast between the meandering lock-free Daw End cut with its graceful red brick, round-arched Riddian Bridge, and the purposeful straight line of the Rushall, falling through nine locks and passing under engineering brick and steel decked bridges.

Never industrialized, the Rushall Canal fell through an open landscape between the 473ft (144m) Wolverhampton and the 408ft (124m) Walsall levels. Exposed to easterly winds, it was a place where boatmen would put on extra clothing, leading to the nickname for the flight, 'Ganzeys', from the Guernsey jumpers worn by watermen of all kinds. A boaters' rhyme named the lock flights on the trip from the top of Rushall to Birmingham: 'Mosses Two, the Ganzeys Seven, the New Thirteen and the Lousy 'leven, with a boat coming up, a boat coming down and another one a-standing in the 'ospital pound'. Aston Locks were 'lousy', as it was where dossers would get in the boats to sleep, so steerers coming to collect one in the morning might throw a bucket of water into the cabin first, in case.

A 'Cause of Immense Benefit': Netherton Tunnel

Dudley Tunnel had long been a bottleneck for traffic passing between the east and west of the Black

Country. The restricted nature of the bore meant that one-way working was necessary, with convoys of boats passing through during alternating four-hour slots. Men lay on their backs on the cargo and legged boats through, pushing with their feet against the tunnel walls and roof. A typical transit would take about two hours, there could be waiting times of several days, and a traffic survey recorded the passage of 41,704 boats in 1853, an average of 800 per week. The merger of the Dudley Canal with the BCN in 1846 led to wholesale improvements west of the watershed.

Following a request in June 1854 from the Iron & Coal Masters and other traders of South Staffordshire for a new tunnel under the Rowley Hills, the Committee resolved on a special report into the state of the Dudley canals and the resultant actions to be taken. John Freeth and agent Mr Thomas presented their report on 28 July. It described a well-used canal running partly through a heavily mined area that would benefit from the kind of development the Company had been actively pursuing for the past thirty years. Where there had been no mining, the canal was in a 'tolerably fair state', but in other places the banks were very weak and the puddles very low: 'They require immediate attention and more vigilance than heretofore to keep them at all times at a proper height.' Some lengths were made up mainly of banks and curves, including the much complained about Bumble Hole Turn, and long lengths of the towing path were used as wharves, where 'the inconveniences and hindrances caused thereby, can hardly be described'. The area around Parkhead running up to the end of Dudley Tunnel had been 'much sunk lately by Mining Operations' and some of the bridges were dilapidated for the same reason.

The solution (apart from more vigilance than heretofore!) was to involve altering the canal line in places, strengthening banks, building the Two Lock Line (proposed in the 1830s but never constructed), rebuilding the nine locks at the Delph, widening bridges and, critically for all the rest, building a new tunnel. The cost for all these works was estimated at £238,000. James Walker, now senior partner in the firm of Walker, Burges & Cooper, had overall responsibility for the latter, designing the tunnel and new canal and steering the Bill for the works through Parliament. The directness of the cut and the sheer scale of the tunnel, with a length of 3,027yd (2,768m), a width of 27ft (8m) comprising a 17ft (5.2m) channel and twin 5ft (1.5m) towing paths and a clearance of 16ft (4.9m), show the influence and inspiration of Thomas Telford, whom Walker had succeeded as President of the Institution of Civil Engineers. They also show the developments in engineering that had occurred. Netherton is truly a canal tunnel of the railway age.

The Act authorizing the new cut between Dudley Port on the New Main Line and Windmill End on the Dudley Canal was passed in July 1855, the work went out to tender, and that of George Meakin, civil engineer of Birkenhead was accepted, at an estimate of £176,000. James Ralph Walker, James's nephew, was appointed resident engineer with seven inspectors of works as assistants. The first sod was cut by the Earl of Dudley on the site of construction shaft No.7 at Oakham on 28 December 1855, 'in the presence of three or four hundred of the leading gentry, landowners, ironmasters, colliery proprietors &c. of the district'. The spade with which the ceremony was performed bore the following inscription: 'Presented to the Right Honourable Lord Ward, for the purpose of turning the first sod of the new canal and tunnel to be called the Netherton Tunnel'. The reverse bore the names of BCN Chairman Sir George Nicholls, the engineers and contractor.

Not everyone agreed with the name for the undertaking. In the preface to a new edition of his book about the South Staffordshire Coalfield, eminent geologist Joseph Beete Jukes commented on the 'driving of the tunnel beneath the Rowley Hills, which by a rather unfortunate misnomer is called Netherton Tunnel'. This may have been an emotional reaction, as he was rather piqued by not having had the opportunity to visit the works and inspect the Rowley basalt before the tunnel was finished.

Building the Tunnel

Sinking the first shaft started on 17 January 1856 and on 19 March the excavation of the tunnel itself was begun at shaft No.15; there were seventeen in all, the deepest being 350ft (107m). On the surface, the shaft sites were linked by a 2ft gauge railway bringing materials from stockpiles on the canals at both ends. Following shaft sinking, pilot tunnels were driven to link them, before excavating the rest of the material to full section and bricking up the invert, walls and arch. The accuracy and quality of the work meant that no section of the finished tunnel was more than 1in (25mm) out of line. From starting to sink the first shaft to laying the last brick – by James Walker in the arch between No.7 and No.8 shafts – took two years and seven months. The bricks, around 26.5 million of them, were all fired in yards at Tividale, Old Hill and Oldbury, within a mile of the site, and the brickwork itself is nearly 2ft (0.6m) thick in the walls and arch, and thicker where the ground was bad. This was to be expected, as 'the district through which the tunnel went was peculiar, the land was perforated by mines, and liable to sinking and shaking'. A result of this was that the invert stretched the whole length of the tunnel and heavy and massive retaining walls were needed at each portal.

The work was not without its share of accidents. In September 1857, Joseph Smith, one of the inspectors, was killed while ascending a shaft, being knocked out of the skip by a trolley falling from the top. It appeared that 'some men at the top of the pit were putting a skip in readiness to send down the pit when they accidentally pushed it too far'. A verdict of accidental death was returned at the inquest, which noted that the deceased 'when taken up was quite dead, several of his limbs being broken'. Early the following year, the *Wolverhampton Chronicle* reported the death of William Woodhall, accidentally killed when a large quantity of clay falling from the roof 'completely smothered the poor fellow'.

Opening

The tunnel was declared open on 20 August 1858 to the usual round of celebrations. The day itself was not without incident, when, after the formal ceremony, the tunnel was opened to traffic and there was 'a rush of boats to pass through it, each striving to be the first to accomplish the passage. In the contest two boats were sunk and several men thrown into the water, but no accident to life or limb took place'. The opening proceedings had been lavish and were widely reported. Sir George Nicholls with the Committee and 'a large body of gentlemen interested in the undertaking' travelled in the company's 'elegant barge' from Birmingham to Dudley Port Station, where they were met by 'a large number of influential gentlemen invited to "assist" in the ceremony'. The station was 'gaily decorated … with evergreens, flowers and flags'. The party, travelling in eight boats, set off to turn at Dudley Port Junction into the tunnel branch. On arrival at the tunnel mouth, each boat's company gave several loud cheers, 'which were repeated at intervals as the boats progressed'. One of the tunnel's innovations was gas lighting and for the opening ceremony 'triumphal arches and designs in gas

Netherton Tunnel Branch leading to the north portal. The Old Main Line crosses on Tividale Aqueduct.

were introduced, and produced a very agreeable and pleasing effect'.

Continuing, the convoy went towards the Two Lock Line and on to Delph Locks, before returning to Park Head where the boats were left and most of the party walked to the Hotel Dudley, for 'a most sumptuous and recherché repast', comprising every delicacy of the season, followed by more toasts and speeches. Meanwhile, the Company's Clerks and agents were being entertained in the Committee boat 'anchored near the Lodge Farm Reservoir for the purpose', where the evening was spent 'in a most enjoyable manner'.

The last word is left to Sir George Nicholls, whose efforts were fundamental in steering the scheme through to its conclusion. The Tunnel, he said:

> would be the means of bringing into the eastern district the surplus produce of the western district and it would amalgamate the two districts and bring them into effective and active operation. It would be the cause of immense benefit to the enormous population around Dudley, and to the great and important towns of Birmingham and Wolverhampton.

High Bridge.

Blackbrook Junction, stub of the Two Lock Line to left, 1973.

Delph Locks, 1981.

Connected Works

The largest share of the £302,000 outlay on the improvements had been spent on the tunnel, but it needed the other planned works to achieve its full effectiveness. The southern end of the tunnel emerged at Windmill End where the Dudley Canal looped around in the area known as Bumble Hole. Here the solution was to use spoil from the cuttings leading to the tunnel to build up a high embankment for a new straight canal with twin towpaths. Windmill End became the site of a canal crossroads, with the old Dudley No.2 crossing the new line. The short tunnel at Lodge Farm, known as Brewin's after its engineer, was opened out, the tough rocks enabling a steep-sided cutting to be made, above which was built the fine single-span red and blue brick High Bridge.

Nearby, a Horseley Works Bridge still stands to mark the entrance to the Two Lock Line. First planned in the 1830s, it was finally built in 1858 along a high embankment across the Blackbrook valley. Only 3 furlongs (600m) in length and with a lock at each end, it saved the best part of 1 mile (1.6km) for boats not using Dudley Tunnel. The final piece was the rebuilding of the Delph Locks. In use since 1779, the nine locks had been badly damaged by subsidence and their design, with some very short pounds not long enough to hold a boat, caused serious hold-ups. Curving away down the hillside, the middle seven locks were replaced by a new straight flight of six, the top and bottom locks being retained but rebuilt. The pounds were long enough for boats to pass in and were connected to each other by waterfall weirs.

Cannock Extension

The last major canal built by the BCN was the Cannock Extension. The Cannock Chase coalfield made up the northern part of the South Staffordshire coalfield, where large-scale development occurred later than in the Black Country and at a time when the older colliery areas were being worked or drowned out. The Extension ran from Pelsall Junction on the Wyrley & Essington to Hednesford Basin north of Cannock, over 5½ miles (9km) on the 473ft (144m) level, and was fully opened in 1863. It was about 90ft (27.4m) higher than the Staffordshire & Worcestershire's Churchbridge Branch, which terminated about half a mile (680m) to the south-west of Rumer Hill on the Extension line. The two companies agreed to build an interconnecting flight of thirteen locks rising steeply in a straight line to Rumer Hill Junction on the Extension. The cost of the land was shared, but the Staffordshire & Worcestershire paid for the locks, finished in 1860 but not used until the Extension's completion three years later. Around the same time, the feeder from Chasewater Reservoir was rebuilt to navigable standards as the Anglesey Branch to serve mines worked by the eponymous Marquess.

Summary

In 1913, Company Engineer George Jebb summarized the great extent of the BCN, which then had a length of about 159 miles (256km), along with some 550 private basins and short branches, and the various levels were joined by 216 locks. It would grow no more.

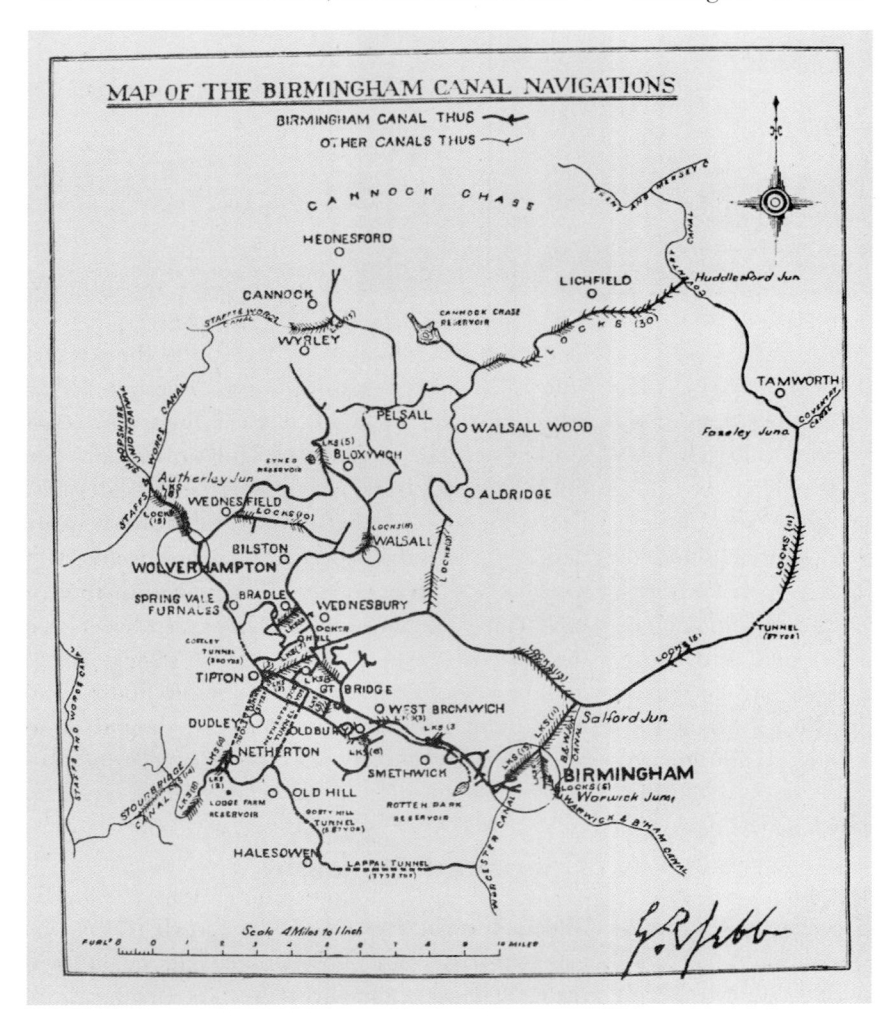

George Jebb's Map of the BCN, 1913.

CHAPTER 4

Water Supply

> 'WE HAVE BEEN FORTUNATE IN AN AMPLE SUPPLY OF WATER FROM THE HEAVENS.'

Unfortunately, the situation alluded to above, in a letter from John Houghton to a gentleman in Bristol in 1797, was not always the case and maintaining an adequate water supply on such an elevated navigation was a continuing problem for the Proprietors of the Birmingham Canal and their successors, who had adopted the Birmingham Canal Navigations name in 1794. The original Act had given the Company powers to take water from all 'Springs, Brooks, Streams and Watercourses' found while building the cut, and from brooks, streams and watercourses within 1,000yd (914m) of the line. It could also build reservoirs within the same bounds. This soon proved to be 'too short a distance'. The June 1768 decision to alter the canal at Smethwick had caused the Committee to send Samuel Simcock scurrying to measure any possible supply for the locks and in the following year's rectifying Act, the powers for making reservoirs were extended to a distance within 3 miles (4.8km) of the cut 'lying between the Two extreme Locks constructed or intending to be constructed between the Villages of Smethwick and Oldbury'. Provision was also included to build reservoirs between Bilston and Aldersley, though this was never taken up.

Reservoirs

Smethwick

In May 1769, Brindley proposed a reservoir on 'Lord Dartmouth's Land on the Summit' to be contained by a 'Bank with waiste Soil from the Canal'. He went on to stress that 'proper means should be taken to enquire into the most expedient methods of bringing ample supplies of Water to the Summit' and, together with Mr Bentley, he would make 'the needful Enquiries' and report back to the Committee. On 25 August, the Committee was looking into securing a mill in Smethwick 'in order to supply the Canal with water'. In November, Brindley was recommending the strengthening and raising of the dam of the 'Pool at Smethwick' and that Simcock should investigate the mills and streams higher up to locate sites for reservoirs. He should also measure the amount of land required 'in case the Damn [sic] of the said pool shall be raised four feet, five feet, or six feet'.

Work was progressing on the Great Smethwick Reservoir by the following February when Dr Small and Matthew Boulton examined it, concluding that 'the Instructions given by Mr Brindley and the methods now proceeding ... are exceedingly proper'. However, progress slowed and Brindley considered that 'as it cannot be finished to be usefull this summer', some of the workmen should be moved to work on the dam head or anywhere else on the canal that needed them. In July 1770, it was recorded that the summit 'is Daily some Inches under Level, The Feed Drain from the reservoir, & the reservoir itself not near finished'. A month later, the situation was improving with a request that 'the feeder be finished with all possible Expedition in order that the Water from the Reservoir may be brought into the Canal'. This was followed by a resolution that 'Bannister do set his own men immediately' to work on the feeder and a final plea that 'Bannister do immediately get all possible assistance to finish the feeder'. Although finished, the reservoir not entirely a success and, in May 1771, Brindley was advising 'that for the better stopping the Leakages in the Reservoir, that Cattle be put to Graze about the Edges of the pool to tread in the Soil, and muddy the Water, as the only temporary means to stop it'. It was never a complete solution and the leaks continued to prove problematical.

The new reservoir was large enough to drown a track leading from the main road to the Church, School and Old Chapel Inn and so it was necessary to build a replacement; in July 1771, the Committee resolved that 'the Road at the tail of the Reservoir up to Smethwick Chapel be immediately finished'. The Great Reservoir held 1,514 locks' worth of water and its smaller neighbour 100. Both appear on William Wright's 1773 map, with a feeder from the small to the Great reservoir and another running from there to the summit above the sixth lock.

Smethwick Reservoirs

From a survey of Smethwick made by Henry Jacob in 1828 and re-drawn, with plot details added, by Smethwick Local History Society.

Smethwick Reservoirs.

> **FISHING**
>
> Water always attracts people and in June 1774 the Committee thought it necessary that 'Notice be given in the Church at Smithwick that all persons Fishing in the Reservoir … will be prosecuted as the Law Directs'. Perhaps the offenders were not churchgoers, as by September they were resolving that 'Handbills be published and dispersed about Smithwick' offering a five-guinea reward for the detection and conviction of anyone found fishing. Several people were prosecuted for the offence the following January. It was a continuing problem and, in June 1787, after Bull reported that the reservoirs had been frequently fished by poachers, he was instructed to apply to the magistrates for warrants and notices warning against fishing and trespass were put up.

Smethwick Reservoir continued to give problems. In a report submitted in May 1773, Samuel Bull stated that the 'Weir at the Grate Pool wants properly fixing with Stone and a Gate 4 foot Wide properly fix'd to Check and Lower the water when wanted'.

Following Telford's improvements, the Great Reservoir was no longer needed, being drained and the land let in 1833. The site of the dam is still apparent on the 6in Ordnance Survey map of 1890, when there was a gravel pit in its bed, but building work was under way by 1905 and it was largely covered with houses by 1921. Walking up Smethwick High Street away from the town centre, the lie of the land behind aptly named Watery Lane still conjures up an impression of where it once lay, while Millpool Way harks back to even earlier times. The Small Reservoir fared better, named as such on a map of 1828 and surviving still as a pool in a park at Stony Lane.

'Improper Liberties'

One problem was caused by the canal itself bringing water into an area not notably blessed with natural supplies. It was not too difficult to build a 'trunk', a pipe or channel by which water could be drawn off the canal. This was especially the case in the proliferating private basins where 'plugs' were inserted to drain the basins for maintenance or cleaning, but could also be used illicitly as a free water supply. In July 1772, Bull was instructed to stop up and secure a trunk under the canal feeding into Mr Hipkiss's graving dock so that no water could go that way. He was also instructed that 'Mr Morgan's Letter relating to the abuse of water there be carefully preserved in the Office'. At the same time, Mr Tomkys was informed that if he tried to 'drive a sough to the injury of the Canal, he must take the Consequences'. The problem did not go away and in December 1777 the subject of 'Mr Tomkys having injured the Canal by making a Dock and a valve' was raised. He had used it to send water to his mill, having availed himself even when there was a great scarcity, while the following July it was reported that Messrs Bourne and Co. had made soughs from the canal by which they took water into their works 'at pleasure … much to the prejudice of the Canal'.

In July 1785, with the Committee already concerned about the taking of 'improper liberties with the Company's Water', the illicit removal of a plug at Aston's Basin at Tipton Field resulted in a great loss. The Committee reiterated that plugs had been put in 'merely for the purpose of occasionally cleaning the Canal and such Basons, which can now be done without such plugs' and resolved that all those in the canal banks would be taken up. In the case of plugs in basins, they should be removed and any refusal to do so would result in the stop gates into the basins being shut up. It was further decided to put a notice in the paper offering a twenty-guinea reward to anyone giving information leading to the discovery and conviction of any offender.

Titford Pools

The notion of another reservoir, about a mile south of Oldbury at Titford, was raised by Brindley in January 1772; the landowner was approached in October, a survey ordered in November and a contract arranged for the land on the first day of 1773. Negotiations rumbled on for a couple of months, but by May work was in progress for there had been complaints about 'the imperfect manner of executing the Dam'. Robinson, the contractor, was to finish the work, but it would need to be examined by 'some proper person' to make sure that it had been 'executed in a perfectly Workman like manner,

Titford Pumphouse.

before the water is let in'. In July, the Committee was inspecting the works so that they could give orders for its completion and it was in use the following year. Covering an area of 9 acres (3.6ha) and fed by rainfall from the Rowley Hills, the reservoir supplied water along a 1½-mile (2.4km) long feeder to the summit 80ft (24.4m) below.

There were times when the reservoirs struggled and on May Day 1775 water was low and the reservoirs exhausted. A plan and estimate for enlarging the reservoir for £706 19s 6d was submitted to the Committee in April 1777 and was referred for future consideration. Proper control of water was essential, but not always practised. In September 1782, Richard Robinson, who 'was intrusted with that business', was brought before the Committee to explain why water had been drawn out of the reservoir in such quantities that the summit was more than 2in (51mm) above level, by which 'a very great waste of Water was occasion'd'.

A new feeder, from Titford to Rotton Park Reservoir, was built at the time of Telford's improvements, replacing the original, and in 1836–7 a new canal. Rising 38ft (11.6m) from the Old Main Line through six locks, the branch met the widened feeder by a new engine house constructed to recirculate water between the Wolverhampton level and the 511ft (156m) Titford level. Now using electric pumps, this still functions, back-pumping water up from below the locks to augment the feed from the Pools to Rotton Park.

Recreation

On 21 July 1783, *Aris's Birmingham Gazette* contained an advertisement warning of prosecution 'of the utmost Rigour' for persons found trespassing, including 'ANGLING, and otherwise fishing', bathing, or sending dogs in the canal at Titford and Smethwick Reservoirs. The situation had changed by the early twentieth century, when the Pools were used for recreation until the First World War.

The site was reopened by the Titford Lake Company in 1933 as Titford Pleasure Park and restocked with 10,000 fish. They built a refreshment room, putting green and shooting range; boats and punts could be hired and motorboat trips were laid on. Concerts and boxing matches were held, often presided over by Jack Judge, local music-hall entertainer, best known for writing the song *It's a Long Way to Tipperary*. Rumours of a monster in the Pools surfaced a year or so before the Lake Company folded at the start of the Second World War. According to the local news, a Professor from the University of Inverness, an expert on

> **Fishing! Fishing! Fishing!**
> **Titford Pool, Langley, nr. Birmingham.**
> Langley Green Station, G.W.R., 10 minutes walk. Rowley Station, G.W.R., 20 minutes walk. Oldbury Station, L.&N.W., 25 minutes walk. Tram Cars, 10 minutes walk.
> Terms:—Angling 1/- per day. Half-day, after 1 p.m., 6d.
> Day Tickets issued for PIKE.
> THE BOWLING GREEN IS NOW OPEN.
> Mineral Waters and Light Refreshments provided at the Pool.
> Admission to Pool and Grounds, 2d.
> **M. COMLEY & SONS, Proprietors.**

Titford Pools advert.

'Nessie', was to visit. The truth was only revealed a quarter-century later when a local man admitted being behind the ruse. Mind, there had been a clue in the so-called academic's qualifications – Professor Hamish McGreig, I.S.A., L.I.A.R.

In 1948, the West Midland Group on Post-War Reconstruction And Planning, which included worthies such as a real Professor, the geographer Sir Laurence Dudley Stamp, along with scions of the Cadbury family, including George, a member of the Docks & Inland Waterways Executive of the British Transport Commission, produced *Conurbation, A Survey of Birmingham and the Black Country*. Contrasting the war- and industry-ravaged landscapes of the region with their vision of the future, one section, a 'Design for Oldbury', highlighted the authors' aspirations for Titford Pools, which were to become 'water gardens, designed for calmness and quiet prospects … adapted from the canal and its disused basins'.

What might have been – Titford Pools possibilities, Conurbation.

In Titford Pools, 2016.

This never came to fruition and instead, in the early 1970s, the M5 Oldbury Viaduct planted its concrete legs in the Pools and deposited increasing amounts of silt from surface water drainage, rendering them difficult to access and navigate. Efforts have been made over the years to encourage boating up to the Pools, including Inland Waterways Association (IWA) National Rallies in 1978 and 1982.

In July 2019, the Canal & River Trust began a two-year project of dredging and vegetation management to open the Pools and encourage more wildlife to the area in order to develop 'a thriving nature reserve with lots of animals and insects flying and fluttering around and with colourful boats in the pools'.

Further Reservoirs

The BCN also inherited reservoirs from its constituent canals. The 1840 merger with the Wyrley & Essington brought the ones at Sneyd and Cannock Chase. The former, built to the west of the locks and in use by early 1795, failed in early June 1799 following a period of heavy rainfall, requiring 'compleat and substantial repair' to the dams and feeders. The extension of the Wyrley Canal with its long flight of locks down to Huddlesford increased the demand for water, and Norton Bog, as the name suggests, was a suitable location for the company's next and main reservoir, begun around 1796. A mile or so north of Brownhills, Norton Pool was formed by damming two streams to cover 81 acres (33ha) of land. Like Sneyd, it too failed in June when the water 'swept everything before it … through Shenstone, Hopwas, Drayton &c, till it fell into the Tame at Tamworth'. Rushing down the valley of the Black Brook, the deluge destroyed a newly built bridge, drowned sheep and cattle, and caused damage 'calculated at many thousands of pounds'. Had it not been for early witnesses riding to warn farmers so they that could move their stock to high ground, it could have been much worse.

Messrs Bradburn and Pitt, Canal Company Proprietor and Surveyor, were requested to attend 'a meeting of the respective persons having sustained injury by the Dam of the Reservoir having given way … in order to hear their account of damages and to endeavour to treat with them for the value'. This included compensation for damage caused to Blackbrook Bridge. The dam was rebuilt wider and thicker, with the inner walls being lined with limestone. It had been a bad year for canal reservoirs, as one on Charnwood Forest, belonging to

Mid-nineteenth century solidity – Anglesey Bridge.

the Leicester Navigation, had failed three months earlier, again causing extensive damage.

Following the amalgamation of the companies, largely brought about by the BCN's ever increasing demand for water, Sneyd was enlarged and a steam engine built in 1854 to pump water from the 473ft (144m) level. When built, the reservoir had been level with the Wyrley Bank Branch at 503ft (153m), but subsidence had lowered it considerably. Although the Wyrley Branch was abandoned in 1954, the reservoir remains and is now a Local Nature Reserve.

The BCN enlarged Cannock Chase Reservoir, adding a second dam, by Norton at the western end, almost tripling it in size. In the mid-nineteenth century, when the landowner, the Marquess of Anglesey, began to exploit his coal reserves in the area, the feeder running to the top of Ogley Locks was enlarged and straightened in places between 1848–50 to create the BCN's Anglesey Branch.

Some of the land occupied by the original feeder was given up to the landowner and some to the new South Staffordshire Railway Company. A steam pumping engine was installed by the main dam in 1855 to pump water up from the Branch. As mining activity on the Cannock Chase coalfield around the reservoir increased, so did the threat of damage. In November 1894, the Norton dam had subsided and was being strengthened, while a couple of months later the reservoir had overflowed and flooded part of a nearby farm. Ordnance Survey maps show that Mr Prince, the farmer, never did recover his land and the Company agreed to pay him £1 10s a year in compensation.

In 1900, more work was being carried out and BCN Engineer George Jebb purchased a steam launch, *Bee*, for £100 for 'tugging boat loads of stones across Cannock Chase Reservoir, large quantities of stones being required for facing the new Dams'. The pumping station worked heavily until 1922, being closed in 1937. Still fulfilling its original purpose, Chasewater is now also the centre of a popular country park supporting angling, water-skiing, sailing and the Chasewater Railway, a heritage line on a section of former colliery railway. Between December 2010 and April 2012, the reservoir was lowered by 26ft (8m) to allow repair work to be carried out on the main dam. A new bridge, weir and spillway were constructed, the total cost being £5.5 million.

Not So Jolly Millers

Looking at the area covered by the BCN now, its streams largely invisible, trammelled and culverted, it is difficult to envisage the numbers of watermills existing when the first canals were being built. The now largely hidden headwaters of Tame, Stour and Rea were used to turn mill wheels, over forty on the Tame in Black Country Staffordshire alone. Most began as corn mills, but by the eighteenth century blade mills were grinding and sharpening edge tools and bloom smithies were hammering iron to rid it of impurities. There were also slitting mills, wire mills and forges.

The Birmingham Canal diverted or intercepted many of the Tame's tributaries around Oldbury, but water supply to the mills was protected by the original Act, which recognized that although the water 'must be diverted for the Use of the ... Navigation', overflow weirs were to be made 'at or near the Top of each Lock', so that water would run off when they were full into the mill pool rather than over the locks. This arrangement was never entirely successful, as there was insufficient water to support the competing needs of millers and boatmen. Brindley had been conscious of the importance of maintaining supplies, as his early decision, later altered, to make locks of 3ft (0.9m) depth at Wolverhampton was, partly at least, due to his considering that water supplies beyond Bilston would not be sufficient 'without distressing the Mills'.

Although problems with millers continued, they lessened with the development of steam engines, which could turn heavier machinery and produce a more effective blast for the iron furnaces than waterwheels could provide. Some mills did continue into the nineteenth century and a very few into the twentieth. The BCN purchased Dunkirk Mill near Ryders Green along with its watercourses around the time of the construction of the New Main Line. It remained a corn mill until 1835, when it was converted to operating a trip hammer, continuing to exist until the 1870s.

What Supplies the Two-Thirds: Steam Power

Coal-mine drainage could supply the canal with water raised by 'fire engines' from the pits. Thomas Newcomen's first successful atmospheric steam engine had been built for Lord Dudley's Coneygre Colliery near Tipton in 1712. During a busy day in April 1756, when he had already visited Bedworth to look at a steam engine, James Brindley rode to Birmingham and on to Wolverhampton, possibly passing Coneygre on his way, and maybe subconsciously making one of his 'occhilor surveys or a ricconitoring' of the route he was riding. It would certainly have proved useful a decade later. Brindley suggested 'Fire Engines' as a way of helping the water-supply problem at Smethwick Locks in June 1768, but nothing was done until 23 August 1776 when Committee Chairman Henry Henn was 'requested to have some Conversation with Mr Boulton about the erecting of a Fire Engine ... between the Third Lock & Shenstone's Mill to raise the Water Eighteen Feet and return it into the Feeder to go into the Summit'.

This was to be the first of many engines built to recirculate canal water from a lower level. In February 1777, it was to be 'forwarded with all expedition under Mr Boulton' and next month, Samuel Bull had been directed to draw a plan and Mr Lee had written to the landowner, Mr Watson of Hull. Despite some reluctance on Watson's part, with Commissioners being called in to settle the matter, and a report in February that 'the Engine at Spon Lane is very much neglected', it was working by April 1778. The following month, Committee Minutes recorded that the Wolverhampton summit was 3in (76mm) down and 'the working of the Engine thought to be injurious to the trade'. Bull was ordered not to work it anytime when the level was 1in (25mm) or more down. In July 1779, there was an accident at the engine by which Richard Robinson was very much scalded. He was claiming 10s 6d that a doctor had charged him for 'attendance and applications'.

Smethwick Engine

Any early problems there might have been with the Spon Lane engine did not stop the Company from deciding to build a further one at the Smethwick end of the summit and, in July 1778, the Committee resolved that 'one be Erected upon Mr Boulton's Construction'. The latter required dimensions and Hateley and Bull recommended a pump of 24in (610mm) diameter. Timbers and iron work, as well as Cumberland Slate, were ordered and, in agreement with the landowners, the feeder was to be culverted. As well as John Wilkinson, whose boring machine had greatly improved the efficiency of Watt's engine cylinders, the Coalbrookdale Company was also approached about parts for the machine. Whether or not this was an attempt to encourage Wilkinson to lower his prices, the Company stayed with their original supplier. On 2 July 1779, Bull was asked for his opinion of the 'new Engine erected by Messrs. Boulton & Watt'. He was fulsome in his praise, reporting that 'the workmanship is exceedingly perfect in every respect and that He thinks there is not a more compleat Engine anywhere', and a fortnight later Boulton and Watt were paid £210 for its licence.

It was a sophisticated piece of engineering, the first engine to introduce expansive use of steam to Watt's other improvements, the separate condenser and valve gear. In the meantime, the engine had begun working in late May and there seems to have been a celebration as the Committee, presumably asked to foot the bill, resolved, in October, 'that Wright and Popes Bills for entertainment of the Workmen at the New Engine be returned to them and they informed that the Committee don't consider the Company accountable for such demands'. The effect of the two engines meant that 250 boats could pass the summit in a week, enough, along with feed from the reservoirs, for the traffic at the time. The engines were almost constantly at work and needed maintaining. In November 1781, Boulton and Watt were invited to inspect the engines and see 'that they be kept in proper order and well Managed'.

John Smeaton's Opinion

However well managed the engines were, they could not compensate fully for the increase in traffic so, by September 1782, Meredith was writing to 'Mr Smeeton' canvassing his opinion on water supplies for the growing canal. In a detailed report, the engineer largely dismissed natural supplies, reckoning them 'very inadequate … in dry seasons'. During the previous summer, the canal had been so low that the vessels could only go with 'a burden of seventeen tons instead of twenty four'. The reservoirs had been of minimal use, as their feeder streams were supplying the mills with little to spare. In conclusion, as the Company's engines were providing two-thirds of the supply, 'what supplies the two-thirds may just as well supply the other part'. This was to be the future for the Company.

In June 1786, it was instructed that the 'Old boiler lately taken up at Smethwick Engine be repaired & put down under the direction of Mr Bull & that Spon Lane Engine Boiler be sold'. Following the lowering of the canal, the Spon Lane engine was no longer required and, after failed attempts at letting it and moving it, it was sold for use on the Dudley Canal. Water only now needed to be raised up three locks, but with the duplication of the Smethwick flight, the engine there was fitted with a larger pump to lift more to the summit and, with an increase in traffic, another engine was installed in 1804 and was working the following May. The pumps continued, sometimes working twenty-four hours a day and, about 1850, the first engine was overhauled while retaining its original appearance. Following Telford's improvements at Smethwick, and with pumping capacity still required, the feeder, enlarged in 1825 to make the Engine Branch, was carried on a graceful Gothic-styled Telford Aqueduct to join the Old Main Line above the locks. All the iron components were cast at the Horseley Ironworks in Tipton.

Preservation

The original Smethwick Engine was moved by the BCN to Ocker Hill in 1897 for preservation as it was believed to be the oldest working Watt engine in the world, and the engine house demolished. In 1919, on the centenary of James Watt's death, it steamed again, but, following the closure of the Ocker Hill workshops in 1954, the engine was presented to Birmingham City Council and preserved at the Museum of Science and Industry, where it celebrated its bicentenary by steaming in 1979. It is now located at Thinktank, the Museum's

CAST-IRON BRIDGES

The Horseley Coal & Iron Company, developing from coal mining to iron making and, by 1815, into engineering on a site by the Toll End Branch, is chiefly remembered for its fine cast-iron bridges. Galton Bridge is its prime canal example, but there are many more. The company's earliest seems to be a swing bridge built at the East India Docks in London in 1816, while one dated 1820 still spans the Grand Union Canal on its approach to Brentford. In the same decade more were built around the BCN, particularly in connection with Telford's improvements. They are of a fairly standard design of two arched castings linked by a central locking plate and decked with smaller flanged plates bolted in place, but there are variations. The Horseley Coal & Iron Co. was bankrupt in 1843, subsequently reforming as the Horseley Company and continuing to supply canal bridges, including three dated 1858, at Delph Locks and both ends of the Two Lock Line.

Early Horseley Bridge on the Wyrley & Essington.

'Standard' Horseley design, Blackbrook Bridge refurbished 2020.

As well as the Horseley Ironworks bridges still extant on the BCN, there are half a dozen 'Toll End Works' ones, while another example, by 'Thomas Astbury Smethwick', straddles the Main Line at Rotton Park Junction.

Demolition of the Old Smethwick Engine House, which was built for the Birmingham Canal Co. by Boulton and Watt in 1776.

Pumping engine built for the Birmingham Canal Co. by Boulton and Watt in 1776 Regularly working until 1892 Now re-erected at Ocker Hill Tipton

successor, and is steamed several times a year. Although the original engine house, in Bridge Street North, was demolished in 1897, the foundations are preserved.

New Smethwick Engine

In July 1891, George Jebb, in his monthly Engineer's Report to Committee, had recommended replacing the two Smethwick engines, 'now almost past further repair' with a new plant on a new site below Brasshouse Lane Bridge. It was to consist of a pair of Centrifugal Pumps capable of pumping 200 locks a day from the New to the Old Main Line. The total cost would be about £2,800, compared with an estimate of between £600 and £700 for repairs to the old plant which would then be able to pump 160 locks per day, but the saving, by the installation of the new plant, would be at 'least £75 per annum'. Plans and estimates were prepared by the end of October and the following February rough castings and forgings for the pumping engines were ordered from Drysdale & Co. of Glasgow for £390.

Finishing and erecting the engines was left to the BCN's Ocker Hill Department. The plant was completed in August except for the upper 30ft (9m) of the stack and the engineer reported that everything was completed and 'the Engines are working satisfactory'. The New Smethwick Pumping Engine closed in the 1920s as traffic was declining, but worked for a time during the Second World War. The building remained empty and deteriorating, the stack removed, until it was restored in the late 1980s. It now serves as the Galton Valley Canal Museum, giving an insight into the history of the waterways of the area and is staffed by volunteers.

Ocker Hill Engines

In August 1783, Mr Henn was asked to speak with James Watt 'respecting the Engines to be built upon the lower level' and in December the engineer was asking for dimensions. The Broadwaters extension then being built passed close to the end of the Ocker Hill Branch. This had been included in the original Act and in August 1771 John Meredith had been instructed to write to Brindley 'signifying the Committee's desire that the Collateral Branch to Ocker Hill be immediately set about'. The branch, opened by 1774, was on a level 65ft (20m)

New Smethwick Engine, 1992.

above the later extension and, when the latter was under construction, it made sense to dig a shaft and connecting tunnel so that water could be pumped up to the ever-thirsty Wolverhampton level. In his report, Smeaton had commended the idea as 'very effectual'.

In July 1784, the Company was sourcing plates for the boiler and the engine was running and 'competent to the drawing off 2 feet 4 inches from the surface of the lower Canal', though this was before the Broadwaters canal had been finished. It opened as far as Ocker Hill the following year and to Broadwaters colliery in 1786. A second engine had been added by 1792 and Ocker Hill eventually had the greatest concentration of pumping engines on the BCN; by 1900 there were six. In 1892, George Jebb had recommended the use of mechanical stokers on the four high-pressure boilers at the plant. These were capable of being fired on very fine slack, as opposed to the 'rough slack that is at present used', bringing a saving of £50 per year. Boilers were inspected regularly and in January 1893 this included sixteen at Ocker Hill.

Mine Drainage

John Smeaton's report had listed various mine pumping engines along the canal, the main ones being 'Lord Dudley's Old Engine' and 'the patent engine' at Bloomfield. In total, he calculated that the nine he noted could provide 478 locks-full a week. Arguing that, as the Broadwaters cut was being built to serve new collieries, the Company should include a clause obliging them to 'turn all such engine water as is delivered above its level' into the canal and giving them authority to raise water from the mines themselves. On the existing line and acting on Smeaton's advice about utilizing a 'judicious application of the colliery engines' water', Bull was requested, in May 1783, to examine the engines owned by 'different Persons who are willing to accommodate the Company with Water'. In April the following year, Lord Dudley built an engine at Tipton Pieces, below canal level and the Company was willing 'to throw the Water into the Canal' at its own expense. It speaks of the Viscount's importance that the Committee decided a letter to him would not be suitable and so a request was made for a small deputation to 'wait upon his Lordship … when it will be agreeable to his Lordship to be waited upon'. All went well, the Company agreed to pay for the alterations and additions and his Lordship's request 'reserving to Himself the liberty of diverting or otherwise disposing of said Water whenever He pleases'.

Other engines followed, at Bradley Moor and Dudley Port, while, in June 1785, Mr Gibbons of Wolverhampton was offering the water from his Tividale engine in return for 'Water from the Canal when the Colliery happens to be on fire'. In 1820, the BCN was supplied from nearly seventy mines and a decade later thirty-four engines were pumping into the Wolverhampton level alone. Water was a negotiable commodity. In April 1892, the Engineer reported that 'I have been able to get the Cannock Lodge Colliery Co. to accept 4d a Lock instead of 6d a Lock for water pumped into the Wyrley Bank Branch'. At 503ft (153m), this was one of the highest sections of the BCN.

Ocker Hill Branch

This early branch neatly demonstrated the effects of coal mining on the canal. Although the original canal was built on the level for over half a mile (680m) from Summer Hill, as the thick coal was mined, the ground subsided and the canal had to be banked up. By the time the branch was abandoned in 1955, it stood on a high embankment, above the land it had once run beside.

At its western end was the Moat Colliery, which showed something of the dichotomy surrounding the BCN and the mining districts it passed through. Taking the coal caused subsidence, but water in the pits could be used by the canal if it could be pumped out. In 1812, the colliery, covering 171 acres (70ha) of low-lying land between the western end of the branch and a loop of the main line, installed two Boulton and Watt engines to pump water into the canal. By the 1870s, with depression in the iron trade affecting the price of coal, many pits were closed and many others flooded, drowning millions of tons of coal and iron ore in the district. The South Staffordshire Mines Drainage Commission was sanctioned by Parliament in 1873 and later operated a pumping station on part of the Moat Colliery site. A large beam engine, capable of raising water from a depth of 620ft (189m), operated between 1893 and 1902, raising over 7.3 billion gallons. With a reduction in coal mining, the problems increased while drainage decreased and by 1920 the Commission described the Tipton mining area as lost.

Ocker Hill Branch, 1898.

C.E. MAXWELL, WATER RENTS AND THE KYNOCH CASE

Around 1888, when C.E. Maxwell was the BCN's Chief Clerk, he was asked to take charge of the Company's rent roll. At the time there were no 'Water Rents' as such, only a few agreements for pipe connections with the canal, bringing in 5s to £1 a year. Maxwell soon discovered that although water was being taken from the canal for industrial purposes, it was often not returned, so that a 'very considerable' quantity was being lost. He proposed that a suitable charge be made for the water used and, after studying the various Acts relating to the BCN, Birmingham Corporation and South Staffordshire Water Company and finding no clauses relating to the matter, Maxwell decided to prepare a scale of charges, based on those of the local water authorities. There was, not surprisingly, strong objection from users of canal water, who claimed a statutory right to it, 'until the specific conditions in the Company's Acts requiring the water to be returned were pointed out'.

The BCN therefore took Kynoch Limited, a major Birmingham manufacturing company that had premises by the Old Canal at Soho, to court over the matter. Kynoch claimed a prescriptive right, having been using the water for over twenty years, but the judge ruled in favour of the BCN. The Company furthermore pointed out the large sums of money it had to pay out annually for water supplied to the canal and the water users 'admitted the equity of the Company's claim to compensation and signed the Agreement'. As a result, nearly 700 works along the canal were visited and their existing pipe connections reviewed, 'shewing an incredible quantity of water being taken without permission or payment'. Maxwell afforded himself a little self-congratulation, stating that the number of agreements up to 1907 had doubled and the rents receivable had likewise increased from £10,000 to £20,000, 'such increase arising mainly from Water Rents'.

Jebb's Conclusions

In his evidence to the Royal Commission on Canals, begun in 1906 and reporting in 1911, George Jebb stated that most water was supplied by mine pumping, either by the Commissioners or private engines, while the BCN itself had thirteen stations, mainly to recirculate water, and maintained reservoirs at Cannock Chase, Rotton Park, Sneyd and Lodge Farm. The cost was probably greater than for any other canal in the country. The average outlay for pumping alone was £11,000 a year and the Company's pumping stations were capable of raising the equivalent of 4,080 locks daily.

In 1913, he further outlined the water supply situation to a meeting in Birmingham of the British Association for the Advancement of Science. The BCN's reservoirs held a total capacity of 1,202,000,000 gallons, supplied by streams and by water pumped from the canals in rainy weather, and further supplies came from mine water and feeders and streams running directly into the canals. Jebb stressed that water from these sources would be inadequate were it not for the recirculatory pumps capable of raising 100,000,000 gallons per day. Even so, in exceptionally dry spells, only by setting 'old pumping engines at work ... to pump water from the mines ... and by causing boats to meet at certain locks, technically called "pairing"', was it possible to keep the canals open.

Water Supply Now

Chasewater remains the main supplier to the BCN and is the Canal & River Trust's largest reservoir, capable of holding 4,500 million litres, while the pumps at Bradley can lift up to 32 million litres per day. The Titford Canal, on the highest current level, can also supplement the supply with water from the Pools and pumped up from the Old Main Line.

CHAPTER 5

Traffic

King Coal

'Wheras the Utility of a Navigable Cut or Canal from this Town thro' the Coal Works to Wolverhampton …' is the opening phrase in the Birmingham Canal's first Minute Book and it set the tone for the next two centuries. In July 1768, the Company surveyors had been ordered to take a sketch and fresh levels of the Gentlemen's estates near the coal works so that the canal could be laid out to cut through the greatest number of estates containing that most desired mineral. Coal was the foundation of the canal's success, much as it was the basement of swathes of the area through which its ramifications would run. It would also bring recurring and ultimately insoluble problems. Opening the canal to Wolverhampton was of secondary importance to securing the coal from Wednesbury by way of a collateral cut.

'The Canal is Full of Boats'

From the first three boats to unload at Friday Street on the canal's opening day, the trade grew quickly. It was important to organize the coal traffic, the

Cooper's Coal Wharf, Smethwick. One of scores located around the BCN.

Committee wishing immediately to find 'two proper persons' to be in charge of the boats between the collieries and Birmingham, so that regularity could be established and loss of time and water minimized. Before the end of the month, two extra lock-keepers were needed at Smethwick to work with the two already there, 'alternately day and night, that no delay or Irregularity may be occasioned in the passage of boats'. At the beginning of 1770, eighteen boats had been built with two more mostly finished. Constantly carrying coal from the Wednesbury pits and returning to reload may have been stretching the canal to capacity, as an order for making fifty boats was suspended. In a letter to Lord Dartmouth in February 1770, Committee man Dr John Ash wrote:

> Success attends us … The Canal is full of Boats belonging to the Company & private owners; that is the Term; & Coals are daily hawked abt. the Streets for purchasors, the Town is fully stocked & the Country Teams increase on the Wharf so that the Waggons are very few indeed very few on the road. Three Hundred Tons at best are brought daily by the Navigation which is 100 Tons more than the Town has demand for.

John Ash's letter pointed out that the trade was carried in canal and privately owned boats and he went on to state that it was necessary for the Company to carry coals on its own account to keep down the price. If it did not, 'the private owners … would never have sold Coals any cheaper than the Waggons'.

In order to prevent the coal masters from gaining a monopoly in the trade, it was determined that the Company should take on a mine, but not to work it unless or until such a restrictive practice developed to threaten the security of the public.

Suppliers

John Wood, a Wednesbury coal and ironmaster, had been the first to supply coal by canal to Birmingham. In March 1770, the Committee decided his price was too high and his contract would not be continued, though they 'shall at all times be open to receive reasonable proposals from him'. Meanwhile, other coal masters were to be asked what price per ton they would be willing to charge. Following a report that someone had bought a load of coal cheaper from the wagons than from the wharf, it was resolved to cut the price to 4d per hundredweight at the wharf and place an advertisement accordingly in the next paper. In June, a special General Meeting considered it necessary to appoint a special committee of eleven to take charge of the coal trade and in October it was agreed that the Company's coals should continue to be sold at 6s 8d per ton. As it was vital that the amount of coal being carried could be ascertained, boats were to be marked for the purpose. Another mine owner, John Bickley, supplied coal once the canal had reached his pits in Bilston, though in July 1771 John Meredith was writing to the gentlemen of the Coal Committee 'requesting their opinions of the propriety of continuing the Contract' with him.

FOWNES & ASTON

Some coal masters became involved in building the canal as they saw the benefits it would bring them. Messrs Fownes & Aston owned pits at Tipton but were working on the canal in July 1769, when Clerk of the Works George Holloway was instructed not to pay them, as 'they do not appear to have perform'd their Contract with the Company relative to Cutting that part of the Canal set to them'. The following month, after Brindley had inspected their work and found that it let out water in several places and was incomplete, the Company's Surveyor, Mr Wright, was ordered to mark up the defective places so that they could be made good after the water had been let out. The situation had not been resolved by the following June. Fownes & Aston had refused to make good the defects and it had fallen on Wright to repair 'that part of the Canal … which was defectively executed'. The partners were to pay the full cost of repairs to two lengths of cutting undertaken by them and not completed according to contract, or the Company would take legal action.

By September, Fownes & Aston had built a 'Collateral Branch … from the Canal to their Colliery', but had not signed an agreement acknowledging that it had been made with the Canal Company's consent. It was 'absolutely necessary' that they should do so and if

> they did not 'immediately execute such Agreement', the stop gate between their cut and the canal would be 'forthwith shut up & continued so stopped till such Agreement and Acknowledgement is Executed'.
>
> Although the partners may have been uncertain in their approach to canal building, they understood the law and how it affected mining in relation to the Navigation, sending notice, in August 1770, that they had got the coal and worked up to a distance of 12yd (11m) from the canal 'in a certain pit ... at Tipton ... & that they do intend to get the coal under the 12 yds. and also under the Canal'. Meredith replied that they were at liberty 'to proceed to get that part of the Coal mine contained in their Notice not injuring the Canal & towing paths thereby'. Fownes & Aston were profiting from their proximity to the canal, but were not necessarily playing fair, for in October, along with Mr Dixon and Messrs Nock of Oldbury, they were threatened with prosecution unless they 'Immediately deliver a true account of' and pay the tonnage on the coal they were carrying.

Following full opening, the demand for coal continued to grow at both ends of the canal and there was money to be made in all aspects of the trade. At the end of 1776, the Company's loaders at the Brickiln Piece Wharf may have been involving themselves in some freelance work, as they were informed that they would not in future be allowed to take money for loading wagons or carts on pain of being discharged.

The following May, coal dealers at the Wolverhampton Wharf were complaining that they were suffering from the lack of a fence around the wharf and that they needed a small office in which to transact their business. In February 1778, night watchmen were being sought for the Paradise Street Wharf. Coal was 'in great Demand' in November and in reply to Mr Barbor, a collier who had informed the Committee that he could not supply the Company with more than eight boatloads a week, John Houghton stated that fresh steerers had been engaged and that they expected their boats to be loaded immediately when sent to his mines 'notwithstanding any other Contracts He may have entered into'.

End of the Company's Involvement

In March 1780, an application from the Bloomfield Company for a contract to deliver coal led the Committee to consider their own continuation of the trade. They reached the conclusion that it was no longer financially beneficial and that it would be 'more advantageous to the Navigation Company and the Publick that the Coal Trade be discontinued' and the boats 'Lett to Hire'. They passed their decision to the next General Assembly meeting, which passed it back. It was eventually agreed to discontinue the trade by a later General Assembly

Loading coal at the wharf.

Brickiln Piece Wharf was also known as Paradise Street and later called Old Wharf.

and to 'signify the Resolution to the several Persons interested therein to prevent any inconvenience arising therefrom'. The Company's direct involvement in the coal trade came to an end on 1 July 1794.

Not all coal masters shared in the success. Many were small-scale operations, often undercapitalized, and bankruptcies were not uncommon. In October 1824, a report in *Aris's Birmingham Gazette* stated that the half share of William James in Toll End New Colliery was to be auctioned off to pay his debts. More usual, though, were advertisements for mines where proximity to the canal was an obvious advantage. The notices also show how the Black Country was developing industrially at the time. One, from the same issue, for 'Valuable Staffordshire Mines', advertised:

> forty-five to fifty Acres of Coal and Ironstone Mines, situate within a mile and a half of five large and populous towns, upon the banks of the Birmingham Canal, which runs through the estate. These Mines are most advantageously situated, being within from two to three miles of twenty-two blast furnaces, now in work, upon the same canal ....

The benefits were reaching out beyond the growing towns. In the same month, a correspondent describing himself as a country gentleman explained how he lived in a place that was 'ill supplied with fuel before a canal was made some years ago by which Wednesbury coals are brought to us at 10d. per hundred'. By then, the canal was an established part of the local scene: 'There pass on the canal about fifty boats a day from the direction of Birmingham, and, of course, as many towards that place, without exciting attention.'

At the Peak and Beyond

The middle decades of the nineteenth century saw the peak of coal production in the Black Country, having risen steadily from around 800,000 tons annually at the end of the eighteenth. The Birmingham & Liverpool Rail-road Company's 1824 prospectus had estimated that the coal raised annually in the South Staffordshire field amounted to 2,300,000 tons. This grew to around four million by the end of the 1830s and about five million tons in 1854, but the pits were increasingly being worked out. A haphazard approach to sinking and working new mines, combined with the sheer abundance of the thick coal in many places led to 'a mode of working ... of which we have no reason to be proud'. This was written in the 1870s, the author continuing that 'the rapid exhaustion of the pits renders it probable that in a few years the working of the thick coal will be a matter of history'. There were still the lower seams such as the Heathen and New Mine to be exploited but the focus of operations was moving north to Cannock Chase.

During the 1880s the quantity of coal carried into Birmingham by canal had been decreasing, while that transported by the London & North Western Railway (L&NWR) was rising. In 1880, canal carriers had brought in 770,000 tons as against the railway's 365,000, but by 1890 the corresponding figures were 677,148 by canal and 728,200 by rail. The BCN's share was slowly falling, while that of the railway had virtually doubled during the decade and was over 800,000 two years later, the balance switching in 1887. Also significant was the increase in coal coming from the Cannock Chase, Essington and Brownhills Districts. Even with the Cannock Extension Canal open the BCN's share of traffic from that lucrative area had decreased by 86,000 tons while the railway had almost doubled, increasing by 262,867 tons.

'Up to Edgeford Basin for Thirty Tons of Coal'

The Cannock Extension, founded on coal, subsided with it, and two-thirds, virtually the entire length north of Watling Street, including its terminal basins at Hednesford, has disappeared. In its heyday, Hednesford ('Edgeford' to the boatmen) Basin was noted for its 'mid-day tide'. The movement of all the boats heading towards the basins and pushing the water before them was said to raise the level by 18in (472mm). Following the demise of Hednesford Basin, coal loading passed to Anglesey Basin under the Chasewater Dam. The railway

Old Wharf.

Anglesey Basin coal chutes, 2019.

bringing in the coal closed in the early 1960s and an overhead loading gantry was replaced by chutes used by lorries to tip coal into boats. The last train of boats left Anglesey Basin in the middle of the decade and the wharf was abandoned in 1967.

A pair of basins, built to serve the Brownhills Colliery's Grove Pit, survive on the Extension by Wyrley Common Bridge. In 1922, it produced 159,044 tons, falling to around 100,000 tons per year in the 1930s when it was also supplying water to the BCN at a rate of 420,000gal per day. Although the colliery closed in 1950, water was still pumped from the workings for several more years. Another basin survives on the original Wyrley & Essington line at Short Heath. In 1841, the BCN had built a tramroad from pits in the Essington area to Coltham Basin, later known as Short Heath or Holly Bank Basin. The sinking of Hilton Main Colliery in the 1920s increased production and the basin was in use until the late 1960s and the closure of the mine.

The Big Four Pits

Hilton Main was one of the last four large collieries on the South Staffordshire coalfield, all sunk to great depths outside the boundaries of the exposed Black Country mining area. The others were Baggeridge, Hamstead and Sandwell Park, with the latter two also making extensive use of the BCN. Sandwell Park Colliery, on the Earl of Dartmouth's estate in Smethwick, was proposed by Black Country mining engineer Henry Johnson, who was convinced that the thick coal would be found under the sandstone beyond the coalfield's eastern boundary fault. The pit was located to take advantage of canal and railway transport. The first sod of the shaft that reached the thick coal at a depth of 418yd (382m) in April 1874 had been turned nearly four years earlier by the eminent geologist Sir Roderick Murchison and the colliery proved successful, raising about 300,000 tons a year into the 1900s. It was connected to a wharf on the Old Main Line by a tramway, operated by an endless chain system, capable of moving 600 tons a week. The wharf could deal with eighteen boats at a time and a self-acting slack store with a chute loaded a boat in ten minutes. Most of the colliery's output was carried from the wharf, where fifteen men, five boys and three ponies were employed in loading them. In 1909, a new pit, Jubilee Colliery, was opened about 1¾ miles (2.8km) further north and coal transported in tubs to Sandwell Park for processing. A large new loading plant was constructed on the canal wharf in 1937–8, surviving the closure of the pits in 1960.

Sandwell Park coal drops, built 1937–8.

One of the last tangible remains of Black Country mining, its ferro-concrete structure, deteriorated and it was demolished in 2006, 'despite having significant local connections with the now abandoned Sandwell Park Colliery, and all the industrial and social relevance that coal mining and canals have in the West Midlands'. A display board about the history of the wharf was later erected on the site.

Domestic Fuel

Much coal was carried for the domestic market to scores of coal yards around the BCN. One still with a canal-side location, the Wulfruna Coal Company, was first established in 1850 at Bridge Wharf by Bilston Road Bridge, Wolverhampton. In the 1930s, they acquired another site, Minerva Wharf off Horseley Fields, where a new 'Half Basin and Wharf' was built, with a concrete bottom, by the BCN for Wolverhampton Corporation which was also responsible for its maintenance. Wulfruna was a major distributor of coal to local industries, such as the nearby Chillington Iron Works as well as to the domestic market. Coal came from the Cannock Mines, being loaded originally at a landsale wharf near the Globe Inn at Hednesford Basin. Deliveries by boat ended during the 1960s. Several boats were abandoned at the end of a long basin stretching under Minerva Lane and, according to Wulfruna's current manager, 'they're still there', buried under industrial units.

Generating Trade

Much of the traffic from these large pits was destined for electricity generation. In the middle of the twentieth century, the Black Country landscape was dominated by the cooling towers and chimneys of power stations as it had been by pitheads and blast furnaces a century before. The last three were at Ocker Hill, north of Tipton, Birchills, near Walsall, and Wolverhampton, but there had been earlier canal-side power stations alongside Farmer's Bridge and Aston Locks in Birmingham. As the demand for power increased, more and larger stations were built using coal delivered by boat and canal water for cooling purposes.

Wolverhampton

The Wolverhampton Power Station, which opened in 1895 on Commercial Road, stood by a busy length of canal, surrounded by iron and nail works, wharves and basins, sawmills and corn mills. Most of the coal burnt in the station came from Hollybank Colliery, amounting to 30,000 tons in 1909.

> **A GOOD DEAL**
>
> In September 1918, an agreement with Wolverhampton Corporation came to an end. The Corporation had been paying the BCN £350 per year for using 511 million gallons of water, of which about 10 million gallons was lost through evaporation. The Company estimated the current annual use to be 717 million gallons, with about 14 million lost, and negotiated a new agreement whereby the Corporation offered to increase the annual water rent to £500. Not only that, 'As the Corporation are now turning into the Canal about 38½ million gallons of town water a year which is 24 million gallons in excess of the total quantity of Canal water lost by evaporation … the Clerk considers the offer a very good one.'

Increased demand led to extensions to the power station; a telpher was used to unload coal from boats and in 1922 the Corporation was applying to the BCN to extend it across the canal. There would be no objection from the Company if a 'Coal Guard or other suitable means for preventing Coal from falling into the Canal from the Grabs' was erected. A decrease in the BCN's revenue in the late 1930s was put down to 'the closing down for long periods of Local Electricity Generating Stations' during the industrial depression. A fleet of twenty boats was in use at Wolverhampton until the mid-1950s, when road transport took over, and the station closed in the late 1970s. One of the generating halls still stands beside the cut, but the single cooling tower was demolished soon after closure.

Birchills and Ocker Hill

Birchills Power Station, above Walsall Locks and near the junction with the Wyrley & Essington Canal, was opened in 1922 with a pumping station for cooling water on the Anson Branch. The water was returned to the Wyrley, which also supplied coal. In 1949, a large new plant with six cooling towers and six chimneys opened, again supplied with slack by canal. The station closed in 1982 and was demolished five years later. Ocker Hill's cooling towers, two from 1947 with a third added in the mid-1950s, dominated the heart of the Black Country for nearly four decades. Built near the junction of the Walsall and Tame Valley Canals, the first station opened in 1902, being supplied with coal to a basin that could accommodate eight boats.

Birchills Power Station, 1972.

Coal Boats

The British Electricity Authority, later the Central Electricity Generating Board (CEGB), had its own fleet of boats to supply the power stations and it was still taking new, locally built boats into its fleet in 1949. In January 1951, Wolverhampton was receiving 4,000 tons per week, equating to 160 boats or 23 per day. Figures for March that year show that Walsall was supplied with 2,850 tons a week by canal against 5,450 by rail and 150 by road. In 1959, Walsall received canal-borne coal from Hilton Main, Cannock Wood and Coppice Collieries and a comparison was made between canal and rail transport by the CEGB's Regional Fuel Supplies Officer, who stated that 'the throughout transport and handling costs by canal compare favourably with rail'. He concluded that 'canal transport to your Station continues to be an economic proposition and may even suggest that water-borne supplies may be increased in the future'. This optimism would not last long and canal transport to the power stations had ceased by the middle of 1965.

Putting the Gas into Gas Street

Gas Street Basin is probably the best-known place on the BCN. The original intention had been to name the track passing John Gostling's new gasworks, opened in 1817 and the first in the Midlands, Netherton Street. No doubt this was because it received its coal by boat delivered to the Dudley Canal's Netherton Basin, just through the Bar Lock, but it must have picked up the Gas Street name early. It was soon discovered that Black Country coal was inferior to others for the production of gas and by the middle of the century coal was brought in by rail from further afield, although local coal was still used to fire the retorts producing the gas. Coke was a valuable by-product of the gasworks and was usually carried by boat to ironworks and furnaces around the system. Other by-products included gas tar and gas water, which also made use of the BCN for carriage. More than a dozen gasworks were established around the BCN, with the largest of them surviving into the 1960s and the introduction of natural gas.

Wolverhampton Gasworks, 1950s.

Swan Bridge Junction, early 1970s.

In 1825, the Birmingham & Staffordshire Gas Light Company was formed to produce and supply gas to Birmingham and several neighbouring towns, including West Bromwich. On completion in 1829, the works, at the bucolic sounding Swan Village, were the largest in the country, being supplied with coal by a basin cut from the Ridgacre Branch close by its junction with the Old Wednesbury Canal.

All those Basins

The opening of gasworks along with other industrial activities increased the need for off-line basins and, in its prime, the BCN had hundreds of basins and arms, serving a multitude of works, mines and factories. They had been built from the early days of the Navigation as in August 1787, when Matthew Boulton applied to the Committee for 'a small Canal adjoining to the Lock near Livery Street for the purpose of enabling Him to land any Commodity He may have occasion to bring along the Canal immediately upon a Wharf intended by Him to be made there'. He was willing to pay all the associated expenses and ensure that the work was carried out 'by or under the direction of the Company's Engineer'. His request was agreed to and James Bough instructed to see it through. These basins were built after the canal, many of them on the towpath side, where their construction would interrupt the everyday flow of traffic when boats were hauled by horse.

Smethwick Gas Works was built on a piece of land off Rabone Lane and adjacent to the Soho Foundry, following the setting up of a Gas Committee in April 1877. The Local Board of Health was responsible for this initiative and in order to cope with the influx of large quantities of building materials it was decided to build a basin from the adjacent Birmingham Canal, which meant cutting through the towpath. The basin was subsequently used for bringing in coal. The agreement between the Local Board of Health for the District of the Hamlet of Smethwick in the County of Stafford and the Company of Proprietors of the Birmingham Canal Navigations lays out in detail the responsibilities of each party.

The Local Board was to pay the BCN a yearly sum of £1 by equal quarterly payments. It was to give seven days' notice of commencing excavations to the Canal Company Offices in Paradise Street. During the work, the Board was to provide a good and sufficient temporary road, or way, for horses and others using or trading along the canal. It was to be as near to the towing path as could be and maintained in good condition until the towpath was made passable, so that traffic on the Canal could be conducted in safety with as little hindrance as possible.

The bridge over the end of the arm was to be built of good, sound bricks and other materials on sound and solid foundations of bricks and stone to the approval of the BCN's Engineer, and the approaches were to be covered with a proper coating of 'good cinder or other such materials as were generally used in the neighbourhood'. It was the Local Board's responsibility to repair the bridge and keep it to its original level. If the bridge or its approaches should sink or were deemed unsafe and the Board failed to make repairs within seven days, or if the Board failed to pay its quarterly dues, then the Canal Company was empowered to remove the bridge and stop up the communication. The Local Board was to give the BCN three months' notice of discontinuation and was to restore the towpath when it ceased using the basin. Like most of the rest, these basins have been filled in and the side bridges demolished, their position only now marked by a length of concrete edging the towpath.

THOMAS CLAYTON OF OLDBURY

A name synonymous with gasworks and carrying, Thomas Clayton of Oldbury specialized in liquid cargoes transported in a fleet of flat-decked narrowboats known locally as 'gas boats'. Beginning as a general carrier in Birmingham in 1842, William Clayton's business grew and Clayton boats were soon carrying tar from as far afield as London to Birmingham. Gas water, an ammonia-rich by-product of the many canal-side gasworks, was used in making fertilizers and became another valuable cargo. By the time that his son, Thomas, took over in 1882, the business was well established. In 1889, Clayton's general carrying business merged with Fellows, Morton & Company to form what became the premier canal carrying firm, Fellows, Morton & Clayton Ltd, and the fleet, of around seventy boats, was divided between the two concerns. Thomas maintained the liquid side of the business, moving to a site in Oldbury on the Old Main Line by the foot of Oldbury Locks and just around the corner from Springfield Tar Works. Thomas Clayton (Oldbury) Ltd was formally incorporated in 1904.

Evolving from an open hold carrying barrels covered by canvas, the liquid-carrying craft later had a fixed weatherproof deck, with the hold being divided into two large wooden tanks separated from each other and the ends of the boat by sealed bulkheads. Most Clayton boats were named after British rivers and from 1916 newly acquired boats were given names beginning with the same letter on an annual basis. The 1916 boats were *Alde* and *Adder*, 1917 following with *Blyth*, *Bourne*, *Bannon*, *Boyle*, *Brent* and *Beaver*. This continued until 1939 with *Usk* and *Umea*. The latter is a Swedish River, perhaps no one at Clayton's had heard of the Yorkshire *Ure*! Most traffic was handled by horse boats, even on long-distance routes such as the fuel oil carried from the Shell company's refinery at Stanlow on the Manchester Ship Canal to their depot at Langley Green on the Titford Canal. The 160 miles (258km) round trip took about a week.

By the early 1950s, Clayton's fleet had grown to over ninety boats, sixty being horse-drawn, along with sixteen motors and their butties. The Stanlow traffic amounted to nearly 30,000 tons of fuel and gas oil in 1949, but had fallen to 5,666 tons by 1955, when it was ended with the development of pipelines. The last significant traffic was in gasworks by-products. In 1964, Clayton boats moved 10,561 tons of tar from Wolverhampton, but the trade finished in 1966 with the imminent switch to North Sea Gas. That, and the construction of the M5 over the Oldbury boatyard, brought Clayton's canal carrying days to a close, though, by then, the company had developed a road oil-tanker business. The last boatload of all was carried from Walsall gasworks by *Stour* on 31 March.

Clayton's yard, 1965.

Passengers, Philosophers and Craft of Renown

Over a period of about thirty years, passenger boats plied the Birmingham Canal. Around 1820, boatbuilder Thomas Monk constructed the packet boat *Euphrates* to carry passengers between Factory Bridge, Tipton, and the Wagon and Horses, by Friday Bridge in Birmingham. Two classes were accommodated in separate cabins and the fare was 1s 6d for first class and sixpence less for second, with the journey taking two hours and operating on Mondays, Thursdays and Saturdays. An omnibus was laid on to convey passengers from Dudley to join the packet where the turnpike to West Bromwich crossed the canal at a place that became known as Dudley Port. *Euphrates* was a fly boat, built with a keel and rounded sides for speed. Even taking into consideration the fly boat's priority, it says much for the design of the boat, the state of the towpath and the quality of the teams of horses used, that the journey could be so quick, especially on such a busy route.

As well as running a regular service, *Euphrates* could also be hired, a popular excursion being to Dudley to visit the castle and limestone mines. One was advertised,

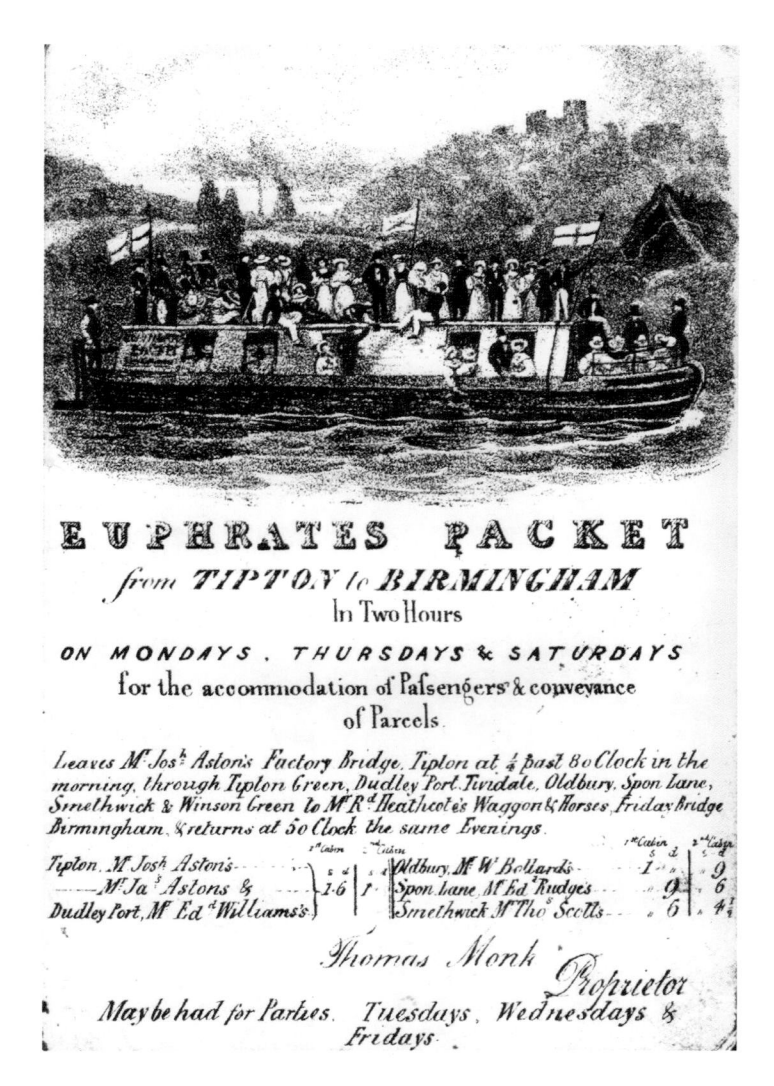

Euphrates Packet Poster, c.1820, with Dudley Castle behind. An early hen party off to Broad Street, Birmingham, for the night?

in August 1832, as a 'Private Aquatic Excursion to the Ruins of Dudley Castle by the Euphrates Packet' and included a 'short VOCAL and INSTRUMENTAL CONCERT in one of the caverns, for which that ruin is so celebrated'. The 'caverns', in reality limestone mines, also attracted scientists. In September 1849, Sir Roderick Murchison, pre-eminent geologist of the mid-nineteenth century, addressed a large crowd of geologists, ethnologists and antiquarians in one of the caverns with 'the aid of a powerful speaking trumpet'. Three hundred of them had travelled from Birmingham in the 'swift packets plying on the ... canal' and were conducted directly to the magnificently illuminated caverns. As the BCN's last Chairman, George Taylor, pointed out in a valedictory speech at the Company's final General Assembly in 1948:

> ... never before or since, did the canal bear such a precious freight ... It was customary ... for the captain of each boat to carry a 'manifest', to show the Company's weigh clerk, that the proper dues might be charged on the freight. On the first of these occasions ... the return made for one of these boats to the surveying officer ran thus:- 'Draught, 13 inches, weight, 3½ tons; cargo PHILOSOPHERS'.

DOLLARS

An unusual cargo was mentioned in a letter from Matthew Boulton to the Canal's John Houghton in June 1804:

> I have finally completed the Coinage of Silver Dollars for England and for Ireland and intend to begin to load the Irish in two of Mr Bradley's boats on Thursday morning about 5 o'clock at the Soho Wharf. I expect we shall start about nine and arrive at the Cresent about ten, and from there proceed to Liverpool under a guard of 12 soldiers and two Bow Street Officers etc where one of the King's armed ships will wait to receive our cargo and convey the same to Dublin.

Boulton went on to ask for preference over coal boats at the locks on the run to Fazeley as the cargo 'is worth between 2 and 3 hundred thousand pounds and I wish their passage to be as quick as possible. The names of the two steerers are William Barlow and Richard Britain'.

Swift Travel

In 1830, a daily service between Wolverhampton and Birmingham had been introduced, but, on Thomas Monk's death in August 1843, this may have ceased, for a new service was advertised, run by James Shipton, an established carrier in the town. The Swift Packet Company used lightweight iron boats towed by two horses, the lead blinkered and the second ridden. The boats were purchased from Scotland, where they had been developed by James Houston and used on the Glasgow, Paisley & Johnstone Canal. Carrying between thirty-six and forty passengers, they could reach a speed of 10mph (16km/h). The journey along the New Main Line from Wolverhampton to Birmingham, including eight stops and, passing through the three Factory Locks at Tipton, was timetabled for two hours and ten minutes.

In 1845, the Swift Packet Company's boats were given precedence over all others at locks, but, two years later, the Company's annual toll for five daily trips was increased by the BCN from £800 to £1,000 as a result of the 'great injury which is being done to the canal works' by the boats. The service finished towards the end of 1851 and an advertisement appeared in the *Wolverhampton Chronicle* for an auction 'upon the premises at Mr Shipton's Timber Wharf, Union Mill Street' on 17 December. The items included from fifteen to twenty 'well-seasoned harness horse, a useful horse and cart', saddles, bridles, horse clothing, weighing machine with weights, straw engine and bean mill with measures, other equestrian paraphernalia and 'a quantity of old Boat Lines'. Also to be 'disposed of by Private Contract' were two of the Swift Packet boats, the reason being that the Company had 'discontinued working the Packets'. With the opening of the Stour Valley Railway a few months away, Shipton must have seen the writing on the wall.

This was not the last attempt to introduce passenger traffic on the BCN. In April 1919, a letter from Fellows, Morton & Clayton was received, stating that they had been approached by the Dunlop Rubber Company about the possibility of providing

Dunlop workers' boat.

a motorboat to carry workpeople from Gravelly Hill, Aston, to their new works, Fort Dunlop, at Bromford, a distance of about 2½ miles (4km) with no locks. There would be three double trips Monday to Friday and three single ones on Saturday, 'for the present – perhaps more later on', at a charge of 1½d each journey. The boat, fitted with a 10hp engine, would travel at 4mph (6.5km/h). A trial had been carried out which showed that no damage from wash would occur to the banks. A charge of 5/- per journey would be levied by the BCN, plus £26 per year for use of the landing place at Gravelly Hill. The Clerk had met a representative from Dunlop, who seemed keen 'to make good use of the Canal for the transport of partly manufactured material between the firm's two works at Aston and the large new works at Erdington'.

The service was introduced on 28 April, but by October Dunlop was asking for a reduction, 'pointing out that the number of passengers carried on many of the journeys is considerably less than was anticipated', on average only thirty-two per boat, leading to a loss to the firm of about £80 a week. At the end of the month, it was reported that a winding hole had been dug near Brace Factory Bridge so that the boats had no need to go on to Tyburn Basin to turn, but in June the following year the service was discontinued as the tramway had been opened. In the fourteen months the scheme had operated, the Company had received £1,018 in tolls and Dunlop proposed retaining the boats 'for the carriage of goods'.

A Year in the Life

The mid-nineteenth century saw buoyant traffic on the BCN; 1850 ended with reports of a good supply of available water and traffic in January 1851 was 112,000 tons up on the previous year. At the time, the number of boats passing Golds Hill Stop on the Tame Valley Canal near its western junction at Ocker Hill, and those passing along the Rushall Canal, was being recorded in Committee Minutes.

Each month in 1851 saw an increase in trade on the same month from the previous year, of between 7,500–112,000 tons, and February's totals of 474,633 tons, 'exceed those of any corresponding month in any previous year'. Even though there had been water shortages in the autumn when 'the trade had suffered much in consequence', September's figures still showed an increase of 50,000 tons and October's of 60,000 tons. Monthly totals of the traffic carried, peaking at 514,706 tons in May, emphasized the importance of coal, generally amounting to just over 50 per cent, followed by ironstone, lime and limestone and general merchandise.

Boats Passing Golds Hill Stop and on Rushall Canal 1850–51

		Golds Hill Stop	**Rushall Canal**	**Revenue**
1850	Dec	1,148	319	£15,515 13s 0d
1851	Jan	1,252	426	£14,575 2s 3d
	Feb	1,144	412	£13,584 10s 8d
	Mar	1,233	542	£14,924 15s 9d
	Apr	1,334	564	£14,394 15s 5d
	May	1,463	584	£15,301 8s 4d
	Jun	1,207	541	£13,480 13s 1d
	Jul	1,377	647	£13,404 14s 7d
	Aug	1,280	608	£12,934 4s 4d
	Sep	1,222	497	£13,238 18s 1d
	Oct	1,553	655	£14,313 9s 5d
	Nov	1,570	699	£13,956 15s 1d

Lime Kilns at Dudley, now part of the Black Country Living Museum.

Quantities of Commodities Navigated on the Canal during November 1851

	tons	cwt	tons	cwt	tons	cwt
Coals for supply of Birmingham			53,510			
Coal via Worcester Canal	25,493	10				
Coal via Warwick Canal	8,736	6				
Coal via Coventry Canal	708					
Coal via Staffs & Worcs Canal	2,308	10				
Coal from Mr Brook to Fazeley	238	6	37,484	12		
Coal for supply of works in Mining District			145,878	10		
Total coal					236,873	2
Ironstone					47,521	10
Lime & limestone					32,939	
Sand					6,919	
Bricks					15,816	
General merchandise incl. building stone					109,419	17
Road materials & manure					12,016	10
Total					**461,504**	19

Sweet Smell of Success?

A fair amount of the manure carried was night soil, that is, human waste. In 1868, Wolverhampton Corporation took over responsibility for sewage disposal, which included the removal of night soil, in pails loaded on to carts, from houses around the town, and four years later bought a piece of land beside the canal at Crown Street. The Public Works Committee built a 'canal basin and stabling on it, for the accommodation of this department. Your Committee expect great benefit from having premises so convenient, and such improved facilities for getting rid of night soil, besides which, from its situation, they will effect a great saving in canal dues.' The night soil was distributed to farmers using the Corporation's boats.

The benefit did not stretch to the BCN's lockkeeper occupying the cottage by the tenth lock, who complained of the 'nuisance caused by the loading of night soil from the Corporation pails into boats at their Crown Street Wharf', and George Jebb wrote to the Town Clerk in May 1895. He was still writing two and a half years later after more complaints from 'J Davis the Lockkeeper at Fox's Lane Cottage ... of the nuisance caused by the loading of Night Soil, Stable Manure & other refuse in the basin'. Jebb considered the annoyance 'a very serious one & I think ought to be abated', but in any case the Corporation should pay for a replacement cottage. He did not see any objection to the Corporation renting the existing house, 'but I do not think it is fit that anybody should live so near the Night Soil Wharf'. An agreement about the cottage was signed between the BCN and Wolverhampton Corporation in June 1898. Given the proximity of the gasworks, a galvanizing plant and an artificial manure works, this must have been a particularly malodorous stretch.

CHAPTER 6

Working the BCN

Working for the Company

Necessary Officers

The first General Assembly of Proprietors outlined the roles and responsibilities of the Company's officers who were 'deemed essential for the Conduct of the Undertaking':

- **Clerk:** to attend General Assemblies and Committees, to keep an account of Proprietors' names, shares and addresses, 'and to enter the Transfers, and all other the Acts, Proceedings and Transactions of the Company'. John Meredith was appointed on a salary of £100 per annum.
- **Treasurer:** to receive all monies and pay the Clerk of the Works according to the Committee's orders. For such a financially responsible post, John Kettle deposited sureties of £5,000.
- **Surveyor:** to level and set out the works and to superintend and inspect their execution. James Brindley received a salary of £200.
- **Clerk of the Works:** to ensure that the works were carried out according to the Surveyor's directions, to measure the works, enter all contracts and act as intermediary between contractors and Committee. George Holloway, having given sureties of £1,000, was to be paid £140.
- There was also to be an Under-Clerk to assist the Clerk of the Works and a Book-keeping Clerk.

John Meredith, who had been involved with the Navigation from the very beginning, remained in post as Clerk, company secretary or chief administrative officer as he would be called now, for nearly twenty years. Part-time and probably overworked, Meredith was informed in June 1771 that the Committee expected his punctual attendance at their meetings while, sixteen years later, they noted that the Company's business was 'much retarded for want of the regular attendance of Mr Meredith' and that they expected him to inform them, 'in writing whether He will regularly attend … or not'. John Houghton was his successor in 1787 when Meredith took on the role of Secretary with an allowance of two guineas a day for attendance at Committee and General Assembly. Houghton, who had begun his career with the Company as a Book-keeping Clerk in 1774, remained in post until his death in 1825, when he was in turn succeeded by his deputy John Freeth. Son of the balladeer, he worked for the Company throughout his career, starting as a Writing Clerk and retiring in November 1842 due to ill health. By then his salary was £750 and because of his 'long, valuable and faithful service', he was awarded a gratuity of £375 for life.

BCN COMPANY CLERKS	
John Meredith	1768–87
John Houghton	1787–1825
John Freeth	1825–42
Robert Thomas	1842–76
W.W. Pilcher	1876–88
William Hutton	1888–1907
Richard Altham	1907–18
T.A. Henshaw	1918–26
Albert H. Pearshouse	1926–8
Percy Nadin	1928–46
George B. Lakin	1946–8

'Proper Persons to Steer and Stow'

With the canal's opening approaching, advertisements were placed in October 1769 for a superintendent at the wharf in Birmingham and 'for persons to have the conduct of the Boats'. At the same time, William Bentley was to look out for 'proper persons' to attend to the locks. Among their duties was checking the loads carried by each boat, for no boat carrying under 20tons was to be allowed to pass a lock without consent. They were also to report any offence committed against the Company's by-laws or Act of Parliament, 'that the Offender may be fined', and were to deal with the bills of lading carried by the boats. The role of employees at the wharf was laid out in detail in May 1770 when the Committee thought it necessary that a 'Person of Character and weight' should be appointed immediately as Superintendent to take charge of the whole conduct of the wharf and weighing machine. As he would be 'Cashier General', he had to give security of £300 'for the due & faithful execution of his Affairs'. He would receive a salary of £50 and supervise a wharfinger, two weighers, two Clerks and two watchmen. Part of the remuneration of the wharf staff would be paid by charging the 'private boats' for night-time security.

With the extension of the canal towards Wolverhampton, more Under-Clerks were taken on and, during April 1770, Brindley expressed confusion over the way that the Company's 'Clerks and servants' were being transferred from one job to another, a situation by which 'no Clerk or Agent seems to be responsible for a neglect of duty or inattention of his proper sphere of business'. It could be resolved by ensuring one piece of work was fully completed before the responsible Clerk was moved and that the Committee members received 'a particular account of the state of the business', so that they could clearly see the progress made. Another result of extending the cut was Holloway's application at General Assembly for a pay rise. 'The Business of the Canal now lay so distant, he was obliged to be almost constantly out at considerable Expences' and unless his salary was increased he would have to leave the Company's service. The Committee was given the power to raise his salary 'as they think necessary'. In May, two 'Walking Surveyors' were to be appointed, but by October this had increased to three and their remit was to be 'walking Surveyors and Stock takers'. In the end, William Foster and Richard Smith were taken on at twelve shillings per week each. One of their responsibilities was to give notice to anyone riding on the towpath that it was not allowed without written permission from the Committee. With the appointment of John Brookes in March 1771, they were dismissed.

John Brookes

A busy man, and versatile; during the first week of May John Brookes was involved in sorting out undersized boats and finding 'a proper person' to receive bills of lading, organizing eight boats for repairing towpaths, supervising the building of a wooden bridge, attending a meeting with Lord Dudley's agent, inspecting levels, preventing leakages and examining the state of a road damaged by a leak. The following week saw him finding suitable locations for 'Stops' where boats could be checked, inspecting Beswick's work 'where the Canal is defective in his Cutting' and ordering him to make repairs, and measuring up 'Solid yards

Wolverhampton Top Lock. Thomas Clayton boats Umea *and* Leam *returning from the gasworks, early 1960s. Nearly two centuries after being built, Littles Lane Bridge remained fairly steep and too narrow for the bus to cross.*

of Clay'. By the month's end, he had also worked on further land measurement and valuation, water supply to the canal and millers, and fencing in a piece of land. In June 1772, Brookes was appointed Collector of the tonnage at Wolverhampton with the additional responsibility for the 'care of the Canal from the Bridge in Fennywell Lane to the junction at Autherley'. He was soon negotiating for land for a road 'through Mr Walls garden' to make a convenient entrance to the planned wharf and preparing a plan of the wharf, adjoining land and showing the most convenient place for a house.

In June 1773, Brookes was to be 'consulted relating to the propriety of erecting of Cranes at Autherley for removing goods from 1 Boat to another', an early reference to trans-shipment. In November the following year, he was seeing to repairs to the bridge by Wolverhampton Top Lock, which had been 'scarcely passable' because of its steepness and the road was in a bad way. In January 1775, having asked for a coal allowance for his office, he was allowed £1 per year.

Lock-Keepers

With the canal nearing completion, lock-keepers were needed at Wolverhampton and the first one mentioned, in July 1772, was carpenter John Brown, who was to be employed in that role 'when the Junction to Autherley is Compleated'. Applications followed in August from Samuel Hyde, who could also assist with carpentry and expected 14/- a week, and blacksmith John Grigg, who was looking for 15/-. It seems that they were not taken on, but Thomas Jones was appointed that month, at 10/-, and John Birch also, ten days before the junction opened. A year later, John Brown, having been found to be 'very negligent and deficient in his duty' was discharged. He was not alone, for in January 1787, George Gutteridge, keeper of the Wolverhampton upper locks, was dismissed for attempting to defraud the Company and ordered to quit his house within three weeks.

There seems to have been a steady turnover of keepers on these upper locks for, at the end of the year, John Woodhouse was being appointed 'to succeed Kennedy', on the same wages. At Smethwick, following 'some suspicions respecting the manner of his Death', the Overseer of the Poor was paid one guinea for calling out a jury to enquire into the accidental death of William Hawksford, lock-keeper at the first lock house. Edward Bate was appointed as his successor and notice was given to Hawksford's widow to vacate the house 'on Monday or Tuesday next in which case one week's wages to be paid her but not before she has quitted the premises'.

'Of Essential Service', Surveyors and Superintendents

The main officer in charge of works along the line was originally the Surveyor of Works, later called Superintendent. In March 1774, applications were invited for the post of a Surveyor to superintend repairs to the works 'through the whole course of the Canal', with the stipulation that 'No person need apply who has not been Conversant in Works of this kind and cannot give sufficient Testimony of his Capacity for such an Undertaking'. John Cope filled the role part-time, being given a contract in April with a salary of £52 10s, for which he was expected to 'give up two entire Days in each Week' to inspecting locks, bridges, culverts, aqueducts, reservoirs, feeders, towing paths and fences 'through the whole course of the Canal'. He was to report any repairs needed to the Committee and to direct the work. The following August, the Company was again advertising for a Superintendent, now as a full-time post, as the Committee felt that such a person 'will be of essential service to the Company', and Mr Lowden was appointed in November. In April 1778, Lowden was found to have 'employ'd Himself in Business not belonging to the Company' and was discharged, to be replaced by Mr Denham in September.

The Company's Superintendent certainly had a varied workload, for as well as the day-to-day task of looking after the Navigation, often along with Samuel Bull, in August 1780 Denham was called on to deal with the problem of a new public house opened by the side of canal near the road between West Bromwich and Dudley. An opening had been made on to the towing path by which the Company's fences had been broken down and more damage was 'likely to be daily incurr'd unless such communication … is stop'd up'. He was to ensure that the publican mended the fences and to threaten legal action for any repetition. Following that, he was to 'dispose of one of the Ricks of Hay upon the Farm at Oldbury for the best price that He can get and reserve the other till spring'. His application for a salary increase the following January 'in consequence of his devoting the whole of his time to the Company's Service and the great expence He is at in the keep of his Horse', was granted and he received a further £30.

Bough and Bull

James Bough, with Samuel Bull as assistant, worked together on several schemes for the BCN during the latter part of the eighteenth century, most notably the Birmingham & Fazeley Canal and the summit lowering at Smethwick. Bough had been working as a mason for several years on the Birmingham Canal following employment on the Stroudwater Navigation. In March 1771, he was to 'employ his Men at Gornal in getting Stone for the use of the Locks beyond Wolverhampton' and in September he was supplying the bricklayers with stone to finish the locks.

At the end of November that year, the Committee was asking the overseer of the Bromsgrove road 'in what Capacity and at what wages Mr Bull hath been employ'd in the Oxford Canal'. The reply must have been favourable, for the following week they resolved that he be retained to look after the canal between Birmingham and Bilston and Birmingham and Wednesbury at a salary of £70, and by the end of the month he was 'to attend to the execution of such repairs as he hath himself reported … as necessary to be done'.

Following the passing of the Act for the Birmingham & Fazeley, the Company advertised for a Superintendent for the works and James Bough, having written to the Committee 'an Account of what He conceives to be the general Duty of a Superintendent', was invited to discuss the matter with John Houghton before attending a Committee meeting with him. In January 1784, he was appointed to the post of Superintendent at a salary of £120, 'considering the £20 as a recompence for keeping a Horse the more expeditiously to proceed in the Company's Business'. It seems that Denham and Bough were both employed until March 1786, when, following Denham's failure to keep the Navigation ice-free and 'that business being put under the direction of Mr Bough', he was called before the Committee. This may have been a final straw, as the members concluded that 'Mr Denham is not competent and qualified to discharge the duties of His important Office' and gave him six months' notice. In October 1786, the Committee commended Bough in a letter to their counterparts of the Trent & Mersey Canal, saying 'we much approve of the abilities of James Bough as an able Engineer and very capable of directing the execution having found that what He has heretofore done for this Company has been approved and scarce ever altered by Mr Smeaton, Watt and others who Survey'd it'.

Bough and Bull continued working together until the former's death in 1796; a letter from John Houghton to Mr Wall of West Bromwich Hall in March had noted that 'Mr Bough has for some time past & is now confined to his house by indisposition'. Bull was responsible for completing the aqueduct carrying the canal to Walsall at James Green, now called James Bridge, in 1797. Bough's replacement, Hood, stayed till 1809, when the work was divided between two superintendents.

MOLES

One of the more unusual roles, though probably necessary in the continual battle to keep the canal watertight, was mentioned in Committee Minutes during August 1774: 'That the Molecatcher do every week draw up the Stop Gates & that he have Satisfaction for his Trouble'. A scribbled memorandum beneath goes on to say that Mr Cope has 'undertaken the Above the Molecatcher not being able'. Perhaps he was too busy with a sideline in making trousers and waistcoats. Moles continued to be a problem and in April 1901 their burrowing in an embankment at Ogley Locks caused the loss of all the water over a distance of 56 chains, not far off three-quarters of a mile. The Engineer noted 'leakages from this cause are of common occurrence' and had the embankment not been 'composed wholly of sand', it would have been stopped before any damage had been done. In the event, the canal was closed for over a week.

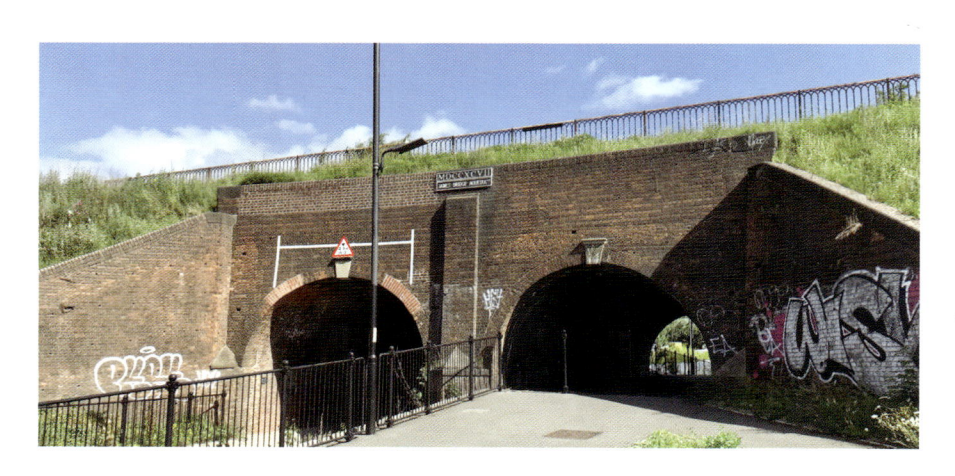

James Bridge Aqueduct. When built, the road went under the left-hand arch and the River Tame beneath the right.

Canal Cottages

The Company provided accommodation for its employees from the earliest days. In February 1770, it was minuted that 'the wages of the Lock-keepers be reduced to 10/- per week after their houses shall be completed'. These were to consist of a lower room, a chamber and a pantry. Other employees were provided with accommodation. At the end of 1772, Richard Hipkiss, who had been appointed wharfinger in Birmingham, was 'to live in a part of the Octagon Building Rent free', but this did not suit everyone. At the start of 1785, Spencer the Machine Clerk at the wharf in Birmingham, having complained that his 'present accommodations at the Office are very uncomfortable', was provided with a kitchen, lodging room and cellar on condition that he gave them up should the Committee need them. This arrangement did not last long, as he was dismissed in May for neglect and irregularity.

Early in 1787, it was resolved to build a house at or near 'Monmoor Green', about 1 mile (1.6km) from Wolverhampton Top Lock. It was for a Clerk whose main responsibility was 'to make out and enter numerical Cheques of the Ladeing of all Boats which pass'. Many other houses for Toll Clerks followed, along with lock-keepers' cottages and accommodation for lengthsmen, reservoir keepers, engineers and labourers. They were constructed at different periods and, in the early days, some had been built by the Dudley and Wyrley & Essington Companies. A numbering system to identify the houses evolved from the Districts that the BCN was divided into during the latter part of the nineteenth century:

- District No.1 included the Birmingham area, Birmingham & Fazeley Canal, Rushall Canal, parts of the Tame Valley Canal, Smethwick, Spon Lane and Ryders Green
- District No.2 covered the Wolverhampton and Tipton areas
- District No.3 comprised the Dudley, Oldbury and Rowley Regis areas
- District No.4 the Walsall, Cannock Chase and Lichfield areas.

At first, there were separate numbering schemes for each district, but these were combined in the mid-1920s, when the numbers still visible on surviving cottages were given. At the beginning of that decade, 273 properties were listed in the BCN's Cottage Rent Journal.

BCN cottage beside the Haines Branch at Great Bridge, 1972.

Nos 258 and 257 at Bodymoor Heath by Curdworth bottom lock, Birmingham & Fazeley, 1971.

Improvements were made to cottages, particularly by the provision of a piped water supply, such as, for example, to the one at James Bridge in August 1891. As part of the agreement, the BCN was to pay the L&NWR five shillings a year for a pipe crossing their land. In April 1897, the following was agreed, due to:

> sanitary arrangements at the house at Aston Top Lock having been found to be very defective and there being a difficulty in providing a Water Closet in consequence of the distance of the sewer from the house the Corporation have agreed to provide a Pan Closet the Company paying 10/- per annum.

Not all Company houses stood singly or semi-detached in canal-side locations. The Rent Journal lists terraces of six houses on Rood End Road and five on Birchfield Lane, Oldbury, with a further eight on Bridge Street, Smethwick. As well as providing accommodation, the Company also rented out Garden Land, the 1921 Journal recording fifty-six pieces, mostly near locks. Although it is hard for the modern eye to imagine garden plots at Ryders Green and adjacent to Factory Locks, one at Parkhead was still being used until 2016 and the vestige of a garden at the foot of Wolverhampton Locks, reverting to nature, can still be traced.

Neither did all employees live in Company houses. In 1873, an Officers' Conference discussed complaints, coming from Toll Clerks, that the weekly allowance of three shillings for accommodation 'is not sufficient to provide a respectable

---

ENGINEER'S REPORT TO COMMITTEE. FEBRUARY 23RD 1894

THE HOUSE OCCUPIED BY W. MATHERS THE WHARFINGER AT SMETHWICK WHARF IS IN SUCH AN UNSANITARY CONDITION THAT I RECOMMEND THAT IT BE PULLED DOWN. DURING THE PAST 15 YEARS MATHERS HAS LOST SEVEN CHILDREN, THE HOUSE IS NEAR THE ENTRANCE TO THE TUNNEL WHICH CARRIES THE FEEDER COURSE TO ROTTEN PARK RESERVOIR FROM WHICH FEEDER THERE IS OFTEN A VERY OFFENSIVE SMELL & IT IS PROPOSED THAT MATHERS REMOVE INTO ONE OF THE HOUSES ADJOINING SMETHWICK OLD PUMPING ENGINE NOW OCCUPIED BY A COMPANY'S WORKMAN & THAT HE REMOVE INTO THE HOUSE IN BRIDGE ST OCCUPIED BY THOMAS LEAVESLEY NOT A COMPANY MAN.

LONG SERVICE

Several early Company servants, such as John Houghton and John Freeth, had long careers with the BCN. The former served for just over fifty years and Freeth, who had intended to retire in 1839 on his own half-century, stayed on for a further three years. Meanwhile, a portrait of him, discovered among the effects of absconding Company Cashier Mr Bridgens, was to be 'purchased and placed in the Committee Room as a mark of respect for his character and long & confident services as principal Clerk in the Company's Office'. Another would appear to be the naming of Freeth Bridge on the Tame Valley Canal.

Robert Thomas, John Freeth's successor, was Clerk for thirty-four years and his career partly coincided with that of C.E. Maxwell, who compiled an *Index Rerum* where he noted down facts and figures pertaining to his own forty-eight year career with the BCN. Starting work at the canal office on 4 April 1870 as a Tonnage Clerk, Maxwell then also took on the duties as a Ledger Clerk before progressing to be the Company Correspondence Clerk. Later promoted as the Clerk's Chief Clerk and assuming the duties of Estate Clerk, he became Company Cashier, a post he held until retirement at the end of June 1918. Maxwell listed several long-serving employees in the Traffic Department. John Jones, Toll Clerk, had retired aged eighty after sixty-eight years working for the Company and enjoyed three years of retirement, while D. Pitt worked as a wharfinger until he was eighty-three, retiring after sixty years, though no length of retirement is recorded. Perhaps he had none to enjoy.

Long Service Awards were presented to employees during British Waterways' tenure of the BCN.

FRONTISPIECE: *On the Grand Union Canal near Watford*
LEFT: *Near Pollington Lock on the Aire & Calder Navigation*

home'. The Officers agreed and recommended that instead of the allowance, the Company should pay the rents of houses taken by the Clerks, 'care being taken that premises above their several positions in life are not occupied'.

Gauging

It was necessary that the Company should know the weight of cargoes carried on the canal in order that the correct tolls could be collected. At a Committee meeting attended by James Brindley on 11 November 1769, the engineer gave his recommendation:

> that all persons navigating with any Boat or Vessel upon the Canal, shall have a piece of Lead or other proper metal fixed at each end of the Boat marked and divided into inches, that so it may appear, not only what Burthen such Vessel is laden with, but also what water she draws.

In March 1770, Drs Ash and Small were to see to the method of weighing the boats and affixing the index.

In November 1772, notice was given to boat owners whose craft had not yet been gauged or had not had the 'Index's' fixed on them, to send them to the dock at Birmingham Heath to have the work done or take the consequences. They were also to ensure that their names were put on the outside of their boats in white capital letters. In case of a difference over the weight of goods, toll collectors had the power to 'stop and detain' any boat in order physically to weigh or measure the cargo, a time-consuming process which a later Act, of 1811, accepted caused 'great Delay, Expence and Inconvenience'. In future, it was made lawful to charge according to the gauge or graduated index of the boat.

A further Act, in 1835, authorized the BCN to gauge boats, compile books containing the information and affix a gauging number on a metal plate to each boat. This was carried out at an indexing station on an island in the new line in Smethwick cutting. Traffic could still pass on either side, while boats to be gauged would enter an open dock in the middle. Here, weights were added to the boat and its freeboard, with different loads determined and entered in the book. The system was further refined in 1873, with the rebuilding of Smethwick Indexing Station to accommodate two boats under cover, along with a new station that had two internal basins, beside the top lock at Tipton Factory Locks, at a total cost of £5,077. In May 1889, there were 12,430 boats on the register, with 475 gauged between 1886–8.

Among the earliest to be gauged at Tipton, this nameless open wooden boat was typical of the thousands on the BCN.

Tipton Gauging Station.

CONSTABULARY DUTIES

In November 1918, the BCN was employing Thomas Martin, 'this Company's Police Constable', who, with the help of a boatman, was involved in rescuing a young man and woman from the canal at the top end of the second of the Factory Locks. On questioning the parties afterwards, they said that they had 'walked into the canal in the dark'. In June 1920, the Clerk reported that Martin, then aged fifty-two and with twenty-six years' service, had tendered his resignation and that there was no one suitable on the staff to take up the position. It was suggested that the police work on the BCN could be undertaken by the L&NWR on behalf of the Company, as had already happened for the Shropshire Union Canal. As an aside, 'Mr Henshaw declined to order Uniform for Martin each year because he rarely used the clothes supplied by the Company'.

Smethwick Indexing Station was used until the 1920s and the buildings demolished in 1945, when brickwork from it was used to fill in the central channel. Tipton continued gauging boats until the early 1960s and the dilapidated building with its filled-in basins remains awaiting a future.

Boats and Boatyards

Company Boats

In April 1769, the Committee, meeting at the Navigation Office for the first time, resolved to acquire ten boats so that the 'undertaking may be forwarded with all possible dispatch for which purpose … such boats are essential'. George Holloway was sent to timber merchants at Lichfield and Worcester to discover the price of timber suitable for boat building delivered to Birmingham or Bromwich. In August, the Committee was ordering the Company's boatbuilders to get on with building fifteen boats, 'that number deem'd essential for the Company's use', and two months later they were ordering Holloway to provide 'temporary rudders, upright polls, and polls with spikes & hooks for ye boats', as well as seeking 'persons to have the conduct of the Boats'. Accordingly, *Aris's Birmingham Gazette* of 30 October carried an advert which specified that the boatmen must produce 'Certificates of their Sobriety and Honesty'.

Four days after the canal's opening, an official was sent to Shropshire to try to 'procure two proper persons to steer, and three to stow the Company's Boats'. Holloway was to see that a stage was built in each boat 'for the steersman to stand upon' and was also to obtain 'haling lines … and other necessities without delay'. The Committee wrote to John Gilbert, the Duke of Bridgewater's agent, to see if he could 'lend the Company a Boy or two to steer the Boats'. By 17 November, trade in coal was busy on the canal, with a dozen boats being used, timed so that a loaded and an empty boat would cross at the locks to save water and prevent loss of time. In October 1770, two dry docks were ordered to be built near the bridge at Birmingham Heath for cleaning and repairing the Company's and private boats, 'the latter paying an acknowledgement for each boat that goes into them'.

Although the Company finished with its own trading boats in 1794, it kept a fleet of maintenance craft. This expanded with the growth of the

---

EXTRACTS FROM 'INDEX TO ICE BOATS &C', 1902

DISTRICT NO.1 ICE BOATS : *PEARY, ARCTIC, ANTARCTIC, BAFFIN, MCCLINTOCK, NANSEN, PARRY II, POLARIS* AND THREE FLATS.
DISTRICT NO.2 ICE BOATS : *LAPLANDER, NORTH STAR* AND ONE FLAT.
DISTRICT NO.3 ICE BOATS : *NARES* AND *SPEKE*, A TUNNEL DREDGER AND A FLAT.
DISTRICT NO.4 ICE BOATS : *BALTIC, ESQUIMAUX* (OLD & NEW), *EMPRESS, ICEBERG, PANDORA, ROSS* AND *FRAM*
OCKER HILL ENGINEERING AND STORES DEPARTMENTS : *ANGLESEY*, ENGINE BOAT, LOCK PUMP, YACHT *SELENE*, THREE TUG BOATS, ONE FLAT, ONE NEW BOAT, A PONTOON FLOATING DOCK, NEW MOTOR PUMP BOAT, MORTAR BOAT, *NEPTUNE*, NO.A1, HOPPERS, STEAM DREDGER NO.1, STEAM DREDGER NO.2, STEAM UNLOADING PLANT NOS. 1 & 2 AND BOATS GENERAL.

Spoon dredger at Salford Junction, 1900s.

Spoon dredger on Eustace. *Black Country Museum, 1992.*

network until, by the start of the twentieth century, the Company had over 150 boats listed in a Boat Repair Book, which continued in use until 1947. By that time, the BCN was divided into the four geographical Districts previously noted, each with its own allocated maintenance boats, while the Engineering and Stores Department at Ocker Hill was accounted separately.

Dredging, to remove material washed or thrown into the channel, was an important maintenance task. As well as the steam dredgers, the BCN also used manual spoon dredgers, which, though more basic and heavier to work, could reach less accessible parts.

Committee Boats

In January 1770, the Committee members considered 'If a Boat should not be built for the Committee's convenience to inspect the Works', and a Proprietors' Meeting in September resolved to build two boats to be used by them, stressing that they were 'at no time to be used either by the Committee or any of the Prop'rs but upon the publick business of the Canal'. Perhaps this had been flouted or there was insufficient 'publick business' to attend to for in June 1779 it was further resolved that the 'Companys yatch be converted into a Coal Boat and the Windows and other spare materials be sold'.

Selene at Halesowen with members of the BCN Committee c.1920. (T.W. (Will) King Collection. Courtesy of Ruth Collins)

In the late 1830s there is mention of 'the Company's barge', *Amphitrite*, named after the sea goddess of Greek Mythology, and another of a Committee boat at the opening of Netherton Tunnel. A later inspection boat was used during the latter part of the nineteenth and early decades of the twentieth century. Bought second-hand in 1870 and named *Selene* by the Company, she was initially steam-powered and described as 'yacht Selene' in Engineer's Reports. Her boiler was regularly inspected; nine times between 1895 and 1900, when her value was put at £288. She was converted into a motor launch with a petrol engine at Ocker Hill in 1907 and three years later valued at £358. *Selene* was still on the books in 1939, though by then motor vehicles were being used for inspections.

Dayboats and Joeys

The ten boats ordered by the Committee in April 1769 would be the first of thousands to be built as the canal expanded. Most craft on the BCN were open and flat-sided, with blunt lines and a straight stem and stern. Used to take coal, pig-iron, sand, bricks and other materials to basins and wharves around the system, they were generally called dayboats, as they lacked the permanent living accommodation as well as the fine lines developed on long-distance narrowboats.

Many boatyards and docks were set up to construct and maintain these ubiquitous craft, one of the earliest and most successful belonging to Thomas Monk, who started a yard in Tipton around 1790. The site, by the entrance to Lord Ward's Branch, was still labelled Monk's Boat Dock on the large-scale BCN plan of 1895 and the business survived into the 1930s when it was run by another Thomas Monk, the founder's great-great grandson. Between 1788 and 1806, Thomas and his wife Sarah had eight sons and a daughter, all of whom were involved with boatyards. As well as building them, Thomas had a fleet of around 130 boats trading between the local canals, the rest of the Midlands and London and introduced the passenger carrying *Euphrates*. He is said to have first put cabins, originally a simple shelter also housing hay and corn for the horse, on canal craft, which developed into a small day cabin with a stove and bench. The family name is commemorated in the term 'monkey boats', sometimes applied to narrowboats.

Advertisement for George Hale.

In the same fashion, wooden 'joey' boats are said to be named after Joseph Worsey, another prolific boatbuilder with a number of docks. One, below the locks at Toll End, was operated by Worsey's during the first quarter of the twentieth century. The changing industrial fortunes of the Black Country saw the site later occupied by a firm manufacturing baby and invalid carriages, while a modern street, Worsey Drive, now stands nearby, apparently the only such naming in Britain. Other Worsey yards existed at various times in Tipton, Aston, Icknield Port and Walsall.

Some businesses that started with boatbuilding developed in other ways. An advertisement of 1851 shows that Stephen Thompson of Highfields Wharf, alongside the Birmingham Canal near Bilston, was making steam boilers, canal boats and water cisterns along with all kinds of wrought-iron roofing. In 1868, under the name William Thompson and Son, the range of products had expanded to include blast and stovepipes, colliery air pipes and wrought-iron girders, but still included iron boats. The 'son' was John, the driving force behind an expansion of the business and specialization in boilermaking, including some, in the early twentieth century, for Fellows, Morton & Clayton boats. The works had moved in 1870, to new premises by the cut near Catchems Corner Bridge at Ettingshall. Developing into one of the largest industrial concerns in Wolverhampton and with worldwide connections, the Ettingshall Works lasted longer than most other traditional Black Country firms, finally closing in 2004.

Catchem's Corner, *a striking painting by Joseph Fereday.*

Some joey boats were nicknamed according to the goods they carried or the traffic they were involved with. Rag boats carried Rowley Rag from the quarries, while Tow Rags were boats belonging to the Severn & Canal Company Ltd and towed on the river. Railway Boats worked the boatage services between the works and interchange basins and 'ot 'olers ventured into the basin by the blast furnaces of Stewarts & Lloyds Springvale Steelworks.

The manner of working the dayboats on regular runs was normally to have a boatman and a horseman. Father and son pairings were not unusual, so the experience passed through the generations. The boat was basically an empty shell, with all the movable parts going with the men when they moved from boat to boat. Having delivered, say, a load of coal to a canal-side factory, the towing mast, tiller and 'ellum' (BCN name for the rudder), shafts, lines and fire bucket or stove were transferred to an empty one for the return to wharf or pit. If the destination was a basin with no towpath access, the horse would be unhitched and the boat shafted through the bridge 'ole.

Examples of 'ot 'olers at Springvale Furnaces.

Birchills was among the last wooden dayboats to be built on the BCN, at Ernest Thomas's dock above Walsall Locks in 1954. Restored, she is the only surviving joey with a day cabin. Black Country Museum, 1998.

DISTANCE TABLES

The BCN's volumes of Distance Tables, measured in miles, furlongs and links, and compiled in the early years of the twentieth century, give the lengths of the various canals and branches, locating bridges, locks, junctions, wharves and basins, the position of works, furnaces and factories, and also boat docks. Nearly sixty of these are listed and although not all would necessarily have been working at the same time, they give another indication of the busyness of the system in its heyday.

6

	5	7	885	Slater's Coal Wharf
Portway Road and Shidas Lane Brick Works =	5	7	755	
Hay Wharf	5	7	545	
Whimsey	5	7	405	Bridge
Hay Wharf	5	7	225	
Park Hall Wharf—Morris' Brick Works	5	7	125	
Whimsey Bridge Coal Wharf, Tonks =	5	6	925	
Accles & Pollock's Tube Works =	5	6	885	
W. E. Chance & Co.'s Glass Works =	5	6	755	
	5	6	735	**JUNCTION OF OLD CANAL** (Pages 23 and 24)
Radnalfield Brick Works =	5	6	670	
Churchbridge Brick Works, Valentia Wharf, = Chance & Hunt's Boat Dock	5	6	545	
Seven Stars	5	6	035	Bridge
	5	5	735	= Basin
Chemical Arm—Chance & Hunt, Albright & Wilson, and Park Lane Iron Works	5	5	175	
Thompson's Malthouse	5	4	565	
Stone Street	5	4	525	Bridge
T. Clayton's Wharf	5	4	445	
Roving	5	4	115	Bridge
JUNCTION OF TITFORD BRANCH (Page 21)	5	4	045	
Anchor	5	2	945	Bridge
Hale's Boat Dock	5	2	720	= G. Hale's Lime Kilns Basin

6

Distance Table extract – a busy stretch in Oldbury.

Les Allen and Sons – One of the Last

Les Allen had followed his father into the boat-building business, becoming foreman boatbuilder at Spencer Abbot's Gravelley Hill Dock by Salford Bridge. In 1949, Les was interviewed by a local paper on the state of the business and spoke about the boats. The design hadn't changed in the last half-century, he said:

> We still make them of English elm and English oak, the elm for the bottom and the oak for the sides. They're carvel built with caulked seams.

Their size hasn't changed either, they're still the regular 71ft. long with a 7ft. 1in. beam, and they draw 10in. empty and about 2ft. 6in. loaded.

Les thought that the only difference was the oakum used for caulking seams: 'It used to be picked by prisoners but now they don't do it any more for punishment so we have to use machine-picked oakum and it's not so good …'.

In 1950, Les Allen moved to T&S Elements' boat dock in Oldbury, where the firm, continued by his sons Bob and John, remained, making fine-lined, traditional style steel leisure boats until closure in 1997, one of a handful of yards to span the change from commerce to leisure.

Sunken Boats

Boats can sink through accident, negligence, overloading and, occasionally, on purpose. If they are causing obstruction or inconvenience, they need to be recovered. A note in the Company Minute Book in March 1770 reported that Mr Fford's Boat was sunk and that he 'had requested that Water might be let off to get up the same'. The Committee declined for many unspecified reasons, but particularly 'as it will injure the Mills'.

One of the earliest private carrying concerns on the canal was the Birmingham Boat Company, which had been granted permission to build a shed on the Company's Wharf in August 1770. The following February, they were given leave to let off the water at the Wednesbury stop gate to raise a boat sunk there, and they were asking again, in June, to let off three or four inches to raise a further one, a request that had risen to six inches for another in November. By March 1772, the Company was informing boat owners that water would no longer be let off for that purpose.

By the twentieth century, a system had been established that involved the Company keeping bound books of 'Raising Boat Accounts'. Ninety-seven boats were raised during 1912 at a cost starting at £1 2s and increasing with the amount of work needed; for instance, the charge for raising a boat at Snow Hill Lock and removing it to Farmer's Bridge was calculated at £1 6s 2d. Owners could also be charged for mooring up or tying up loose boats, for 'removing out of the way of trade' and for 'scoping' – baling out water with a wooden scoop. Some incidents proved more expensive. In March 1916, Stewarts & Lloyds of Coombs Wood were charged £11 13s 4d (equivalent to around £1,250 currently) for 'Expenses incurred in lowering water in the Gosty Hill Tunnel to raise your boat'. As traffic decreased, so did the number of boat raisings and by 1939 it had fallen to twenty-seven.

Pleasure Boats

The question of pleasure boats having been raised by the Committee, a General Meeting of Proprietors, held at the end of September 1770, had voted that none should be allowed to use the canal. This seems to have come about from information that Messrs Grew and Co. had been using the cut for that purpose, so John Meredith was to write to Mr Grew that he should desist from this under the threat of prosecution. The Proprietors also gave notice that no navigation whatsoever was to be allowed on Sundays. As has been noted, passenger boats, sometimes used for special occasions, were seen on the system over the years.

'For the Good of the Souls'

Concerns about the moral welfare of workers on the canals and their effects on others had long been expressed. In September 1826, 'A Friend To Order' had written to *Aris's Birmingham Gazette* complaining about 'the great number of bricklayers and labourers at work on the new Canal Bridge at Birmingham Heath' on a Sunday. This was no doubt Lee or Winson Green Bridge, which both carry the date MDCCCXXVI. The correspondent was mostly concerned about the effects of this on:

> from fifty to one hundred young persons that pass this road from School to Church, with a Clergyman at the head of part of them, who are obliged to

witness this breach of decorum – besides a great number of working people who take an idle walk to waste away the important hours of the Sabbath.

Later in the century, concern became focused on the boaters themselves. Philanthropist George Smith of Coalville published *Our Canal Population* in 1875, mainly to draw attention to the miserable lives of many long-distance boaters. He included a description of 'the Worcester Wharf' – Gas Street Basin:

The visitor passing the gates lands in a strange region, which partakes of the nature of docks, carriers' yards and a small Dutch port. The mysterious windings of the canal are quaint, and side by side lie some dozens of boats, huge coal heaps, piles of timber, trusses of hay, sacks of corn; and such cargoes slightly enliven the dreary waste of cinders and watery lines. It is a desolate and wild place, especially on a dark muddy Sunday evening ….

Boatmen's Rests

Although largely aimed at the crews of long-distance 'cabin boats', the 'Missions' built around the canal system also catered for the men operating short-haul traffic around the BCN who might find themselves away from home overnight or waiting hours for loading or to go through locks. A small red-brick building, close by Tipton Top Lock and now used for light industry, gives its past away by the finials decorating its gable ends and the stub of a tower on its roof. This once held a bell, while a tell-tale change in the brickwork by the towpath wall shows where an arch surmounted by a cross once led to the Boatmen's Mission. Its foundation stone was laid by Mrs Legge, wife of the Bishop of Lichfield, in 1892.

The Diocese sponsored an active industrial mission to the 'barge population on the canals, and to the slums of the large towns in our midst, to spread the Gospel and rescue the fallen'. In 1904, three services were held at Tipton Mission each Sunday and one on Saturday evening. Other missions were established by the Incorporated Seamen and Boatmen's Friend Society in Birmingham in the early 1860s, as well as at Hednesford and Walsall. The last came about after a supporter had visited Walsall one November:

on a very stormy and rainy day. He saw a great crowd of men with their horses standing on the towing path side, exposed to the inclemency of the weather. The friend walked alongside the eight locks, through inches of mud, towards Darlaston, and he felt there ought to be a 'rest' for boatmen at the top lock at Walsall.

Designed by George Jebb, it was built at Birchills beside the top lock and opened in 1901. Described as a 'coffee and reading room and a mission room', it was built at a cost of £350 with the aim of acting as 'a new centre of mission work in connection with the society'.

The Society's missions were busy places, with 16,754 visitors, 'chiefly boatmen', to the coffee

Birchills Mission, 1993. The adjacent cottage was built in 1841.

rooms in 1909, rising to 17,690 in 1912. This had increased, in 1914, to 26,000 at Birmingham and 13,000 at Birchills. The latter closed around 1948, but for several years was involved in a mission of a different sort, being opened as a canal museum between the mid-1980s and 2003.

Poor Old Horse

As the prime mover on the BCN for most of the canal's working life, thousands of horses worked around the system and stabling was provided by the Company at key locations. Unfortunately, the horse was not always well-treated. Historian William Hutton described horses on the original Birmingham Canal as little better than skeletons covered with skin: 'whether he subsists upon the scent of water, is a doubt; but whether his life is a sense of affliction, is not; for the unfeeling driver has no other employment but to whip him from one end of the canal to the other'. From the 1830s, measures were introduced dealing with animal protection, but there were still reports of cruelty a century later; two boatmen were each fined £1 and ordered to pay costs at Walsall in November 1931.

A CRUEL BOATMAN : *Birmingham Post* **26 March 1891 Wolverhampton**

At the Police Court yesterday, Thomas Lowe, canal boatman, was summoned for cruelty to a pony. Inspector Luckings spoke to finding a pony on the canal side in an emaciated condition. There were a number of people standing around it but no one admitted the ownership. A little later, however, he found the animal attached to a boat laden with 19 tons of coal, and the defendant was urging it along. When served with a summons the defendant said the pony died a few days after the witness had seen it. The Stipendiary pointed out that if the defendant had been previously convicted for such an offence he would have been committed to prison. A fine of 40s and the costs was imposed.

Equine Friends

The Incorporated Seamen and Boatmen's Friend Society involved itself with the welfare of horses, building stables at Walsall, Hednesford, Rushall and Great Bridge with the help of donations from individuals and groups. At the end of 1891, George Jebb reported the receipt of a letter from the Boatmen's Union requesting that the Company

Stables and cottage at Titford Top Lock, 1970s.

provide 'a shed' at the top and bottom of Ryders Green Locks for boat horses to stand in while waiting their turn. He submitted a sketch for a shed that would 'accommodate 10 or 12 horses' at a cost of £82. This was on a busy stretch of canal for, although it had sixteen locks, it was a shorter route between the Cannock pits and the Main Line than that through Wolverhampton, and it also received traffic coming off the Tame Valley Canal. In 1851, over 15,000 boats were recorded passing through Golds Hill Stop near the junction of the Tame Valley with the Walsall and this had increased to 40,580 in 1898, while Ryders Green Locks passed 63,635 boats the same year.

Bad winters created extra problems and in January 1892, although the canals were kept open during a severe frost, 'very great difficulty was experienced in hiring horses. This difficulty seems to increase every Season, Farmers & others being very unwilling to hire horses for such a dangerous occupation.'

In 1900, Jebb considered that 'it would be in the interest of the Company to have a stable for one horse to be built at Factory Locks, Tipton, as occasionally a horse is wanted for an emergency and has to be fetched from Ocker Hill, a distance of 1½ miles where No.2 District horses are stabled'. The cost would be about £30. Care of horses was important and, following an outbreak of Parasitic Mange in April 1918, BCN Engineer Willet, at the request of a representative of the Board of Agriculture, had ordered the cleansing, whitewashing and disinfecting of the Company's stables and horse shelters.

At the boatage depot established at Ninelocks Wharf in Brierley Hill, there was extensive stabling and from the 1920s the London, Midland & Scottish Railway (LM&SR) employed its own

Remains of a horse shelter at Ryders Green Top Lock, 1982.

farriers, ostlers and a veterinary surgeon who had use of an equine sickbay. Although no trace of this remains, a late nineteenth-century stable block still stands down the flight, by the third lock. In the latter days of working, men and horses would meet loaded boats brought by tug to the top lock and take them down the flight and the Stourbridge sixteen locks, returning with an empty boat.

Horse boating continued long on the BCN. Clayton's boats and rubbish boats were still being horse-hauled in the 1960s and Black Country boatman Caggy Stevens carried on until the mid-1970s.

Thomas Clayton's Mole *with Jack Taylor on Farmer's Bridge Locks, 1958.*

Thomas Clayton's Gifford *under repair at Ken Keay's yard, Walsall, 1973.*

Gifford restored.

Working boats at Titford. Tug Caggy and Thomas Clayton tar boats Stour and Gifford at the BCN Society's 2006 gathering to mark the 40th anniversary of the end of Clayton's Oldbury-based carrying company.

CHAPTER 7

The Railway Connection

Steam on the Twenty-one.

Rumours

It is believed that the first wholly iron rails were produced by Richard Reynolds at Coalbrookdale in the same year that James Brindley was presenting his plans and estimates for the Birmingham Canal. At first, railways were seen as a useful adjunct to the Navigation and the Birmingham Committee was resolving in November 1769 that they be made 'at the Collierys as expeditious as possible for the more convenient loading of the Boats'. The Wyrley & Essington Canal was involved in a dispute with colliery owner Henry Vernon at the end of the eighteenth century when he proposed building a railway from his pits directly to the Staffordshire & Worcestershire Canal, a serious threat to the Wyrley concern. In the end this never materialized and a line was built to the latter's Lord Hayes Branch.

The next inkling that the railway might be a competitor rather than just a supplier came in 1810, when William James, a Henley-in-Arden solicitor and land agent to the Earl of Dartmouth among others, proposed a scheme for a canal and railway to join Walsall and Fazeley. It was possibly part of his wider proposal for building a national network, a General Railroad Company. This came to nothing but, in 1822, after hearing of material plans for the Liverpool & Manchester Railway, the Birmingham Committee resolved to 'neglect no opportunities or endeavours to protect the Company's Interests and Property from innovation or injury'. Opportunities were soon presented. In June 1823, Thomas Eyre Lee, the Company's solicitor, had written to James Loch, agent to George Granville Leveson-Gower, the Marquis of Stafford and inheritor of his uncle the Duke of Bridgewater's canal interests, 'to ascertain whether rumours industriously circulated ... have any more solid foundation as connected with the Marquis ... than I have found them to be when connected with the names of other respectable Noblemen. One would have thought that the age of wild speculation had passed away.' Lee was afraid that aristocratic support of railways might lead to the establishment 'as a Parliamentary principle the propriety of running railroads parallel to old canals'. According to Loch there was nothing to the rumour.

This was still a time when an article in the *Quarterly Review* could dismiss 'those persons who speculate on making rail-ways general throughout the kingdom, and superseding all the canals, all the wagons, mail and stage-coaches, post-chaises, and, in short, every other mode of conveyance by land and by water, we deem them and their visionary schemes unworthy of notice', and could go on to describe as 'palpably absurd and ridiculous' the idea that locomotives would move 'with twice the velocity, and with greater safety' than coaches. However, it did point out the disadvantages of canals regarding water supply, weather and speed, conceding that the contest between canals and railways 'will speedily be brought to issue'.

Birmingham to Liverpool

At the end of April 1824, the *Birmingham Chronicle* was reporting that 'a meeting was held at the Swan Inn at Wolverhampton ... when it was resolved to ... form a company to establish a Rail Road, with locomotion Steam-engines, from Birmingham to Manchester and Liverpool'. In September, *Aris's Birmingham Gazette* reported on a meeting of the Committee of the Birmingham & Liverpool Rail-Road Company at the Royal Hotel, Birmingham. It was, they resolved, to run from Birmingham, through the Staffordshire Collieries and Iron Works, by Wolverhampton, Nantwich and Chester, to the Mersey, with branches to Dudley and Stourbridge. The object was 'to establish a more direct, expeditious and cheap communication' and, with a dig at canals, the motive power of locomotives and stationary steam engines, would be able to 'transport the heaviest Goods with certainty and security, by day and night, at all times of the year, in periods of frost or of drought, at a rate of at least eight miles an hour'. The line would be able to carry goods at a cost a third or even a half cheaper than currently, as the capital required to build and maintain it would be 'much less than that employed by any existing establishment for the conveyance of Goods'. The trade of the country, they claimed, had increased in such an astonishing way that 'sufficient employment therefore may be found both for the Canals and Rail Roads', but as the latter 'can carry with undeviated punctuality, security and celerity', it would both provide good profits for its supporters and 'create a competition highly advantageous to the public'.

Not to the BCN, however. Lee, 'as Chairman of the Birmingham Canal Navigations', had written to his counterpart at the Wyrley & Essington soliciting support 'in opposing and counteracting the Project', which might 'tend to the Establishment of similar undertakings in other Districts and Directions and deteriorate the Property invested in Inland Navigations'. The canals were joined by other interests in opposing the Bill, including landowners 'aware of the serious inconvenience and injury to their property' arising from the scheme. Lee was soon once again writing to Loch suggesting that the scheme was 'a Banker's manoeuvre', supported 'by few people of real importance' in Birmingham. However, at the same time plans were being made to scupper the railway by building a new, direct canal between Wolverhampton and the Mersey.

Railway or Canal?

The usual flurry of correspondence broke out across the pages of the Birmingham press, including the still fairly novel cries about locomotives frightening the horses and cattle not grazing where 'steam engines are continually smoking and moving with a great noise', being countermanded by attacks on the BCN's monopolistic aims and an accusation that the Company had employed one of its agents to assure 'those that would listen to him', that no gentleman would be able to cross, or presumably hunt across, 'the rail-road, as it was intended to erect a WALL on each side of it FROM END TO END!!' A correspondent from London, 'a considerable holder of canal shares' could see that the 'introduction of locomotive engines may be considered a new era in the annals of this commercial country' and urged Canal Proprietors to realise that it 'cannot be prevented by the machinations of a few interested individuals'. He went on to mock the Birmingham Company with its improvement schemes and 'delegates from other dirty waters' who had met to 'cook up the opposition to the Rail-way', with sarcasm:

> Is it not obvious that two lines of canal will be kept in repair at less expence than one? That two or three towing-paths will be cheaper than one? Is it not obvious to the meanest capacity that the tonnage on a short line will be much more profitable than upon a long one? Fear not that we shall soon drown all our competitors.

He had decided to 'take shares in the one undertaking by way of edging out of the other', the rising price of railway shares and the 'falling prices of canal property, are sufficient evidences of the public estimate of their respective merits'.

More Opposition

Although the Birmingham and Liverpool Railway Bill was defeated in 1825, it was quickly reintroduced, with the Proprietors again putting forward their case, stating that the distance from the two towns was between 115–120 miles (185–193km) by canal and the Mersey and only 90 miles (145km) by the proposed railway, while the average time for a fly-boat to make the trip was 'at a very low estimate', sixty hours, but by the railway 'it will not exceed 15 hours'. A load of merchandise of 16 tons, 'the average of a boat's cargo', dispatched by railway from Birmingham at 5am., would arrive in Liverpool at 8pm 'instead of being days and night on the journey'. The railway supporters, conscious of the new canal proposed from Wolverhampton to Nantwich, the Birmingham & Liverpool Junction, expressed their:

> considerable surprise inasmuch as, whilst it proposes to occupy the line of country previously selected by them, it admits the necessity of extended accommodation for the public, and thus confirms the correctness of this part of the case of the Railway, which was so strenuously denied by the Canal Proprietors in the last Session of Parliament.

Having admitted the need for improved communications, Parliament would have to decide which of the two parties had the better case. It chose the canal and the railway company was dissolved in June. The BCN continued in its opposition to railway schemes, coming out against a proposed Birmingham, Dudley & Wolverhampton line. First projected in 1830, it floundered with the Birmingham & Liverpool Railway's defeat, but was resurrected five years later, one of its main arguments being that 'the town of Dudley cannot from its locality have any communication with the Canals, except by a tedious and expensive conveyance by land carriage'. Shares were being traded in December and meetings of local Turnpike Trustees were discussing whether to allow the proposed railway to lay its lines across their roads. All was in vain, for in November the following year, 'having taken into consideration the certain and powerful opposition ... from the Committee and Proprietors of the Grand Junction Railway and Birmingham Canal Companies, and the most influential land owners on the line, together with the manifest indifference of the inhabitants of Dudley and Wolverhampton', the company was dissolved.

Birmingham & Liverpool Junction Canal

The proposal for a Birmingham & Liverpool Junction Canal presented an opportunity to speed up traffic to the north and was partly initiated and greatly supported by the Birmingham Company. Thomas Telford had seen it as a logical extension to his works on the BCN, as in 1825 he had written to the Trent & Mersey Company that he had, 'in the course of my investigations, with the view of rendering unnecessary, the proposed lines of railway between Birmingham & Liverpool, found it advisable to recommend making a canal between Autherley and Nantwich'. Second-generation Birmingham Canal men, including Samuel T. Galton along with the younger James Watt and John Freeth, were on the new company's Committee in September 1825 and Thomas Eyre Lee was appointed as Clerk. The Birmingham & Liverpool Junction opened between Autherley and Gnosall in January 1835 and fully on 2 March, exactly six months after the great engineer's death. Freeth was among the officials on the first boat to traverse the 39 miles (63km) of the canal, commenting later that 'the state of the Great Bank is still very precarious'. This was the massive 70ft (21m) high embankment at Shelmore. The man tasked to complete it was William Cubitt, who, along with others working with Telford on his last canal projects, was soon to turn his skills to railway work.

THE TETTENHALL & AUTHERLEY CANAL

With no direct connection between the BCN and the new canal, boats had to traverse the thousand yards of Staffordshire & Worcestershire water between Aldersley and Autherley and pay for the privilege by a compensation toll at the rate of one shilling a ton. A plan was hatched for the Tettenhall & Autherley Canal and Aqueduct, which would leave the BCN above Wolverhampton's Lock 19, leapfrog the S&W on an iron aqueduct and fall through four locks to join the B&LJ. The threat worked and the S&W reduced its tolls to 4d a ton.

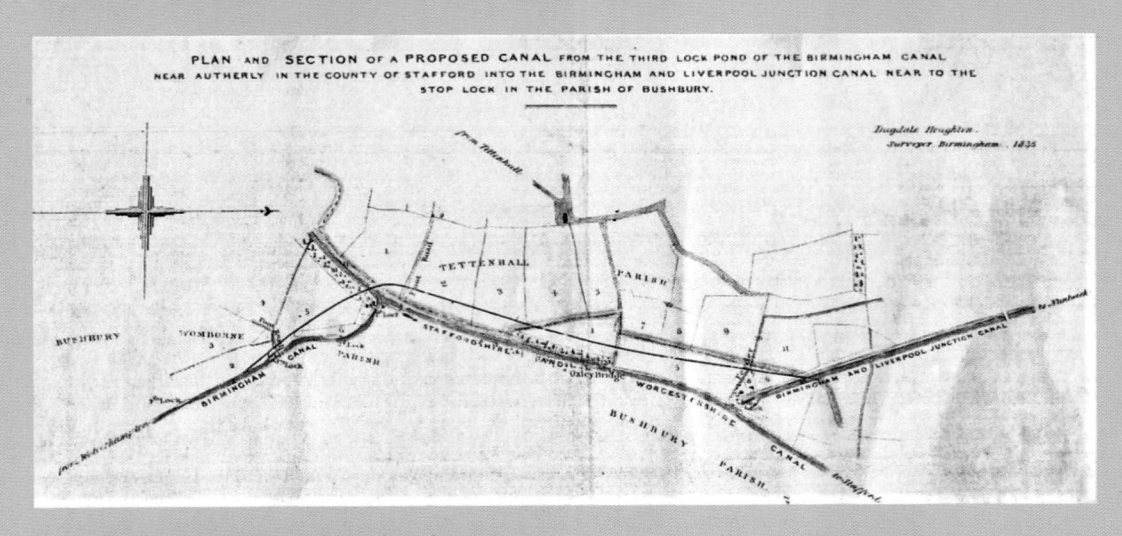

Tettenhall & Autherley Canal and Aqueduct plan.

'It Will Not ... Do to Sleep'

In 1829, James Loch, busy juggling the Marquis of Stafford's canal and railway interests, had written to Lee, both commending the BCN's New Main Line as 'the most magnificent works imaginable', while at the same time warning, 'It will not, I assure you, do to sleep'. While the BCN man agreed and thought that the Navigations between Birmingham and London should join with Telford to build a new canal, he seemed convinced that the companies would not agree, stating: 'I am sure that Mr Telford is fully satisfied that nothing but perfect canals can compete with the power of steam, but if he be not properly supported ... he cannot be blamed for injuries brought on by the blindness of others'. He still doubted that railways would carry heavy goods, claiming that the rails and pistons were simply not strong enough.

However, the opening of the Liverpool & Manchester Railway in September 1830 would soon prove the inevitability of railways and on 6 May 1833 the Birmingham & Liverpool's successor, the Grand Junction Railway, together with the London & Birmingham Railway, were both sanctioned by Parliament. When complete, they would form a trunk line from the capital to the north, passing through Birmingham. In 1830, the BCN had initiated a Subcommittee to examine the effects of railways 'on lines parallel to the Birm Canal', and despite approaches from other companies, began to pursue a policy of defending itself 'upon its independent merits against such Railways as may affect its interests'. To that effect, a clause 'for the prevention of Hindrance and Obstruction to this Canal and for the preservation and protection of the rights, privileges and authorities of the Company' was prepared to be inserted into the London & Birmingham Railway Bill. Rather than confrontation with the railways, the BCN seemed content to demonstrate a degree of cooperation and the building of several stretches of the railway line in Birmingham was eased by assistance from the BCN.

Comparisons

'The Most Perfect Canal in the Kingdom'

Having pushed through its own major and expensive modernization plans, and bolstered by the advantages of a concentrated system with a guaranteed and flourishing local trade, the BCN had adopted a decidedly superior attitude towards its neighbours. In 1824, when the Warwick & Birmingham Canal complained that Ashted Locks, leading to the Digbeth junction between the canals, were often closed at night, while the canal to Fazeley was open day and night, the BCN gave the haughty reply that the Fazeley route remained open as it carried urgent Liverpool trade; when the Warwick line was as busy, equal service would be provided. In response to called-for reductions in tolls to meet railway competition, the BCN claimed that the other canal companies could have no claim on it 'until full amends shall have been made by them for the loss and inconvenience arising from their supineness & want of spirit'.

The Company's officers were not above a little bragging. Their own efforts during an unusually dry period, the 'short water season for 1840', when 'the Company's resources, though put to a most severe test, proved sufficient for the accommodation of trade, and ... the humiliating step of compelling Boats to wait turns at the Locks, was not resorted to at any one point throughout the whole of the

---

UNDER THE CUT

The first main line to open through the district was the Grand Junction, in July 1837, just a fortnight into the Victorian Age. Taking a direct line, it bypassed both Wolverhampton and Walsall, passing beneath the Wyrley & Essington, where William Pitt had engineered the canal along the watershed at Wednesfield Heath. This was the railway's Summit Tunnel, where thirsty locomotives were replenished, not from some bubbling headstream but rather by a series of leather tubes connected with a reservoir supplied by the canal. Further south-east, the line passed under the Walsall Canal on a brick and stone aqueduct built at Bentley while the canal was diverted. The cast-iron liner was found to leak in several places and was only made watertight with difficulty. This delay meant that Bentley Aqueduct was the last structure on the line to be completed.

extensive and complicated lines of the Company'. This could be contrasted with the failure of others 'a considerable fall of rain having taken place, and the neighbouring Canals being now navigable …'.

State of the Waterways

On 28 August 1838, John Freeth, in an address to Committee members who were about to attend a meeting of canal delegates and traders, spoke at length about the current state of the waterways. After expanding on the improvements carried out by the BCN, he went on to point out that, except for the 5 miles (8km) of the Oxford Canal between Napton and Braunston, 'the several Canals constituting the shortest existing Route between Birmingham and London … have undergone no shortening or improvement whatever'. He pointed to the 'faulty levels of excessive lockage … remaining uncorrected' and stated that the length of the water route was 'more than 33 Miles' longer than 'the Railway now about to be opened'. This was the London & Birmingham Railway, which started running a full service between its termini at Euston and Curzon Street on 17 September.

The lack of waterway improvement, along with inter-company rivalries and arguments over the rates for tolls, had brought about a decline in 'the vend of Staffordshire Coal' in the southern markets. The total had fallen from 270,181 tons in 1832 to 186,691tons in 1836. Only following a reduction in the Grand Junction Canal's rates in 1837 did they rise again to 212,376 tons, 'still very far short of the pitch to which it attained prior to the Compact of the 3 Companies'. The Warwick & Birmingham, Warwick & Napton and Coventry Canals had 'entered into an engagement' resulting in not only depriving the public of part of the benefit intended by reducing rates, but also in diverting the southbound coal trade 'wholly into the Warwick Route, to the great and manifest injury of the Birmingham Canal Company'. This was evidenced by the tonnages of coal passing through Fazeley, falling from 51,416 tons in 1832 to 9,212 five years later. Furthermore, Freeth concluded, although the BCN's improvements, together with reductions of tolls on coal by 50 per cent at the Worcester Bar Lock and the diversion of trade through the Kingswood Route adding 'considerably to the Revenues of the Worcester & Birmingham and Stratford on Avon Canal Companies', it was the case that neither company had made 'any serious effort to bring about such diversions, but on the other hand, have on every occasion, exhibited the most marked & unaccountable Apathy in relation thereto'.

Joining Forces

As the BCN continued to grow in the 1840s with the Wyrley & Essington and Dudley Canal amalgamations, the building of the conjoining lines and the opening of the Tame Valley Canal, proposals for new cuts were floated. One, first suggested by James Walker in his November 1839 report on the Tame Valley, was to run between Friars Park on the latter and the tenth lock at Wolverhampton. It would benefit 'the general traffic of the country' by saving lockages, up to and then down from the Wolverhampton Level, of sixty-five feet and could be achieved by 'forcing the Walsall Level under the Wyrley Canal to join the present canal upon the same level at Gosbrook'. Although the idea was investigated in June 1841, nothing ultimately came of it.

The system grew, improvements were made and maintenance was non-stop, but profits did not reflect the expansion, nor the huge amounts of capital invested in them. Between 1835 and 1844, the new canals had cost £636,793 and the Company had to raise a further £130,307 to complete them. The first half of the 1840s saw a stagnation in trade, with the price of bar-iron in the Black Country slumping from £9 to £2 10s in three years, accompanied by wage reductions, bankruptcies, strikes and riots. The BCN Minute Book, however, was able to report, on the last day of 1841, that 'Notwithstanding the bad state of the Iron Trade and the depressed state of Trade generally, the revenue of the Concern for last month (November) exceeded that of any of the corresponding month of any preceding year'. It had risen to £11,465. Profits peaked at £42,032 during the half year ending in September 1841, but with interest to be paid on the sums borrowed, dividends could only be paid by dipping into reserves. The BCN found itself in a similar position to its precursor, the Bridgewater Canal. Under its autocratic Superintendent of thirty years, Robert Haldane Bradshaw, The Duke's Cut had fought tooth and nail against the Liverpool & Manchester Railway, but, in March 1833, it had to recognize that 'our trade is very good and doing a great deal of business, but no profit'. Perhaps these northern happenings influenced the BCN's future actions.

The Railway takes Control

A meeting of coal and ironmasters held at the Dartmouth Hotel, West Bromwich, on 18 August 1845 and attended by deputations from the BCN, London & Birmingham Railway and the Trent Valley & Midland Railway, unanimously passed a motion, 'That this meeting approves of the Line of Railway between Birmingham, Dudley and Wolverhampton, projected by the Birmingham Canal Company, in conjunction with the London and Birmingham and Shrewsbury and Birmingham Companies, and pledges itself to give its most strenuous support to such undertaking'. Meanwhile, discussions had taken place between the BCN and the London & Birmingham Railway concerning a 'Union of Interests' and on 11 April 1845 the Canal Company submitted a proposal to the railway by which the latter would guarantee a dividend of £4 10s per share per annum. Any surplus profit from canal traffic would be divided equally between the two companies and they would join 'in making a Railway from Birmingham to Dudley and to divide the profits therefrom arising'. The railway replied that it was 'prepared to take a favourable view of the principle contained therein'.

Railway Rivalries

With the merging of the London & Birmingham with the Grand Junction (supporter of a rival Black Country railway scheme) to form the London & North-Western Railway, the planned railway faltered, with the result that the Shrewsbury & Birmingham eventually only reached Wolverhampton, leaving a gap between the town and Birmingham. As was usual during the time of the Railway Mania, two rival groups were bidding to bridge it. Lord Hatherton, Chairman of the Staffordshire & Worcestershire Canal, speaking for the Birmingham, Wolverhampton & Dudley Railway in October 1845, stated that the 'importance of the Birmingham and Dudley line, in the hands of an independent company, could hardly be over-rated'. He went on to stress that it should be kept out of 'the hands of any party like the Birmingham Canal Company, whose interests must be opposed to the increase of railway accommodation throughout the district'. Another supporter, W. Mathews Esq., added that 'the line of the Birmingham Canal Company was encumbered with too many difficulties to admit of its being adapted to the wants of the district; as well as on the score of its avoiding the localities where the population is most dense'.

The opposite point of view was expressed at a meeting of shareholders in the Birmingham, Wolverhampton & Stour Valley Railway in May 1846. The chairman, R. Scott Esq. MP, attacking the rival Birmingham, Wolverhampton & Dudley line, 'defied any company not in connexion with the Birmingham Canal Company to give the same amount of accommodation to the public', going on to state that it was 'physically impossible that any line of railway could be made to accommodate South Staffordshire not in connexion with the Birmingham Canal' as 'the great and important works' were along the line of the canal.

Arrangement

Negotiations having continued, the London & Birmingham Railway and Birmingham Canal Arrangement Act became law in July 1846, shortly after the London & Birmingham Railway's merger with the Grand Junction, giving the railway company the right to appoint five members to the BCN's Committee. The full independence of the Birmingham Canal therefore came to an end, seventy-eight years after the passing of the Company's first Act. An essential part of the arrangement, from the BCN's point of view, was the railway company agreeing to guarantee a 4 per cent dividend to its shareholders. The BCN was to retain control of its affairs so long as the guarantee was not needed, though it would have to refer expenditure on new works of over £500, as well as alterations in tolls, to the railway company.

Union with the Dudley Canal

The looming railway threat had also finally brought about the amalgamation of the BCN with the Dudley Canal, an idea first brought up in 1813. The Oxford, Worcester & Wolverhampton Railway's prospectus, published in the *Wolverhampton Chronicle* in May 1844, was a direct threat and gave an extra push to a provisional agreement reached between the companies the previous year. The line 'is proposed to branch out of the Grand Junction Railway near the important manufacturing town of Wolverhampton … It will pass then through highly valuable mineral property, and in the immediate neighbourhood of the town of Dudley, containing 31,000 inhabitants, passing several important ironworks'. The following August saw the passage of the Oxford, Worcester & Wolverhampton Railway's Act and a couple of months later agreement between the canal companies was reached, amalgamating the shares and thus extending the railway's guarantee to the Dudley shareholders.

The merger Bill was passed on 27 July 1846 and the Dudley Canal Navigation's final Committee meeting was held three days later. The Subcommittee appointed to carry out the negotiations was congratulated on the success of the measure, by which 'a substantial benefit has been obtained in the perpetual guarantee of the London and Birmingham Railway Company of £4 a Share upon every Share in this Canal'. This would secure a certain income to the canal and confidence was expressed that trade would greatly benefit by the management of the canals 'being under one direction'. Particular thanks were given to Thomas Brewin, long-time Clerk to the company, who 'has devoted the whole of his energies to render the Canal beneficial to the Proprietors'.

MARKING THE BOUNDARIES

The BCN became a major landowner over time and kept records of its holdings on plans and, in places, on the ground. BCN boundary markers came in a variety of styles, including oval-topped stones and the more common cast-iron posts. Some are still in situ, but many more have 'disappeared' over the years. We generally only see the top section, but, iceberg-like, there is more hidden below.

Boundary stone, Hopwas.

A survivor. Cast-iron Boundary Post in its original position.

What lies beneath.

Diversions in Wolverhampton

Railways brought about an alteration of the original canal in Wolverhampton when the site for a station in the town was chosen along its route. The Navigation was realigned to the south into a cutting crossed by a bridge carrying a new carriage drive to the station. This realignment did not happen without a minor drama when the bridge failed. The *Wolverhampton Chronicle* reported the incident in early December 1849, saying that the bridge:

> … recently constructed over the new cut of the canal … suddenly gave way without warning, and fell with a tremendous crash a heap of ruins into the hollow beneath. The bridge had been erected for the purpose of connecting the road leading to the new railway station of the Shrewsbury and Birmingham and Stour Valley Railways with the station itself, about to be erected on the other side of the new cut.

John Williams, a bricklayer, had a lucky escape when the bridge fell: 'He had just passed over it, and found himself in an instant upon the edge of a precipice on the side nearest the intended station, but fortunately succeeded in maintaining his balance and escaped unhurt.'

The centres of the bridge had been taken away more than a month earlier and no crack or other

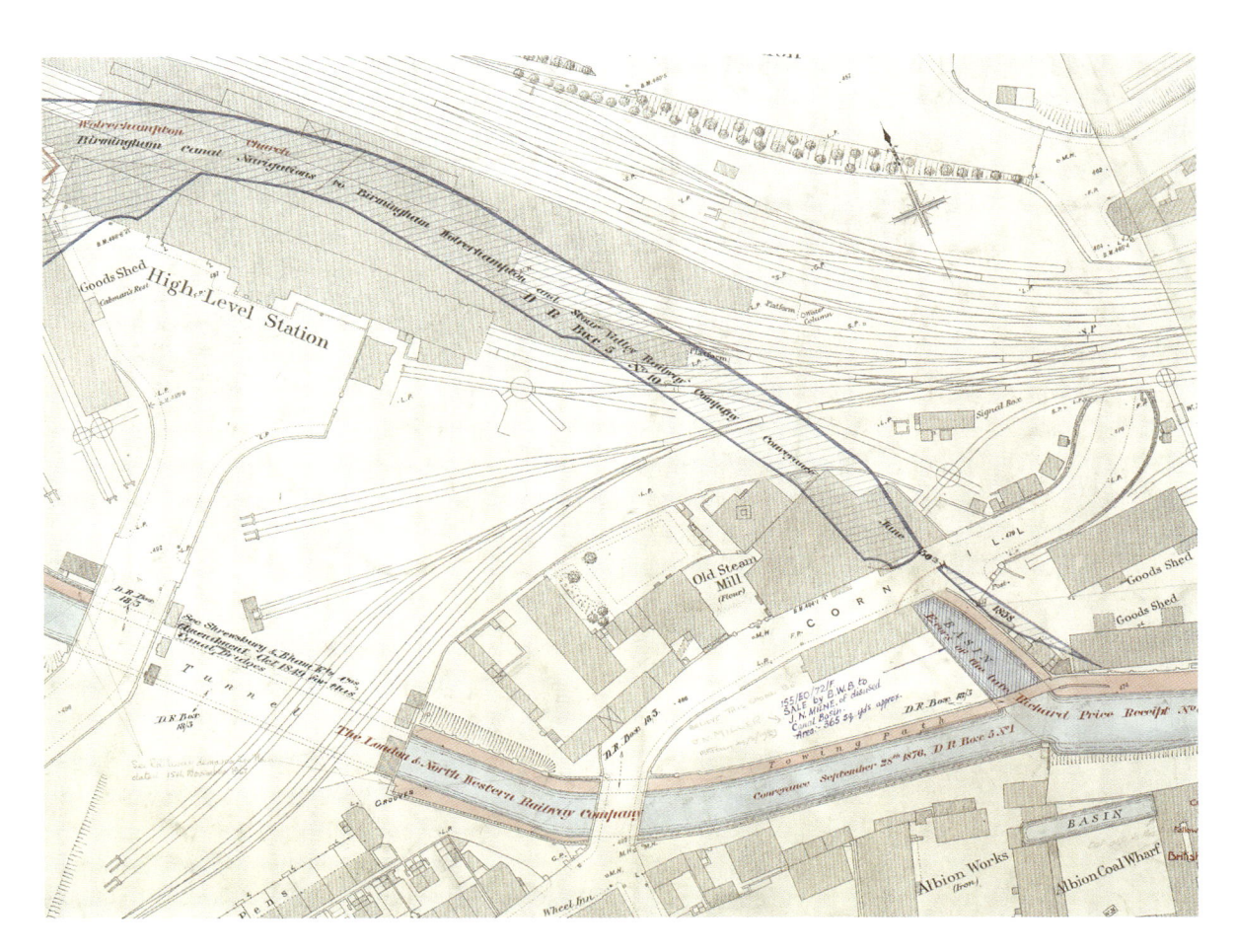

Deviation at Wolverhampton Station.

appearance of instability had been noticed. Fortunately, nobody was beneath the bridge when it collapsed, 'but several men had passed in the course of the day'. The new line of canal was opened in May 1850 and the bridge was extended about thirty years later when sidings were built above. You can still see the join in the brickwork as you walk through Wolverhampton Tunnel.

Reading the Riot Act

A further incident in the town indirectly involved the BCN and was a pointer towards a major part of its future traffic. In April 1850, the Shrewsbury & Birmingham Railway, frustrated by lack of progress on building the Stour Valley line, had arranged for a small basin to be built at the top of Wolverhampton Locks to transfer goods and mineral traffic between its trains and canal boats. Albert Basin was behind a temporary station on the Wednesfield Road. Feeling in Wolverhampton was already running high about the L&NWR's lack of progress in completing the Stour Valley line and on 8 July the mayor had complained that there was 'no town in the kingdom of its size that contributed so largely to railway prosperity, and none that received so little accommodation in exchange'. Four days later, the Shrewsbury company's attempt to lay a siding to its basin was stopped by the L&NWR's Stour Valley contractor.

The following morning a large band of navvies, 'about 300, standing or sitting with spades, pickaxes etc.' had gathered on the side of the embankment, 'apparently for the purpose of preventing any further attempt … to communicate with the canal'. The mayor and chief constable attempted, without success, to calm the situation and 'a train of wagons, containing probably about two hundred navigators' in the Shrewsbury company's employ and identified by the red tape tied around their arms, approached. The two sides displayed no ill feelings towards each other and 'many … exchanged smiles and other signs of familiar recognition'. This only lasted until the men tried to lay planks against the side of the embankment for the purpose of wheeling down barrows of iron cinder from the railway to the boats, at which point the contractor's men threw them down and a riot broke out. The police and a detachment of the military with fixed bayonets was called in and the mayor read the Riot Act. The problems were ultimately hammered out by lawyers rather than navvies and in the meantime the Shrewsbury & Birmingham company decided to build a large canal basin on its own land on the other side of the canal.

Interchange

In an area already entwined with navigations carrying vast amounts of short-distance local traffic, where most of the works had been located so that they could receive raw materials and send out their products by boat, it made sense to use these existing arteries rather than build numerous expensive railway sidings to individual works. The Arrangement Act had recognized this, stating that 'the existing canals … communicate with the … Railway and the mutual transmission of traffic to and from such Canals and railways respectively would be facilitated …' by the amalgamation. The Shrewsbury & Birmingham's Victoria Basin was an early example of a railway/canal interchange, opened in March 1851 and extended two years later, but it was by no means the first. Both early railways in Birmingham had developed trans-shipment facilities near their Curzon Street terminus. The Grand Junction had developed the bottom lock side pound at Digbeth into a small basin in 1838, while the London & Birmingham ran a siding down to an on-line wharf and covered shed by the canal below the lock.

In 1850, there were five interchange basins on the BCN. Albert (later Hay) and Victoria at the top of Wolverhampton Locks, Curzon Street Basin in Birmingham and two in the Black Country, at Darlaston and Great Bridge. By this time, the London & Birmingham's Curzon Street Wharf had disappeared beneath railway rebuilding and extension works. The numbers increased greatly with the expansion of the railways and a dozen or so more interchanges were in use by the end of the 1850s. By the time of the First World War, there were over

London & Birmingham Railway Curzon Street Wharf. The engine shed, excavated in 2020 during preparatory work for HS2, is seen in the background of Edward Paget-Tomlinson's artist's impression drawing based on Ackerman's 1845 perspective of Birmingham.

'Working Days at Horseley Fields' by A.F. Moseley. Midland Railway Basin, Wolverhampton, by the Wyrley & Essington Canal.

Under LM&SR control, the basin worked until 1938.

thirty, a greater concentration than anywhere else on the canals. Boatage services were established by the main railway companies to transfer goods from wharves or depots where merchandise could be collected locally for transfer to railway goods yards and distribution further afield.

Resting under the Shadow

In 1878, the BCN's Chairman gave his opinion that:

> The company would concur in thinking that the directors had done wisely in placing themselves under the tutelage of the L&NWR, instead of leaving themselves to contend against the continually increasing encroachments of the railways, which were now more than ever going on in the district. They might rest under the shadow of the £4 per share which the L&NWR Company guaranteed to them.

This was borne out by traffic tonnages, which, while they were still around 8,000,000 tons per year at the turn of the century, were not enough to make an operating profit. At the Grouping of the railways in 1921, when the L&NWR became part of the London, Midland & Scottish Railway (LM&SR), the amount carried had fallen to around 3,500,000 tons and at Nationalization in 1948 to 1,300,000. It had proved a most valuable shadow.

Looking east from Steward Aqueduct. Thomas Telford's New Main Line provided a ready-made route for much of the L&NWR's Stour Valley railway line, which opened in 1852 between Birmingham and Wolverhampton.

CHAPTER 8

Trials and Tribulations

The Birmingham Canal and its successors, like any major concern, faced a variety of problems apart from the political and financial ones common to all. These were of both a human and a natural kind and began before the canal was even opened. As early as 20 October 1769, it was reported, at a General Assembly of the Proprietors, that considerable damage had been done to the 'Works of the Navigation by some malicious Person or Persons'. The result of this was an advertisement in the papers outlining the sections of the Act pertaining to punishments and the offer of a reward of twenty guineas for the discovery of the offenders. In June 1770, it was suggested that the Committee would sustain great inconvenience by not following up and punishing persons who in any respect injured the Company. They were instructed to begin with 'the most Capital Offences'.

The Company was not always the victim. With any works of such scale, lack of skill or clumsiness could lead to problems and a Committee meeting a few days after the canal's opening was directing Holloway to 'immediately pay for all the damages and trespasses done by the Company's Agents, where he thinks the Demands reasonable' and where not he was to bring them to the Committee with his opinion so that they could 'see the whole state of Trespasses at one view'.

By-Laws

To deal with some of the difficulties the Company decided to make a list of by-laws. This had been proposed at a General Assembly in September 1769 so that it would be ready for the canal's opening, but, 'as there appears much difficulty in so effectually framing' the by-laws, a Subcommittee was appointed to prepare 'such Rules and Bye-Laws' and report back. Something must have been produced, as the following April it was determined that Mr Aris should print the by-laws in a small book to be delivered to private boat owners and Company employees. This does not appear to have met with total success, as the matter was once more under consideration in June 1770 when it was resolved that a fresh draft should be produced. It was obviously needed, as a terse Minute two months later resolved 'That all persons stealing any thing of the Companys property be prosecuted'. Theft was not the only problem; a week later it was decided to 'advertize and Stick up Bills to prevent bathing in the Canal'. It is one thing to devise by-laws, another to make them effective and much of the responsibility devolved to John Meredith to act 'upon every information' and 'put the Bye Laws in Execution against all offenders'.

By-laws needed updating in March 1775, when it was thought that the penalties were sometimes not equal to the seriousness of the offences and that it would be right to 'enlarge them all to Five Pounds with Power of Mitigation in the Magistrate'. At the same time, a new by-law was introduced to penalize the 'Masters or owners of the Horses which shall break down or Damage or otherwise Destroy the Fences'. Much of the land the canal passed through was still agricultural and in May 1772 the Company was installing a gate and post by Sheepcoat Lane Bridge to prevent Mr Russell's cattle from straying on to his neighbour's land, while two years later a Mr Howell was complaining of the great loss he had sustained by sheep getting on to his land. In May 1776, Meredith was writing to a Mr Pickering 'signifying to him the impropriety of his Sheep being washed in the Canal, and request that in future that he will avoid setting such example'.

Theft was a far more serious concern throughout the BCN's existence. Pilfering from boats and wharfs was common, but in February 1788 John Houghton was reporting on theft of part of the wharf itself as 'a quantity of Lead to the amount of near 30 Cwt hath been lately stolen off the Buildings upon the Wharf'.

Weather: 'Seriously Incommoded by Such a Stoppage'

'The Severity of the Frost'

Frost and ice were a recurring trial, as any stoppage had an immediate effect on income. As early as January 1770, the Committee was resolving that 'all future boats be properly armed against frost' and later in the month it confirmed Bentley's contract with an inventive Mr Ford, who had also recently devised a 'Machine to save water in navigating through the Locks', 'for a Machine for breaking the Ice'. Presumably, it did not answer for the following December a Mr Bache was invited to attend the Committee with his 'Model of a machine for breaking the Ice in Severe weather'. The Committee was impressed, thinking the machine 'very Ingenious and likely to answer the intended purpose', while James Brindley, who was present, also agreed, and was to 'attend Mr Bache … to see if any alteration or improvement can be struck out to render the Model more extensively usefull'. This attempt also seems to have failed, but in the meantime, newly appointed engineer Samuel Bull had mulled over the problem and come up with an icebreaking machine which he thought might be made for '4 or 5 £'.

In December 1774, the Committee was once more resolving that all possible means be used to keep the canal open during the frost but had found a use for the involuntary stoppages caused by it, ordering John Cope to be ready with the 'Stop Gates before ordered that they may be ready to put down the first Frost which impedes the Navigation'. On the last day of 1785, it was deemed necessary to keep a 'proper number of Ice Boats in constant motion in the night', so that the canal could be kept open for the daytime but two days later, with 'the Navigation of the Canal locked up by the severity of the Frost', another opportunity was taken to draw off the water from parts of the canal where repairs

---

FRAUD

From the beginning, the Company took measures to prevent fraud. The fifth General Assembly held in October 1769 resolved that every boatman should, at places appointed by the Committee, report his cargo and where he intended delivering it to so that it could be checked. The following February, a resolution was passed that no boat should go through the first lock from Wednesbury without producing a ticket 'of its lading and place of destination', and the lock-keeper was to make a note of it.

One of John Purslow's duties was to carry money from John Brookes at Wolverhampton to the Birmingham Office. In November 1773, he had received 'Forty five pounds four shillings', but instead of delivering it he had 'secreted it and declared he was rob'd of it' with the intention of defrauding the Company. He was prosecuted. A more serious incident occurred in August 1839 when the Company Cashier, John Gardner Bridgens, absconded with over £7,000. Warrants were procured against him and police officers dispatched to London, Liverpool and Bristol. Handbills offering a reward of £100 'to be paid for the apprehension of the offender on his being lodged in any of Her Majesty's Gaols' were issued. Described as about thirty-five years of age, he was 'usually dressed in a green frock coat and darkish pantaloons, is rather gentlemanlike in appearance, and much addicted to taking snuff'.

could be carried out. In April 1787, John Houghton, the Company's Clerk, asked permission to go to Liverpool for a week or so to 'see his Friends'. This was granted but, while he was there, 'if He finds He can have an Ice Boat made there upon better construction than the same can be made here that he do order one accordingly'. Whether the 'Commodious Cabin' he was asked to design the following year to fix on the largest iceboat, so that it could be used as an inspection launch by the Committee, was to go on a Liverpool or local one is not recorded.

With the coming of railways, ice could be used as a propaganda weapon against the canals, as in the *Wolverhampton Chronicle and Advertiser* in February 1832, discussing the projected railway from London to Birmingham:

> '... we appeal to the recollection of our mercantile readers – how often does it happen, in hard winters, that their trade is very much inconvenienced, their orders unexecuted, and impatient or unreasonable customers offended, because a package of goods lies for weeks – sometimes for months – blocked up in a canal, the ice of which no boat can penetrate?

Icebreaking in Wartime

The problems of bad winters during wartime were multiplied by shortages of men and horses and 1916–17 had seen the BCN unprepared, leading to complaints from traders using the canals. A poor harvest in Britain in 1916 and the resumption of unrestricted submarine warfare by Germany in 1917 contributed to the Government setting up a Canal Control Committee early that year, charged with diverting traffic onto the canals away from the overstretched railways. The Midland Subcommittee, including representatives from the BCN, met over the summer to discuss plans to avoid the previous year's problems, including widening bridges that had caused problems with ice build-up, using exhaust steam from colliery plants to warm canal water, and building an elevator to remove broken ice from the waterway. The BCN was to appoint inspectors to work with foreman boatmen to control traffic and, following a meeting between canal managers and traders, thirty-four agreed to provide horses and men to work iceboats during the coming winter. The Company would also be able to provide eighteen

Iced-up on the Wyrley, January 1940.

iceboats and although they would have difficulties finding men and horses, they had been promised between fifty and one-hundred soldiers from the Transport Workers Battalion.

Lock flights presented particular problems, but the BCN engineer reported that those along the Main Line would be kept ice-free by warm water from adjacent works. The small number of boats using the long flight of thirty Ogley Locks did not warrant the expense of trying to keep them free. Colliery owners were to be instructed to keep their basins free from ice and to moor boats so that the iceboats could pass freely.

Plans can be formulated, but they may not always succeed. A meeting in January 1918 between the traders, colliery companies and the BCN must have been a difficult one for the Company's representatives with numerous complaints being made, ranging from failure to keep the Rushall flight open to a report of an iceboat with a single man rocking it. However, it was pointed out that although traders had asked for traffic to be regulated, they had

T.&S. Element icebreaking agreement.

complained when this was brought into operation. Further meetings considered the provision of iceboats to run at night from the first threat of frost with crews of twenty for rocking. There were to be three experienced boatmen with the numbers being made up of soldiers. Daytime working was to be staffed by Company men assisted by the military.

Eventually it was agreed that different traders were to take on specified lengths and supply men, horses and tugs to keep them clear. For example, Walsall Wood Colliery to Pelsall Junction would be the responsibility of W.H. Matty & Co., A.J. Worsey and A. Johnson, while Chance & Hunt's tug would clear the length between Dudley Tunnel and Deepfields Stop and Bradley Locks.

The unpredictability of the weather was a problem. In 1946, the Company had spent £3,302 on icebreaking, but the following year, one of the worst on record, when boatman Caggy Stevens recalled there being 18in (457mm) of ice under Owen Street Bridge in Tipton and the icebreaker worked by twenty horses, the cost was £20,403 3s 2d.

Iceboats

At the beginning of the twentieth century, the BCN possessed over a dozen iceboats, with appropriate names such as *Arctic* and *Antarctic*, *Baffin*, *Nansen*, *Laplander* and *Esquimaux*. These were horse-drawn, but during the 1920s and 1930s the Company was looking to cut costs. One way was to reduce manpower by increased mechanization and in 1936 the wooden iceboat *Shackleton*, built in 1933, had been converted by providing a counter stern and a Ford petrol engine. In 1938, a new boat, *Byrd*, was built to serve the dual purpose of iceboat and tug for Gosty Hill Tunnel.

As far as the BCN was concerned, the severe winter of 1963 was the worst of all, as the Central England Temperature record, extending back to 1659, noted only two colder winters, both before the canal era. The Big Freeze lasted for weeks and, as more ice was removed from the cut, the water level dropped until it was unnavigable. As the level sank, the thick ice bowed down in the middle, pulling the brick side walls out for hundreds of yards in stretches.

Iceboat at Hawne Basin, 1963.

Piled-up ice, Hawne Basin, 1963.

MORE METEOROLOGY

There are rare occasions when ice can be useful, as in January 1963 when it was reported in the *Sunday Mercury* that the church organist at Curdworth on the Birmingham & Fazeley had skated the 3 miles (4.8km) from his home in Erdington along the canal 'every time there was a service'. It was a mile less than by road and Mr Newnes had negotiated two locks and five bridges 'carrying his music case'.

Another problem was fog, with apocryphal stories of boatmen having to hold on to the horse's tail to find the pub, but a far more serious incident was recorded in the Engineer's Report of December 1898 when George Jebb submitted a letter from the widow of John Holmes, who was drowned during a fog, while on duty at Churchbridge Locks the previous month. She was given a £10 gratuity.

A thunderstorm in March 1900 was of enough note as to be mentioned in the Engineer's Report, for although 'it only lasted a very short time …. One of the Company's new houses at Ocker Hill was struck by lightning, a great quantity of slates were stripped off the roof and the pots were knocked off the chimney.'

The last iceboat to work the BCN canals, *Nansen II*, was built by Yarwood's of Northwich in 1951 as a dual-purpose craft whose main function was as a tug hauling trains of dayboats from the Cannock collieries along the Wyrley & Essington Canal. Originally constructed with a wheelhouse and steering wheel, this was removed to increase headroom under bridges and a conventional tiller and rudder fitted. Latterly based at Bradley and mainly used for towing maintenance craft, *Nansen II* passed into the care of the Heritage Working Boats Group.

That Sinking Feeling

It is impossible to calculate just how much of the Black Country was carried away by boat, but in an area where coal mining and the extraction of limestone, clay and ironstone were the main drivers of development, subsidence presented an ongoing difficulty. The southern part of the South Staffordshire Coalfield with its 10yd (9m) 'Thick Coal', was particularly problematical as it lay close to the surface, outcropping in places. Its very accessibility meant that it was mined early and, in many places, haphazardly, with sad loss of life and great waste of coal. The Company was aware of this threat from the beginning, so, as early as October 1767, the Committee consulted with various coal masters about 'the Propriety of driving headways under the Navigation'. The meeting resulted in clauses being inserted in the Bill then being prepared for Parliament. The main one was the 12yd (11m) provision, preventing miners from encroaching within that distance of the canal without consent. They could be allowed to drive headings under the canal, providing that they were less than 6ft (1.8m) high and 4ft (1.2m) wide. Further clauses ordered miners to give notice of their intention to carry out such work and gave the Company the power to enter, measure and inspect them.

This authority was being used in February 1771 when John Brookes was sent to examine two pits belonging to Fownes & Aston, 'which they intend to carry under the Canal'. Underground surveying, particularly in the small collieries prevalent in the Black Country, was often sketchy and inaccurate. Before 1840, there was no requirement for mining plans to be made and it was a further decade before The Inspection of Coal Mines Act required mine owners to keep a plan at each colliery. An inspection in September 1773 of the canal by Aston & Wright's Colliery at Tipton, 'where the Banks of the Canal are sunk, as Supposed by the Coal being got Under the Canal', found that the coal had been taken from under the canal for 'about 50 or 60 yards'.

Underground fires were not uncommon in Black Country pits and canal water was an obvious means of extinguishing them. Permission was usually granted if it could be done 'without material damage to the Canal'. A Mr Bourne, having asked once, in May 1781, had to apply again as 'the Water with which He Hath been indulged' was not enough, but an additional inch 'from the Canal will effectually answer his purpose'. He was indulged again so long as he undertook to restore the canal 'with all possible dispatch'. It was underground fires in disused workings that led to the closure of the Anson Branch the best part of two centuries later, in 1961.

On the Cannock Extension, subsidence became an increasing and continual problem. Banks had to be raised, often edged with 'Utopia' bricks from the Aldridge Brick & Tile Company, and bridges jacked up. In 1960, opencast mining caused a section to sink 21ft (6.4m), leading to the end of commercial traffic the following year.

Raising Leacroft Bridge.

Breaches

Loss of water was a serious problem on any canal, but particularly so where it was not naturally abundant. As early as 2 March 1770, the Committee resolved 'that proper notice be taken of the loss of water from that part of the Canal near to the swivel Bridge that the same may be remedied'. Breaches were more serious still and in August there was the report of a section of canal bank near Winson Green being 'very faulty and liable (if not prevented) to blow up'. It was ordered to be examined and, if necessary, immediately repaired. Breaches led to canal closures, which could be announced in the local press:

> **BIRMINGHAM CHRONICLE, 30 SEPTEMBER 1824**
>
> Notice is hereby given, that in order to repair certain Breaches in the Canal, which have been occasioned by the working of the mines thereunder. The NAVIGATION between the Deepfields and Rough Hills Bridges, in the parishes of Sedgley and Wolverhampton, will be STOPPED on the 3rd, 4th, 5th, and 6th, and again on the 17th, 18th, 19th and 20th days of October next.

'Great Damage May be Done'

Sometimes the problem was with too much water rather than too little. On 25 June 1771, a culvert had failed by Fownes & Astons' colliery, Tipton, but was quickly plugged by driving piles into the opening. The piling was preventing water from running through the culvert and John Brookes was concerned that 'in the case of hasty Rains, great Damage may be done'. Repairs were quickly put in hand.

It was not just 'hasty rains' that could catch the Canal Company out. A sudden rise in temperature at the end of December 1878 thawed all the snow on the Rowley Hills, causing streams and brooks to rise and overflow. The wharf at the Butterfly Pit of Hallbridge Colliery, on the Old Main Line at Groveland between Dudley and Oldbury, was forced away by the pressure of water, causing considerable damage to property in the area. Spoil banks were swept away and houses flooded. At the site of the breach, the opposite bank had been sucked into the canal, filling it with debris and 'three or four coal boats were drawn towards the vortex while empty ones were broken and twisted in an extraordinary manner'.

9.9.'99

An even more serious breach occurred twenty-one years later and less than half-a-mile (0.8km) away, when a section of the New Main Line burst its banks by Samuel Barnett's Rattlechain Brick Works at Dudley Port. At about 4 o'clock in the morning of 9 September 1899, the embankment gave way for about 100yd (91m) and the water rushed out, 'with a noise like thunder', flooding the 100ft (31m) deep marl hole and surrounding land. The flood, draining the canal for a couple of miles on either side of the breach, carried away several boats that were on the embankment. Stranded boats lay all along the canal bed and some were swept into the clay pit. An apocryphal tale was told of a boatman navigating the cut who realized that his boat was overtaking his 'oss. With great presence of mind, he seized a knife, leapt to the bank, cut the rope and saved the animal while his boat carried on, dragged by the flow! The following day it was estimated that 100,000 people visited the scene.

Different opinions about the cause were quickly expressed, with Barnett attributing it to leakage from the canal, while the BCN alleged that the embankment had been weakened by fires and blasting operations in the marl pit. The *Illustrated London News* cited recent heavy rain, while *The Engineer* commented soberly that 'All opinions as to the reason of the affair are largely conjectural'. Company Chief Engineer George Robert Jebb had been in the west of Ireland when he heard about the breach, but was still able to return to Birmingham by 5 o'clock the following morning and was on the scene soon after.

Work was quickly started to repair the breach. A contract was placed with Messrs Holme & King of Liverpool, who brought in a locomotive and 30 or 40 railway wagons along with 250 navvies.

Rattlechain breach. View looking towards Dudley Port.

Fortunately, the BCN owned a large cinder mound, a slag heap that had been part of one of the many former local ironworks, the Stour Valley Furnaces, only about 150yd (137m) from the site of the breach, and lines were laid along the bed of the canal to enable the slag to be moved. About 1,000 tons a day were deposited in the gap. In March 1900, Jebb was reporting that the work was complete, 'with the exception of coping the waterway walls and a few other matters', but this was not in fact the case, as several more leaks were discovered on refilling.

In May, the *Birmingham Daily Post* reported that, although it had been expected that the damage, though enormous, would have been remedied by about Easter, this had not been managed and a further delay of a couple of months was expected, causing dislocation of boat traffic and serious inconvenience and loss. Fortunately, the BCN had an alternative route by way of the Old Main Line. The article went on to give figures showing the seriousness of the 9.9.'99 breach. The distance across the gap in the embankment was 250ft (76m) at its widest and 80ft (24m) at its narrowest. It was estimated that 35,000cu yd (26,759cu m) of material, including the embankment and bed of the canal, which, in the vicinity of the breach, was ploughed out to a depth of 30ft (9m), were carried away. Virtually all of this, reckoned to be about 40,000 tons, ended up in Barnett's marl hole, half filling it. It had taken until Christmas for the pit to be emptied of water and mud and it was estimated that it would take another couple of years to remove the rest of the debris. The canal itself was reopened for through traffic on 13 June 1900.

Barnett v BCN

In the meantime, Samuel Barnett had begun the process that was to end up in a nine-day hearing at the High Court in Birmingham before Mr Justice Bucknill. On 6 February 1900, he had entered a claim for damages of £7,546 15s 0d against the Company of Proprietors of the Birmingham Canal Navigations. This was supported by his affirmations that the embankment was composed of inferior materials supported by wooden piles which had been displaced by the BCN tipping a large quantity of debris against them, causing the piles to be weakened; that the canal had, for a long time, been allowed to subside and the banks raised without proper measures being taken to strengthen them; that the puddling and brickwork had not been inspected fully; and that dredging had only increased the problems. The Company responded by denying it was guilty of negligence; that the plaintiff had not suffered some of the alleged damage; that he had fired heavy shots of high explosives in the marl close to the canal; and had allowed a fire to spread to the BCN's land. The BCN registered a counterclaim for £15,827 10s.

Fifty-eight witnesses were called, covering the canal spectrum. Thomas Pass, navvy, was examined and cross-examined, as was Sir Edward Leader Williams, Engineer to the Bridgewater and Manchester Ship Canals, while brickmakers, BCN Inspectors, half a dozen mining engineers, boatmen, marl-hole managers and Clerks were all questioned. There were long and ultimately fruitless discussions on the composition of puddle, arguments about the effects of explosives and even a correction of terminology that is still heard today. When Mr Justice Bucknill enquired 'Would that be six barges?', Mr Lawrence of the Defence interposed 'They call them boats.' In his summing up, the BCN's Counsel, Jelf, played upon the evidence of the expert witnesses, commenting that 'no canal engineer is called on the other side', while Mr Hugo Young, for Barnett, opined that the Navigation was not confident in its case, implying that the witnesses were there for show and stressing the good character of his client. The judge's summary, when printed, of this 'most difficult, most intricate, most complicated but interesting case' stretched over forty-eight foolscap pages. It took the jury just under an hour and three-quarters to reach their verdict, finding for the plaintiff.

As a postscript to this episode, in November Samuel Barnett wrote to George Jebb asking if he could buy the shed that had been built for the accommodation of workmen during the restoration work. 'The shed cost £50', stated Jebb, 'and if it is sold to him he should pay this amount and also a ground rent.' Barnett declined to pay the full amount, offering £35, whereupon the Engineer recommended 'that the Company remove the shed and make use of the materials elsewhere'.

READ ALL ABOUT IT!

The local *Dudley Herald*, in an editorial on 11 August, compared the action to Charles Dickens' mythical 'Jarndyce v Jarndyce' in *Bleak House*, opining that:

> ... when the history of lengthy trials before judge and jury come to be written Barnett v the Birmingham Canal Company will find a place. Commencing last Monday it is still dragging along its weary way. The leader of the counsel for the defence (Mr Jelf) with all his experience says he never remembers so many expert witnesses called in a single action. The issue at stake is great and one can understand the length of it. Some of us who have had to listen to it all week feel almost canal experts.

Jelf himself managed to lighten the proceedings at one point when Civil Engineer Sydney Lowcock was witness:

Mr Jelf: Do you agree generally with what all the other engineers have said?

Witness: Generally I do.

Mr Jelf: Then will you be offended if I do not cross-examine you on all the points they have spoken to? (laughter)

Witness: I shall not be. I shall be only too pleased to go.

Wartime

The First World War broke out in August 1914 and the railway-owned canals were taken over by the Government, being placed under the control of the Railway Executive Committee. The Company was soon being asked by the Birmingham Chief Constable to warn boatmen against carrying explosives without authority and against 'conveying passengers more particularly aliens who might come into the City for the purpose of committing an outrage'. In October, the District Scout Commissioner offered the services of boy scouts 'with a Scout Master at every other bridge', to protect the Company's bridges. Their services were offered at a rate of one shilling per day plus food, or two shillings exclusive of food. The Clerk politely replied that the Company had already made all necessary arrangements, 'but in case of need he was sure the Committee would avail themselves of his offer'.

Manpower

Several employees volunteered to join the forces and in October 1914 George Jebb was reporting two men of the Engineering Department enlisting in the Warwickshire Regiment. The Military Service Act of March 1916 introduced conscription for single men aged between eighteen and forty-one. In May, 'in consequence of repeated calls by the Recruiting Staff for men in the service of this Company', Jebb lodged an appeal with the Birmingham Military Service Tribunal for the exemption of 110 employees. The canal's working staff had already fallen from 476 in July 1914 to 360, owing to men joining the army, or looking for employment in coal mines or munitions works, and Jebb considered that the 'reduced staff is approaching the limit with which the canal can be maintained'. In July, he was reporting that several men had joined the Volunteer Training Corps, whereby they were liable to be called out for service 'in the event of threatened invasion or national danger'. If this happened, the Company would be deprived of men whose services were valuable to its maintenance and which might have a serious effect on the production of munitions.

The situation became more serious as the war dragged on, with an additional loss of several experienced Clerks in January 1917 leading the Company Clerk to comment that it would 'tend to impair the efficiency of the work but that efforts will be made to meet the difficulty as far as possible by the employment of youths and females'. In April 1917, the Company was having difficulty in obtaining and retaining lads for the toll offices, as wages were higher in munitions works and the Clerk recommended that the current pay scales be suspended for the duration, with increases to be awarded according to the merits of each case. A further depletion of staff was recorded in June, 'owing to men being called to the colours'. The Military Service Act of 1918 raised the conscription age to include men aged between forty-one and fifty-one, but Jebb applied successfully for exemption for the eighty-four in that category working for the BCN.

The Company suffered casualties among its employees who had enlisted. Noah Longdon, a navvy ganger in District No.4, was reported killed in action in September 1917. He was thirty and had worked for the Company for nearly twelve years before signing up in January 1915. More fortunate was Percy Griffiths, a Clerk in the Accounts Department, who returned to the Company in August 1916 after being discharged from active service following wounds received in France.

TIPTON'S WAR DEAD

Of nearly 900 men killed during the First World War and having some link with Tipton, through being born or resident there or listed on a Tipton War Memorial, over fifty had some canal connection: boaters or from boating families, and labourers on boats or wharfs, loaders and dredgers. One, reported missing in the *Dudley Chronicle* of 19 January 1918, was Private Joseph Taylor of the South Staffords. He had been recorded on the 1911 Census as a fifteen-year-old Dudley Tunnel boat legger, son of another also called Joseph, of Chater's Passage, Tipton.

Air Raids

The First World War witnessed the beginning of air raids, though this was not immediately taken too seriously by the BCN. A Government scheme for insurance against 'hostile air craft', noted in July 1915, was not taken up. The city fire brigade seemed more conscious of the danger and an application was received the same month for manholes to be placed in Saturday Bridge, Summer Row and Tindall Bridge in King Edwards Road 'for the purpose of gaining access to the Canal in case of fire'. These were predecessors of the red fire doors installed on many canal bridges during the Second World War.

The most serious incident occurred on 31 January 1916, when a number of bombs were dropped by a Zeppelin crossing over the Black Country. There were no BCN employees among the casualties, although fourteen people were killed in Tipton and two by the canal at Bradley. The following month, the BCN was in contact with the L&NWR about insurance and a policy was taken out in March.

Following the raid, the Company received a letter from the Chief Constable of Birmingham, pointing out that an inspection of the city from an aeroplane had revealed the distinctive shape of Rotton Park Reservoir with its two projecting arms. A suggestion had been made that these should be covered. George Jebb considered this impracticable and proposed two alternatives, either running a quantity of water off, or filling in part of the arms. He thought the first would be easiest and quickest, but could not recommend the loss of water 'as difficulties would ensue … in the event of a drought'. The second alternative could only be done after a considerable lapse of time and, as ashes and refuse would have to be used, 'would somewhat impair the amenities of the place'. He had visited the Lord Mayor to see if the City Council would make up any loss of water, but with no success and so recommended that 'no steps be taken beyond lowering the water about 2ft or as the necessities of the Canal supply require'.

An extra job created by the threat of air raids was the putting in of stop planks 'when alarms are received of the approach of Hostile Aircraft'. The men were to be paid overtime for this duty and it was to be applied to day men called out at night and 'will include their time waiting until danger is over and the work of removing the planks completed'. The Company's telephone circuit was enhanced in April 1916, so that warnings received at New Street Station could be transmitted to the Inspectors' Offices and the Pumping Stations connected to it. The work had unfortunately been disrupted by a snowstorm the previous month that had brought down many of the wires.

Second World War

The *Birmingham Post* at the end of 1939 reported wartime precautions that included the provision of air-raid shelters and the re-excavation of the canal basins at the Old Wharf, which had been filled in to make a car park a decade earlier, in order to serve as a shelter. Little was said of actual bombing incidents for the sake of morale. Newspapers generalized, with reports of attacks 'on a Midland town', though opportunities were taken to boost morale. The *Birmingham Daily Gazette* reported on the city's 'first war vessel' in August 1940, when members of the near thousand-strong Home Guard's Ladywood Factory Unit, tired of 'falling in the darkness into the oily canal' and constantly busy keeping the canal clear of 'barges inefficiently moored', decided that they needed a boat. Capable of 10 knots, *H.M.H.G.S. Ladywood* was christened with a bottle of Empire wine broken on her prow by Alderman E.J. Denton and was used to help guard the city's canal-side factory areas and 'keep clear a fairway of the canals so that the Fire Brigade motor-floats will have an unhampered journey'.

Birmingham's Blitz

As a precaution against bombing, an island was built in the canal at Old Turn Junction, close to the vital near half-mile long railway tunnels running to New Street Station under the canal just beyond the footbridge. This held movable gates that would automatically close if the tunnels were breached, thus keeping the canal's main line out of the railway's.

The island in happier times. Boats congregating to mark the 250th anniversary of the original Birmingham Canal, November 2019.

In one eleven-hour raid in November 1940, incendiaries started over 600 fires, three-fifths of the city lost mains water and the fire brigade had to use the canals for supplies. BCN plans show several strikes in locations, ranging from Deepfields Junction to Warwick Bar. A concentration fell in Smethwick, with two bombs hitting towpaths on either side of the New Main Line next to the Steward Aqueduct on the night of 19/20 November 1940, another landing on the nearby Old Line towpath near Spon Lane Bridge and a further two 300yd (274m) east of Galton Bridge. One fell in the canal just west of Winson Green Stop during the same raid, suggesting that they were all from one plane following the line of the cut. One effect of the bombing had been the removal of the Committee from Daimler House to 'Temporary Headquarters' at Sneyd House, Bloxwich, by the top lock just above Sneyd Reservoir.

The bombing had a destructive effect on housing stock, as evidenced in April 1945 when the Company was leasing approximately 11 acres of land between the Wolverhampton and Birmingham Levels west of Galton Bridge to Smethwick

Mere yards from the BCN. Fellows, Morton & Clayton boats at New Warwick Wharf, December 1940.

Corporation for twenty-one years for building prefabs. A further area of land, west of Dunkirk Stop on the Main Line, was used for tipping bomb-damage material transported by boat from Birmingham, a tramway being used to disperse it.

> **BLACKOUT BLUES**
>
> A neighbour of mine used to tell of how he was horseboating along the Tame Valley Canal on a dark and foggy winter's night during the blackout when he became aware of a motor coming up behind. As it passed, the steerer called out through the murk 'Charlie, I think there's a boat adrift in the middle, I'll just nudge it out o' the way.' Unfortunately, though it might have looked like the fore end of a boat through the murk, it was one of the Tame Valley's brick islands into which stop planks could be inserted in case of a breach or bomb. Charlie would chuckle into his pint as he remembered the incident, 'Knocked 'is two top planks up.'

Accidents

Canals are potentially dangerous, particularly during times of bad weather or stress caused by war. Monthly Engineer's Reports from the late nineteenth and into the twentieth century include accident reports relating to slips, strains and breaks, but as early as June 1770, the Company Minute Book recorded 'That a Guinea be Given to Benj. Partridge, he having had the Misfortune to be hurt in Launching a Boat this 14th May.' Accidents to members of the public received mention generally in relation to fatalities and when compensation was involved. A series of drownings, 'numerous cases', along an open stretch of canal in Winson Green, led to an 'unclimbable fence' being erected in 1898.

Accidents, Jane Smith's comprehensive account of misfortunes in Wolverhampton during the nineteenth century, sourced from newspaper reports and Coroner's Inquests, gives a graphic account of the times, adding humanity to the bare statistics of over 130 canal-related deaths in the town between 1811 and 1899. Ages of those who died ranged from eight months to seventy-seven years, with almost half being under sixteen. Over a quarter occurred on and around the locks and about a third were related to canal employment, such as steerers, boat children or loaders. Most, over 80 per cent, were recorded as drowned, while crushing by boat or cargo, broken neck, 'thrown from a horse while galloping' and simply 'found dead' are also mentioned.

The youngest was Jane Ball, trapped in the cabin of a boat that suddenly sank at lock seven on the twenty-one locks in 1866, while the eldest, Richard Gray Bartlett, was found drowned near Bilston Road in 1890. At the inquest it was stated that Bartlett was very short-sighted and that the spot where the body was found was very dangerous. A Police Constable stated that six bodies had been recovered from the same place, while members of the jury said that the attention of the Canal Company should be drawn to the matter, one suggesting a gate at this approach to the canal, which was 'a regular death trap on a dark night'. Foul play not being suspected, a verdict of 'Found Drowned' was recorded. Drink, not a factor with Bartlett, was directly implicated in over a third of the cases involving victims aged over fifteen.

CHAPTER 9

Decline

'I Do Not Think it Would Ever Come Back'

In 1913, at a meeting of the British Association for the Advancement of Science held in the city, George Jebb presented a paper on *The Birmingham Canals*. Part of it dealt with the BCN's financial position during the second half of the nineteenth century. From 1846 up till 1874, with one exception, the Company had been able to pay a yearly dividend of 4 per cent on its Consolidated Stock out of its own revenues. In 1874, however, the L&NWR had to make up a deficiency of £10,528 and two years later, of £4,796. From 1876, the deficit averaged £25,000 per year despite increasing tonnages. Many other navigations were in a far more serious state and a Royal Commission on Canals, set up in 1906, recommended widening and deepening the trunk waterways to join the Thames, Severn, Mersey and Humber to a Birmingham hub. Jebb had foreseen the difficulties that widening the Birmingham Canal would lead to and pointed out in his evidence to the Commission that, if the canals were deepened, the puddle in the bed would have to be dug out and, following the work, would need replacing, all of which would take a long time. He did not think it could be done in less than a year, by which time the traffic would have gone to the railway and 'I do not think it would ever come back again'. In the end, no proposals were made to widen the BCN waterways which would rather act as a distribution centre for the improved canals.

Canals and Traders

The Commission's findings were criticized by Edwin A. Pratt, who, it should be stated, was working for the Railway Companies Association at the time, in his book *Canals and Traders*, which paid particular attention to the BCN. He had made a tour of the Birmingham Canal with the help of 'a motor launch, supplemented by a motor car'. As well as inspecting the canal between Aldersley and Birmingham, he made a side trip to the Gosty Hill, Netherton and Dudley districts. He wrote that the increase in traffic envisaged by the proposed improvements to connecting waterways would only lead to further congestion on the BCN with its 'extremely sharp curves'; narrow bridges 'under which only a single boat can pass at a time'; clouds of mist caused by condensing water returned to the canal 'often sufficing ... to obscure the boatman's view'; and 'legging' tunnels. Commenting on Jebb's assertion to the Commission that it would be impossible for the existing locks to carry any more traffic and his opinion that it would be impracticable to build duplicate locks at Wolverhampton or to widen the existing flight, Pratt visited the 'twenty-one' to see for himself. At the top basin there were:

> about fifteen boats waiting to get through the locks, and an animated discussion was going on among a group of boatmen – or, perhaps I should say, boat-women, for the gentler sex seemed to have most to say on the matter – because someone had passed through, or wanted to pass through, out of his 'turn'.

In the end, the Royal Commission came to nothing. By the time the final report was published, in 1909, the Liberal Government was preoccupied with welfare reforms and Irish Home Rule and the cost of the work would have been prohibitive.

Subsiding Fortunes

By the end of the nineteenth century, the problems caused by subsidence were becoming more difficult and the infrastructure of the waterways was ageing. In March 1891, Jebb reported that Lapal Tunnel was in a very bad condition and although he hoped to reopen it to traffic in about two months, he feared that considerable repairs would be necessary annually 'for some time to come'.

The tunnel had long been a cause for concern. It had been closed for repair for two months in 1801, just three years after opening, and double that four years later. Even when open, its length and limited size meant that through-passage was slow. The Dudley Canal's engineer Thomas Brewin had eased the problem in 1841 by setting up a pumping engine and stop gates. Water could be pumped to create a current through the tunnel from west to east, assisting the passage of craft and raising the pound at Selly Oak by 6in (152mm). By raising a paddle in the gate at that end the flow was reversed to aid boats from the opposite direction. This 'contrivance' reduced passage time from three to two hours and Brewin was awarded with £50 in plate for his inventiveness.

In October 1891, Jebb reported to the Committee on the state of the tunnel, noting that 1,787yd was in good condition, 1,211yd was fair, 572 bad but in no immediate danger, 165 very bad 'and must be renewed before traffic can safely pass', while 60yd had already been repaired. By the end of the year good progress was being made and the repairs were progressing at a rate of about 9yd per week. Work slowed in the new year as a bout of sickness spread among the workers, but a 2ft 6in depth of mud had been cleared from the workings and progress was around 5yd a week. Lapal reopened in June, when Jebb reported that it 'is very much damaged & out of shape, although as far as can be judged is not actually in a dangerous condition'. The work had taken a year at considerable expense, which only ended when Mr Tranter of Hole Farm, Quinton, was paid £5 for the use of private roads across his property during the repairs.

The pumping engine at Lapal was shut down in October 1914 and, in June 1917, the tunnel was blocked after a length of side wall collapsed, throwing it and the earth behind it into the canal at a point 105 chains (2,100m) (about two-thirds of the way) from the west end. Adjoining brickwork was similarly damaged and the cost of reconstruction was estimated to be about £800. By September, the damaged section had been propped up to prevent further damage, but the tunnel remained closed. At the end of 1920, Engineer A.W. Willet reported that he had not taken any further steps to repair the tunnel, 'which continues in the condition in which it was left three years ago', the state it remained in until formal abandonment in 1953.

An Inland Waterways Association *Bulletin* the previous Christmas had included extracts from a letter sent in by an explorer of less frequented canal tunnels. Although the brickwork at both entrances and for about 50yd (46m) in was in extremely bad condition, the 'troglodyte' reported, 'the rest of the tunnel right up to the main fall is in excellent condition'. However, it was impossible to pass this from either end as the clay rose to the roof. There was another small fall about 40yd (37m) from the main one and the water level in the tunnel was between 4–5ft (1.2–1.5m).

Two Lock Line

The area around the Two Lock Line had long been prone to subsidence, matters coming to a head in 1893 with a report of water entering the workings of Messrs Cochrane & Co. near Blackbrook Bridge. Careful examination revealed the break to be old, no mining having taken place there for over twenty years, while the canal had been sound for many years. Although Jebb asserted there had been no negligence on the Company's part, Messrs Cochrane had given notice that they would claim compensation for damage. The cracks were filled with concrete and the canal lined with 3ft (0.9m) of puddle for 15yd (14m). More cracks appeared at a point which had been thoroughly puddled two months earlier, and stop planks were immediately put in and the water pumped out yet again, to reveal a new 7in (178mm) wide crack, 'extending quite through the 3ft puddle into the solid rock below'. Eventually the cracks were filled with concrete, the canal bed over them was lined with sheet iron, and the bed and sides puddled to a depth of at least 3ft 6in (1m). In July 1894, Jebb reported that the water had been back in the canal between the top of the Two Lock Line and Blackbrook Bridge at the site of the fracture for about three weeks with only a slight leakage 'on either side of this place, which Messrs. Cochrane say is of no moment'. The cost of investigation would not be possible 'without incurring very great expense'. Repairs had to be continued until March 1909 when the aqueduct carrying the canal over the Black Brook collapsed, closing the Two Lock Line for good.

Two Lock Line remains, Blackbrook Bridge, 2020.

Rationalization of the Wyrley

Following amalgamation with the Wyrley & Essington in 1840, the BCN had made improvements to the line, including rebuilding the long flight of Ogley Locks. Traffic on the section declined during the second half of the century, though the locks were still receiving maintenance. In October 1895, they were closed for ten days for general repairs and again for a week, five months later. Approximate figures collected in 1897 showed a deficiency of £636, rising to £697 the following year. The 1897 receipts from traffic were calculated at £303, with extra income of £120 being generated by rents, including £48 raised by cottage rents and £28 from fishing. Expenditure, including £370 on wages and £603 on repairs and maintenance, led to the deficit. In 1900, 1,213 boats passed through the locks, but by 1909 this had fallen to 866.

Following the First World War, there were serious discussions about the locks and in March 1919 attention was drawn to the heavy losses incurred on the section. For several pre-war years the number of loaded boats passing up and down the flight had not averaged more than three a day, bringing in an annual revenue of £260, while the wages for the staff, usually four lock-keepers and seven navvies, was approaching £1,000. Since 1913, the traffic had further decreased to about one boat a day, bringing in tolls of about £100 a year. In May 1921, 'consequent upon the smallness of traffic passing through these Locks', they were closed between 5pm and 7am daily 'and this had enabled the Company's Engineer to dispense with the services of a Lock-keeper'.

The Wyrley & Essington main line between Ogley and Huddlesford Junctions, along with the Wyrley Bank, Essington Locks, Sneyd and Lord Hayes branches and the greater part of the Hay Head branch, were formally abandoned in 1954. Ironically, as Tom Foxon pointed out in *Number One!*, his evocative account of working the canals as an owner-boatman during the 1950s, had the Ogley Locks remained open they could have saved

Abandoned lock, Ogley.

much time and effort when an extensive coal trade developed between the Cannock pits and London.

Post-War

The First World War had only slowed down the decline in traffic on the BCN, which fell from 6,748,133 tons in 1914 to 6,092,065 in 1918. After a short-lived post-war boom, the period following the war was marked by industrial unrest and a decline in the industries that the canals relied on; 1921 was a particularly bad year. Tonnage fell to 3,489,737 tons and economies in staffing were forced on the Company across the system. Hempole Lane Toll Office, at the foot of Ryders Green Locks, had been closed between February 1917 and February 1919, as the Clerk, J.A. Bywater, had been 'called to the Colours'. The office had reopened on his demobilization but, with only fifteen boats a day being ticketed and the information obtainable from lock-keepers' records or the nearby railway basins, the office was to close again, with Bywater being transferred to Windmill End where the Toll Clerk had retired: 'Approximate saving £209 per annum'. Similar cutbacks were introduced the same month at Wednesbury Bridge Wharf and Capponfield, Blakeley Hall and Gosty Hill Toll Offices.

A miners' strike in 1921 led to the traffic being 'almost negligible'. In January, the total tonnage carried on the BCN was 461,959, but by May it had decreased to 168,459 tons and had only recovered to over 300,000 tons in November. Every month of the year recorded a decrease in trade on the previous year's and the total for 1921 was 3,489,747 tons, the lowest for three-quarters of a century. Foreign competition also affected the BCN. At the end of January 1921, reports came in of large quantities of steel from Belgium arriving in the district by rail. Delivered cheaper than steel from local works, it was rumoured that several thousand tons were expected in Darlaston before the end of March: 'This importation means a heavy loss … in toll upon Coal and other raw material.'

Trade picked up periodically over the next few years and improvements were made in places. In March 1924, following 'strong complaints' from Messrs N. Hingley & Sons and other traders concerning congestion on the Dudley No.2 canal caused by traffic at Stewarts & Lloyds Coombs Wood Tube Works, the latter applied successfully to have the canal widened to provide lay-by accommodation for about twenty boats on the towpath side. The previous month there had been an approach from the Chairman of the Old Hill Mines Drainage Committee putting forward complaints from colliery owners in the area about the continued closure of Lapal Tunnel. This meant that traffic for Selly Oak and the Worcester Canal had to travel a long way round, passing through Netherton Tunnel and the Bar Lock, Birmingham. It would cost between £10,000 and £12,000 to make the Lapal route navigable and, as this was out of the question, a compromise on tolls was reached instead, though this would mean a loss of revenue of around £300 per year.

Paradise Lost

General Meetings of the Assembly of BCN Proprietors continued biannually during the 1920s, with the vast majority represented by proxy. In August 1921, of the forty-two listed, four were present in person. By then, the BCN's headquarters were in Daimler House, further up Paradise Street, the elegant offices at the Old Wharf having been closed in 1912 and demolished the following year. Reductions in tolls in February 1922, although resulting in more traffic, did not increase revenue. The trend continued. In 1923, although tonnage increased by 564,066 tons, the receipts were 'insufficient to compensate for the loss sustained by further reductions in Tolls, which, in the interests of the Traders, it was considered necessary to make'. A fourteen-week strike by carriers' boatmen in the autumn had further reduced income by about £3,000.

The *Birmingham Mail* regularly sent a reporter to Assembly meetings and he generally provided a pithy paragraph. In February 1925, he reckoned that the Proprietors 'are losing their dash. Time was when the annual meeting … could be started on the first of Big Brum's noonday chimes and finished before the last of the twelve strokes had boomed forth'. (Big Brum is the familiar name for the clock in the tower on the city's Council House.) Regular attendees were saying that the two minutes and forty-five seconds of the most recent meeting was the worst for several years!

LIVEABOARDS

One money-raising idea never contemplated at the time was the domestic use of the canals. A Mr Stokes had brought a small old boat onto the BCN from the Worcester Canal at Selly Oak. He had told the Company's agent that it was to undergo repairs at Hughes' Boat Dock by Harborne Bridge and, after some slight repairs, Stokes moored it at the adjacent Gibbons Road Wharf as a houseboat for himself and his wife. Interviews and correspondence failed to move him but, as the Medical Officer of Health had reported that the boat was insanitary, it was decided to take proceedings against him under the Company's Act of Parliament. Stokes was brought before the magistrates at the end of December 1920, when 'the Defendant on the suggestion of the Court gave an undertaking that he would remove the Boat within 7 days'. He was also fined 5/- with a guinea for Special Costs.

In 1926, the February meeting was over in two and a half minutes, 'quite outside the record time of 29 seconds'. Traffic was breaking no records either, with tonnage for the previous year down by 419,120 tons and receipts showing a decrease of £17,707 15s 0d from 1924's figures. Money from rents and property showed a slight increase, but the Proprietors were promoting a Bill to close the Old Wharf and sell the land to Birmingham Corporation.

Nor did 1926 improve the Company's fortunes. The General Strike in early May followed by a seven-month miners' strike meant a decrease in traffic from the previous year of 653,892 tons and in receipts of £22,986. The Company's Clerk and Manager, Thomas A. Henshaw, had resigned due to ill health in June and died in December. He was succeeded by Albert H. Pearshouse at the culmination of his half-century's service. One bright note in a pessimistic year was the completion of the Old Wharf sale, by which 'the Company have materially assisted in the scheme of improvements in the centre of the City', although its use as a car park for many years may not have been what was envisaged. Redeveloped several times since, a bricked-up bridge hole on Bridge Street marks the former entrance to the site of the Old Wharf. Other city-centre arms and basins disappeared around the same time.

Birmingham's Disappearing Basins

Gibson's Canal, a privately built branch, opened in 1812 through a short tunnel and a lock from the original canal's Newhall Branch. Gibson's Arm, situated by his works in Cambridge Street, saw several basins built off it about a decade later, on land formerly owned by John Baskerville. These canyon-like cuts, surrounded by foundries and brass works, were towpath-less and boats were moved around by men wielding shafts. The basins nearest Broad Street were filled in during the 1920s to accommodate the city's Hall of Memory and surrounding gardens in Centenary Square. The researcher in Birmingham Library can take inspiration from the fact of being directly above the site of part of Gibson's Arm!

The remainder of the Newhall Branch, apart from a short stub at the top of Farmer's Bridge Locks, was lost and built over from the end of the 1930s. One length that has survived is the much-truncated

Whitmore's Arm. The mid nineteenth-century building was part of the extensive Elkington's Silver and Electro Plate Works and later of the Birmingham Science Museum site.

Whitmore's Arm running off between the seventh and eighth Farmer's Bridge Locks. Whitmore was 'an Engineer and manufacturer of all kinds of rolling and Flatting Mills, Machines for weighing Barges, Boats, Waggons etc.'. He also designed a boat lift which was proposed, though not built, for the Somerset Coal Canal.

Death of G.R. Jebb and Beyond

February 1927 saw the death of George Robert Jebb, one of the Company's greatest servants, having sat on the Board for thirteen years and acted as Engineer and Consultant for thirty-nine. The Proprietor's meeting in February 1929 lasted a minute and a half, while most of those present remained standing. The early years of the 1930s continued the decline as the country experienced severe depression, 'which has particularly affected the heavy industries of the Midlands'; 1930 was the last year that two General Assembly meetings were held, but even an annual meeting could be dispatched in around two minutes. Receipts for 1933 amounted to £110,499, an increase of £350 over the previous figures, but £60,946 was required from the LM&SR to make up the 4 per cent dividend. Receipts in 1936 were adversely affected by long-term closures of the local power stations and this continued the following year. In 1938, they were down to £87,177 because of the continued power station closures, rationalization by industrial concerns and improved landsale wharf facilities at the collieries.

Second World War and Beyond

At the start of the Second World War there was some growth, mainly due to increased activity at power stations, tube works and other industrial concerns 'consequent upon the National Emergency', but the ice and frost in January and February 1940 led to a downturn and over £90,000 was needed from the LM&SR in 1940. The publication of further accounts was prohibited for the duration of the war and they were published in modified form afterwards.

At the final Proprietors' Annual Assembly on 20 February 1948, held, as all had been since 1940, at the Queen's Hotel, Birmingham, the Chairman delivered a speech lasting for longer than many entire meetings of the last couple of decades. It began, 'On 1st January 1948 the Undertaking vested in the Transport Commission by virtue of the Transport Act 1947 and consequently this will be the last Annual General Assembly of the Proprietors of the Company'. Outlining the Company's long history, G.R.T. Taylor went on to summarize the Navigation's decline, with six Proprietors present to hear the speech:

> From the very early days until recent years the weight of traffic passing on the Birmingham Canal exceeded that conveyed on any other British Canal excluding the Manchester Ship Canal. The great bulk of the traffic has always been local in character, i.e. both loaded and discharged at places on the Birmingham Canal. The tonnage passing over the Birmingham Canal as an intermediate waterway between other canals is very small. The peak annual tonnage of 9,046,520 tons was reached in the year 1882, but by 1913 the tonnage had fallen to roundly seven million tons, by 1919 to five and a half million tons, and by 1922 to four million tons. The downwards tendency continued and by 1947 it had fallen to 1,311,415 tons.

Nationalization

With nationalization by Clement Atlee's Labour Government in the air, a small deputation from the Canal Association had met the Minister of Transport in October 1946, when he had 'intimated that he would be prepared to consider representation, either collectively or individually, on the question of compensation'. Correspondence between the BCN and the Ministry followed, with BCN Chairman Taylor pointing out the Company's 'unique' position. This failed to move the Minister and Taylor made his feelings known during the Proprietors' annual meeting in February 1947: 'Whatever may be the merits, or demerits, of the

> ### A BOATBUILDER'S VIEW
>
> In late 1949, the *Birmingham Daily Gazette* sent a reporter to interview boatbuilder Les Allen at his yard by Salford Bridge, where he was building six boats for the British Electricity Authority. Under the heading 'Our canals: A doomed means of transport?', Mr Allen spoke about the problems he faced, starting with the cost of building a boat. Before the First World War, this had amounted to about £120 but had more than doubled to £250 by 1921 and currently stood between £600 and £650. Considering the decline in traffic, he said:
>
> *I suppose that there's only about a tenth of the tonnage carried on the canals today as there was in 1921. Take my company for instance. Then we had over 150 barges on the water, all in regular use, but today, we're down to three. It's not worthwhile spending the money to repair the old barges; the waterways just can't compete with the road transport people.*
>
> Although boat transport was once the cheapest, this was no longer the case with increases in labour costs:
>
> *Most of the cargo is coal, and it has to be carried to the boats. Then we have to pay a surcharge of 1s 6d a ton to the National Coal Board when the coal's loaded. Modern factories are not built with their boiler rooms next to the canal like they used to be so the coal often has to be unloaded and carried some distance to the coal dump.*
>
> There was also the question of time:
>
> *To make one delivery it takes a barge two days. A day to go and pick the coal up and a day to take it to its destination and unload it. It's true that the barge will carry 26 tons, but four lorries could do that job in a morning.*
>
> When asked if a boat could carry 30 tons, the builder 'smiled sadly': 'They should, but we daren't put more than 26 tons in them today because the canals need dredging and the extra four tons would ground them. That's a loss of four tons a journey for each barge.'

Government's policy of nationalisation … it is evident that the Government intend to pursue that policy with a fanatical zeal which ignores any views other than those of their own supporters ….' The financial consideration went before the Transport Arbitration Tribunal and, at the BCN Committee's penultimate meeting, the Manager, G.B. Lakin, reported its decision, that the 4 per cent Perpetual Debenture stock was determined at £105 per £100 nominal. At nationalization, the total length of the BCN was still 'approximately 156 miles exclusive of private arms and basins of which there are some 500'. The BCN came under the control of the Docks and Inland Waterways Executive, a subsidiary of the British Transport Commission.

A Fading Light

The British Electricity Authority's successor, the Central Electricity Generating Board (CEGB), had the last large fleet on the BCN. In the early 1960s, this still amounted to a total, shown on the books at least, of 104 boats and one dredger, based on the four major canal-side power stations. Nechells was by the Birmingham & Warwick Junction Canal, while Birchills, above Walsall Locks, Ocker Hill at Tipton and Wolverhampton stood on the BCN.

Ocker Hill's thirteen boats, built between 1939–43, were valued between £22 9s 10d and £166 15s 1d, largely dependent on age, and they were all scheduled to be written off between 1964–8, a date that would have been over-optimistic even if Jubilee Colliery had not closed in September 1960, ending the power station's supply of coal from the Sandwell Park Colliery Wharf. Of Walsall's notional thirty-nine, ten had been written off. Wolverhampton had the largest fleet, forty-four boats on paper, although eleven had been written off and a dozen 'Big Severn Boats, which were not really constructed for canal traffic' were to be disposed of by sale or scrapping if beyond economical repair.

An informal meeting was held in October 1960 to discuss the CEGB's local canal-boat requirements. It was noted that Ocker Hill had stopped receiving coal by boat and that Walsall's weekly 3,000 tons and Wolverhampton's 1,000 could be 'adequately covered by 80 barges'. Concern was expressed at the 'length of time some boats were occasionally lost in transit and sometimes damaged' and it was decided to have a pegboard at Walsall to record each boat's movements. A note from May 1961 indicated that eighteen boats were sunk, including two at Hilton Main Colliery Basin, one at Wolverhampton Power Station Basin and one at Keay's boatyard. Fourteen boats were 'to be sunk at E. Thomas' Wharf until September 1961 or thereabouts'. Wooden dayboats could be sunk for periods of time when not in use to preserve the timber. A further seven were in dock for repair, leaving sixty-three in service.

In March 1962, Walsall Power Station still had an allocation of seventy-one boats, according to its Coal and Ash Handling Engineer, of which twenty-seven were in good condition, thirty-five needed repairs and nine were awaiting disposal. He considered that forty-eight would be enough to handle the traffic and suggested disposing of a further twenty boats, perhaps because of the concerns he expressed at the end of the report:

> If, however, it is decided not to further reduce the fleet ... I suggest we seek a less accessible spot than the main canal at Walsall for mooring the surplus, and to avoid the nuisance and damage caused by the children from the nearby housing estate, who in spite of advice and action by ourselves, the Canal Company and the Police, still persist in playing in the boats.

The Big Freeze of 1963 cut short any longer-term plans for carrying coal to the power stations by canal. It was imperative to keep them working and, although both rail and road transport were badly affected, they were not shut down for weeks on end like the canals. Following this, many boats were tied up and left to rot.

Abandoned boats, Conduit Colliery Basin, Norton Canes, 1966.

A final announcement came from the CEGB in May 1965 that no more coal was to be carried by canal to Midland power stations. A spokesman for the Board stated that canal transport was 'totally uneconomic' and that the 'demand at new power stations is so enormous that the canal system could never cope with it'. Unloading coal from boats needed separate teams of workmen, which made it far too dear, and it was 'far quicker and more efficient to have rail links with collieries and bunker trains which just drive and unload automatically'. The last canal supply, to Walsall, was to close in June. The spokesman added that only 500 out of the station's weekly requirement of 10,500 tons came by canal. A British Waterways spokesman added: 'We do not like losing any traffic, but this is just part of a natural regional trend. Many of our canals were linked with collieries but now many of the collieries have either closed down or are producing coal unsuitable for power station consumption'.

The Other Sixty Miles

The BCN shrank most radically during the 1950s and early 1960s. A report in the Inland Waterways Association's *Bulletin* from 1952 had noted that the 'many miles of waterways in this complex system are still maintained in their usual good order and there is evidence of considerable internal traffic', but this was not to last. It was the extremities and the concentration of branches within the Black Country that suffered the greatest losses. In the south, the Dudley No.2 beyond Hawne Basin, where there was still extensive tube works traffic until 1967, was abandoned in 1953, while the subsidence-prone northern reaches of the Cannock

Cannock Extension final cruise about to leave Norton Canes, 21 October 1962. The distant bridge, carrying the A5, is the current end of navigation.

Extension saw the end of commercial traffic in 1961 and abandonment three years later to opencast mining. A final cruise, along the 4½-mile (7km) soon to be lost stretch to Hednesford Basin, was organized in October 1962, by boatbuilder Malcolm Braine and attended by thirteen boats belonging to members of the Staffordshire & Worcestershire Canal Society (S&WCS).

Churchbridge Locks had lasted less than a century, with traffic finishing in 1949 and abandonment following in 1955. The Anson Branch, opened in 1830 to serve collieries and a quarry west of Walsall, was granted a lifeline with the building of Birchills Power Station, supplying cooling water for over half a century. It was abandoned for navigation beyond its junction with the Bentley Canal in 1956, although when the M6 was built across the branch a culvert was provided for a small weed-cutting boat and craft could still reach the culvert until around 1974. The remaining length of the Anson Branch, along with the Bentley Canal, was abandoned in 1961. Much of the latter was subsequently and expensively culverted and part of the route is now a walkway, with only a short stub of the canal that is fast reverting to nature at Bentley Mill.

The greatest concentration of closures occurred in the old industrial heart of the Black Country, where branches had been built to serve mines and works, which, by the 1950s, had already gone or were in decline. The greater part of the Wednesbury Oak Loop, much of it still following the line laid out by Brindley and Simcock, was abandoned in the mid-1950s, along with the Ocker Hill and Gospel Oak Branches, while the Bradley Locks, Tipton

OCKER HILL

At the heart of the BCN, Ocker Hill housed the Company's engineering workshops along with the engines pumping water from the Walsall to the Wolverhampton level. It developed during the nineteenth century with the addition of more engines until, by 1900, there were six and it was the centre of a canal community, with the Company building housing and contributing to the local church and board school. It seems its workshops were not restricted entirely to Company projects. The *Montgomery County Times and Shropshire and Mid-Wales Advertiser* reported that the new Severn Street Canal Bridge, opened in Welshpool in October 1900, used steel girders from Dorman, Long & Co., Middlesbrough and the Patent Shaft and Axle Co., Wednesbury, with the fitting together done at the BCN Works, Ocker Hill.

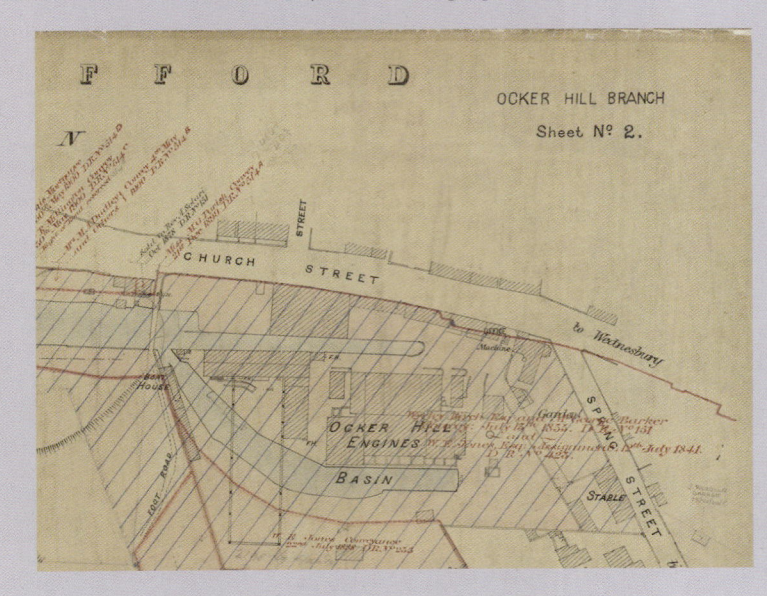

Ocker Hill Deed Plan.

Green, Toll End, Dixons and Haines Branches followed over the next few years. The 'isolated and obsolete' Ocker Hill repair yard, along with certain lengths of short connecting canal, was sold to Tipton Corporation for redevelopment in 1956.

Abandonment of a canal did not necessarily mean filling in, as a piece in the *Birmingham Daily Post* in October 1959 made clear when reporting on the closure of a mile and a half of the Loop. Bilston Corporation was not objecting to the closure, which, a council official explained, only applied to navigation. Many lengths of the lost canals lingered, as linear rubbish dumps or pleasant semi-rural enclaves in the middle of the growing conurbation.

It was the spread of housing that ultimately accounted for the disappearance of much of the abandoned network and there must be quite a number of residents in Ocker Hill who would be surprised to learn that a canal had once passed under their garden or house. The Oldbury Loop was abandoned in sections between 1954 and 1960. By 1963, Oldbury Council was applying to the Ministry of Housing and Local Government for a loan of £2,500 to drain and fill in the length passing under Birmingham Street that had been stagnant and full of rubbish 'for many years'. Nearby residents had complained about the smell and the proximity of 'such a source of disease to shops in the town centre'. Most of the loop was sold to Oldbury Corporation and neighbouring factory owners by the mid 1960s and in April 1968 the short-lived Warley Borough Council's Public Works Committee was applying for a loan for work to drain and fill in the canal through the town centre.

Death Traps

As well as the problems of rubbish and unsightliness, there was the danger of the canals to young children. In October 1953, it was reported that seventeen children had drowned 'in Midland canals' since July; one had been in Oldbury and most were aged 'about four, five or six'. This was mentioned in an article about a local mother, living 100yd from an unfenced canal, who had taken her boy, aged six years, to Oldbury Baths for a swimming lesson. The lad had been refused admission after being measured against 'a chalk mark on the side of the pay box'. He was said to be 'too small for the baths', even though this was at a time when a 'safer canals' campaign had been launched in the Midlands. The following year, a Coroner stated that it was impossible to fence off all the canals while recording a verdict of accidental death on a little girl drowned at Tividale. A decade later, the Wednesfield Safety Organisation was campaigning to fence off a 2-mile length of the Wyrley & Essington around Devil's Elbow Bridge following nine drownings in six years and in August 1968 there were calls to demolish the bridge. The bridge survived, to be shotcreted in shocking pink and long lengths of fencing were built.

How not to treat a canal. Haines Branch.

Devil's Elbow Bridge, 2021. The colour has mellowed somewhat.

RIDGACRE REQUIEM

The last major stretch of waterway to be lost from the BCN was the Ridgacre Branch. Opened in September 1827, it ran from the Wednesbury Old Canal at Swan Bridge Junction for about ¾mile (1.2km) to a basin near Coppice Colliery. Further branches off the Ridgacre, the Dartmouth, Halford and Jesson, opened the following year. The Dartmouth and Halford Branches were partly abandoned in 1947 with Jesson following in 1954, after which it was sold to West Bromwich Corporation, but the Ridgacre remained navigable if commercially unused after the mid-1960s, when tar traffic from Swan Village Gasworks ceased. The Wednesbury Old Canal beyond Swan Bridge Junction had also closed, much of the line being sold to West Bromwich in 1961 and filled in.

These esoteric backwaters at the heart of the BCN were visited by few boaters over the next decades until, in 1992, plans for the Black Country New Road, first envisaged during the 1980s, were altered. They had originally included a navigable culvert beneath the road at a roundabout by Swan Bridge, but, in a cost-cutting exercise, this was not implemented. A protest cruise was held on 3 October 1992, but had no effect on the decision.

Ridgacre Branch protest cruise.

Final Fleets

One of the last firms to carry on trading on the BCN was Thomas Clayton of Oldbury. In 1951, Clayton boats had carried 150,000 tons of gasworks tar and other by-products, but this was down to just over 50,000 tons in 1964. From 1952, when the ninety-strong fleet was at its peak, the numbers had declined to eight operational boats by the time the firm had ceased carrying by canal in 1966. The compulsory purchase of Clayton's yard for the construction of the M5 motorway's Oldbury Viaduct, along with the steep decline in traffic, brought about the decision to pull out of canal carrying, although the firm continued to distribute fuel oil by road.

Alfred Matty & Sons ran a large fleet of dayboats and contracting boats from a yard at Coseley, latterly specializing in carrying chemical waste products for Albright & Wilson from, appropriately enough, the Chemical Arm in Oldbury. The destination was the former Rattlechain Brickworks marl hole, used as a tip between the 1940s and early 1970s. The most obnoxious cargo was phosphorus, transported as a sludge and discharged with the help of a small petrol-driven pump on arrival at the tip. Local memory tells that some was 'lost' overboard during the trip to save time. As a result, parts of the Old Main Line were a milky white colour with no plants, algae or wildlife and the wash from a passing boat could churn up the waste, which ignited on contact with the air or a discarded match.

Caggy Stevens was still boating around the BCN into the 1970s. Although he had the use of his tug *Caggy*, much of his work, especially when flights of locks had to be passed, depended on his horse, Mac, until its death in November 1974. The last traffic was rubbish collection. An empty dayboat would be delivered to a canal-side factory, where a full one awaited collection to be taken to a tip. One

Matty's boats carrying phosphorus waste along the Old Main Line, Oldbury, 1972.

Caggy Stevens on Comet *approaching Sheepcote Bridge, Birmingham, 1974.*

was at Moxley on the Walsall Canal, where a basin ran off into old sand beds and a crane with a grab unloaded them. The site is now grass- and tree-covered, but hidden beneath are the remains of boats abandoned at the end of their carrying days.

Several efforts were made to re-establish commercial-scale carrying, most notably by the enthusiast-driven Birmingham & Midland Canal Carrying Company, set up in March 1965 and based in Gas Street, Birmingham. At its greatest extent, the fleet numbered two dozen boats and cargoes carried included aluminium ingots, bicycles, timber, wheat, tomato puree and coal. The firm was hampered by stoppages and the poor state of the waterways; for example, an optimistic attempt to deliver oil for Duckhams from Ellesmere Port to Aldridge floundered through silting up and rubbish in bridge holes.

The Future of the Waterways – 1963

The 1962 Transport Act established the British Waterways Board, which, following the 1968 Transport Act, defined the future programme and development of all the nationalized river and canal navigations. Waterways were divided into three basic categories – Commercial, Cruising and Remainder. On the BCN, the Main Line between Worcester Bar and Aldersley Junction, the section joining the Main Line with the Stourbridge Canal via Netherton Tunnel and the Birmingham & Fazeley route were classed as Cruising Waterways described as mainly of amenity value with a role of multifunctional leisure use. The rest of the system was classed as Remainder Waterway, 'whose future is currently undecided pending further investigation'.

DECLINE

Last of the 'Ampton Boats, 1970. Also known as wharf boats, these were oversized, up to 86ft by 7ft 9in, and used on the lock-free lengths between the Cannock pits and the Old Main Line. Carrying up to 50 tons, they were often towed in trains of up to five by a tug. This one was owned by E.W. Reed of Tipton and lay abandoned like so many BCN stalwarts.

It's not quite what it seems! One of thirty-five steel sculptures installed along the Dudley No.2 Canal by local artist Luke Perry. The works commemorate the role played by the canal throughout its history. This one stands next to a former toll collector's hovel.

CHAPTER 10

Into a New Canal Age

Rolt and Aickman

The two men who became synonymous with the formation of the Inland Waterways Association both passed through the BCN at different times. Tom Rolt, its first Secretary, took the New Main Line through to Aldersley in 1949 on his way to achieving a long-held ambition of crossing the Pontcysyllte Aqueduct on his boat, *Cressy*. Choosing it as the most direct route, Rolt noted that the old heart of the Black Country was still industrially alive and making use of the canal. *Cressy* passed and crossed many long-distance motors with their butties and even more dayboats. Although some were towed by tugs in trains, most of them were horse-drawn. Rolt also admitted that for the only time in his boating life he nearly went the wrong way, at Bloomfield Junction. It was only with the help of a local, shouting and pointing towards Coseley Tunnel, that he stayed on the right line. Rolt also saw at first hand part of the boatmen's hierarchy, commenting that the long-distance boaters used to call the short-haul men, 'not without a certain disdain', 'joey boatmen'.

During an IWA Grand Canal Cruise in the summer of 1952, Robert Aickman visited the BCN on the converted narrowboat, *Croxley*. After mooring at Gas Street, 'possibly the most picturesque spot in the city', he cruised the Old Main Line where the lock-keeper at Smethwick knew the whole history of the boat. The IWA's Founder and Vice-President considered the old line more varied and interesting than its 'somewhat more direct successor, although the latter was one of Telford's greatest achievements'. Thomas Clayton's yard at Oldbury was 'a particularly picturesque spot, with many painted boats closely packed together'. Eyes must have been focused on the boats rather than the surrounds! North of Coseley Tunnel, at Deepfields Junction, *Croxley* ran into a 'miniature Sargasso Sea'. The Anchor Inn made for a pleasant mooring, 'dramatically encircled by distant but luminous foundries'.

Visions of the Future

The immediate post-war years produced *Conurbation*, the West Midland Group's report on reconstruction and planning. It recognized that the area owed its creation to its mineral resources, but its structure to the canals and railways that remained after much of the industry that fostered them had died or gone. Commenting that the physical amalgamation of the existing urban areas by building development 'would be a disaster', the Group was keen to preserve the character which the Black Country towns retained, citing the canals as one of the barriers allowing them to retain their individuality. The authors also realized the shortcomings of the current canals, stating that they would 'function more effectively by the elimination of certain locks, and by the electrification of the remainder'. This, and the clearing away of bottlenecks caused by low bridges and inadequate tunnels, would enable the existing system of canals to handle more efficiently the coal and quarried minerals traffic carried on between Cannock, Warwickshire and the industrial areas. Although it was recognized that these improvements could only be carried out 'at very great expense', it was concurrent with proposals from the Severn, Trent and Weaver Navigation Boards to increase the width and capacity of rivers and canals connecting the region with the Mersey, Humber and Bristol Channel ports.

Conurbation highlighted the problem of dereliction. Fifteen per cent of land in Dudley and the central districts of the Black Country and 'more than a tenth of the Black Country area' in general, was derelict land that for historical reasons was largely concentrated in areas along the canals. Industry had left a legacy of spoil banks around former coal mines, quarries worked to exhaustion, slag heaps built up from the residues of smelting and puddling furnaces, marl holes from abandoned brickworks, industrial waste and rubbish of all kinds strewn over large areas, while large tracts liable to mining subsidence had been allowed to lie unused and untended.

Canals and derelict land (brown) between Coseley and Tipton.
Conurbation

Solutions involving the canals were proposed. Towpaths 'which are not in heavy use' could form part of a footpath network 'by arrangement with the owners'. Proposals for developments at Titford in Oldbury have already been outlined (*see* Chapter 4), while the 'dismal and flat' area surrounding Bilston steelworks and Deepfields canal junction would be subdivided into factory and housing areas, playing fields, horticultural strips and 'fields for full-scale cultivation'. The latter was to be on land west of the main line canal between Coseley Tunnel and Ettingshall, now occupied by industrial estates and housing. One small part of *Conurbation*'s Bilston plan has materialized, a thin strip between railway and canal main lines north of Deepfields is now covered in woodland, but how much the growth was planned for is hard to ascertain!

A Precious Heritage

In September 1954, Paul S. Cadbury, Vice-Chairman of Cadbury Bros Ltd and former Honorary Secretary to the group responsible for *Conurbation*, published an article in the *Birmingham Daily Post* outlining a possible future for lengths of the BCN. 'These narrow strips of water, which stretch out like a spider's web from the very centre of the city, are a precious heritage. Now is the time to look at them again with new vision.' Although seen by some as 'so many miles of maintained or derelict waterways ... and all too often a convenient drain into which to dump the dirt and rubbish from yards and workrooms', there were helpful developments. The *Norman Chamberlain*, a mobile, floating boys' club converted from a sunken butty boat, could take fifteen boys each week along Midland canals while they received 'instructions from specialists on a wide variety of subjects'. It had taken a party to London in 1953 for the Coronation of Queen Elizabeth II.

Paul Cadbury maintained that much more could be made of the canals for recreation and enjoyment. Even within the town, the towpath offered a pleasant walk – this was at a time when it was closed off, with gates at many bridges. Cadbury considered

NORMAN CHAMBERLAIN

Much of the cost of restoration of a sunken butty boat to be used as a floating boys' club was borne by Miss Enid Chamberlain as a tribute to her brother, Captain Norman Chamberlain, who had done much good work for the boys of Birmingham before the First World War. The work was carried out under the direction of Les Allen at his Oldbury yard, using parties of boys from the city's youth clubs with £2,500 worth of internal fittings donated by over sixty Midland firms.

Norman Chamberlain, *maiden cruise, 1951.*

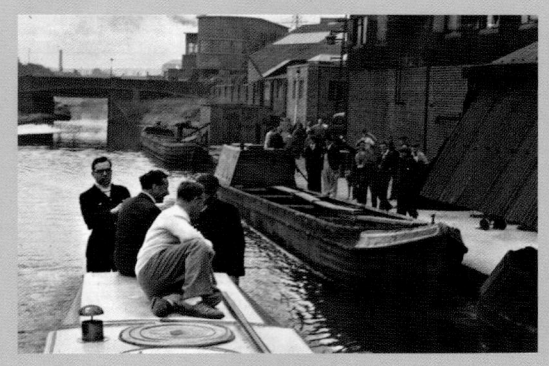

Norman Chamberlain's *'crew' of journalists receives some wry looks, and no doubt comments, while passing through Oldbury, 1950s.*

that developing the derelict stretch of the Dudley No.2 between Selly Oak and Halesowen would be beneficial. A wall could be built at each end of Lapal Tunnel, cutting it off completely, while the remaining lengths could be turned to good uses, especially as 'it is apparently fed by springs, and at both ends of the tunnel it is surprisingly clean and the water clear and sweet'. He suggested that as the Inland Waterways Executive could 'surely have no further interest', then the lengths should be bought by the local councils and developed for boating and fishing.

British Waterways

British Waterways, still under the British Transport Commission, held its first National Exhibition in Birmingham over four days in November 1959. The waterways were by then split into four regions with the BCN canals in the South-Western Division, headquartered at Gloucester. Craft in the Division had carried over one and a half million tons of cargo in 1958 of which 426,000 were coal. There were more than 1,100 boats in the Birmingham area with 300 plying between Birmingham and London and a further 50 between the BCN and the Mersey ports. New engineering workshops were under construction at Bradley, which, when opened, would undertake the whole of the maintenance, repair and construction work in the Midland district of the South-Western Division. Equipment at the new centre was to include an overhead gantry, two covered dry docks – one with a manipulator for upturning boats undergoing repair – petrol and diesel installations and a blacksmith's shop.

The exhibition, opened by the Lord Mayor 'in the presence of about a hundred industrial magnates', also had models of the ports of Gloucester and Sharpness, '51 miles and 67 miles respectively from the centre of Birmingham'; scale models of boats; and a special exhibition devoted to the way in which bantam pusher tugs 'can be used to convey materials between canal-side factories in the Birmingham area, thus relieving congestion on the roads and, it is claimed, reducing transport costs'. Another idea, 'one of the brightest', was the development of canals for leisure: 'Many attractive craft have been fitted out for holiday cruises, craft in which people may cruise from coast to coast without any possibility of sea sickness.'

Dudley Tunnel

'Closed by the Government on Behalf of the People ...'

Traffic through Dudley Tunnel had ceased in 1950, but such a man-made wonder would still witness visitors through the decade. It was mainly kids and cavers in kayaks and canoes who were attracted to its depths but, in May 1952, BCN Toll Clerk and canal photographer Will King organized a through-trip for a party of 200 in three dayboats, possibly the first of its kind since the philosophers' visit a century earlier.

A small notice in the *Birmingham Daily Post* on 22 October 1960 announced a 'protest cruise', against the suggested closure of Dudley Tunnel, to take place the following day. The tunnel was said to be 'no longer of value' by the British Transport Commission, which was seeking to abandon it, but the Midland Branch of the IWA and local enthusiasts wanted to prove otherwise. One of Matty's open dayboats carried ninety passengers on a round trip from Brades Hall, through Netherton and Dudley Tunnels and back, but former Grand Union railway boat, *Saturn*, carrying Robert Aickman along with thirty others, became stuck 200yd in. Filling the bilges 'till the water ran over the floorboards' enabled further progress, but 'after another grating shudder' she jammed again and had to be manhandled back out. Several boat owners who also found themselves stuck 'went to work with saws and axes, reducing the cabin work. One Member hacked off eight inches overall. No complaints were heard: the Tunnel had to be saved.' About 200 people altogether attended the cruise. They set out in around forty craft, ranging from canoes and outboard-motored dinghies to *Saturn*, 'the sweetest-running and most handsome boat present'.

Robert Aickman (in the white jumper) on Saturn.

The IWA *Bulletin* commented that, having spent £250, 'so they said', on clearing rubbish from both portals before the cruise, the British Waterways Divisional Manager had written to the local IWA Branch secretary stating, 'We are, however agreeable to spend this amount for the purpose of you carrying out your cruise, which I am sure will enable you to see the reason why some of these canals should be abandoned to navigation'.

The cruise delayed closure, but two years later the tunnel was sealed with timber baulks while notices forbidding navigation were fixed to the portals and Park Head Locks were rendered unusable.

'… Opened by the People on Behalf of Themselves'

This failed to stop the kids and cavers, canal enthusiasts and amateur geologists who still visited clandestinely, and numbers of them came together to form the Dudley Canal Tunnel Preservation Society at the end of 1963 in response to a threat from British Railways to culvert and fill in the eastern end to replace a railway bridge with an embankment. In the end this proved unnecessary, the bridge being strengthened instead, but the Society prospered, raising money and awareness and running boats trips through the tunnel, giving the participants the opportunity to 'leg it'. In 1970, the renamed Dudley Canal Trust organized the Dudley Dig and Cruise, attracting 50 boats and 600 volunteers who cleared the debris from a lock chamber and two pounds.

Two years later, with financial assistance from Dudley Corporation, the area around Park Head was landscaped and 5,000 tons of mud dredged from the channel. With the restoration of the locks, the way was clear for the official reopening of Dudley Tunnel at Easter 1973, an event attended by around 14,000 people. Two years later, *Electra*, the world's first electrically powered narrowboat, was commissioned to continue the tunnel trips first begun in 1964 with human power. The former British Waterways mud boat was converted at Allen's Oldbury boatyard. The railway bridge was removed in 1997 and the Canal Trust's electrically propelled tug, *John C. Brown*, started hauling private boats through the tunnel. The Dudley Canal and Tunnel Trust continues to run trips into the tunnel, visiting limestone workings revealed by the construction of new tunnels and in 2015 opened a new visitor centre, The Portal.

The Future of the BCN?

At the end of 1963, the newly constituted British Waterways Board published a report on *The Future of the Waterways*, introducing the concept of a 'multi-user' role, but the 'Remainder' status of much of the BCN meant a continuation of slow decline, particularly following the effects of the

Dudley Dig and Cruise.

The Portal and the Tipton portal.

previous harsh winter. *Facts about the Waterways* followed two years later, with the BCN section painting a less than optimistic picture:

- 1964 receipts were £138,769 including £105,246 water sales, £13,780 commercial tolls. £13,290 rents and wayleaves and £934 pleasure craft. Direct costs were £91,358 (£816 per mile). The surplus was £15,862.
- Commercial traffic was about 300,000 tons compared with over a million in the early 1950s, 'and all the evidence points to a continuance of this sharp decline'.
- Revenue from pleasure craft mooring was 'very small indeed'.
- Physically, the network was in a generally fair condition, although there had been considerable pruning and tidying through canal-side businesses needing the sites for redevelopment. Such requests were still being received.
- Financial figures and trends endorsed the Board's views that the 'realistic pattern of future development is likely to add significantly to those lengths which are already "closed to navigation"'. If the system was developed primarily for water-supply purposes, 'there would be substantial savings in maintenance and the surplus would rise to about £24,000 per annum'.
- Present patterns indicated that there was 'a not inconsiderable part of the network from which little or no benefit is derived'. The Tame Valley and Rushall Canals fell into this context. Wholesale elimination would be most unattractive financially, but 'there will be certain spurs and other lengths where culverting or perhaps total elimination would be appropriate'.

Visitors and Explorers

Oozells Loop, Coombeswood and Bumble Hole,
With the plastic right up to your gunnel.
Clean out your weedhatch and put on some coal
Afore Dudley – and Netherton Tunnel (from *BCN Boating*, Bob Bowden)

Redundant boats came on the market following 1963's Big Freeze at a time when there was a developing interest in preserving the BCN's heritage, and the mid-1960s and 1970s saw an increase

Grange End *passes the remains of coal boat* Dorothy, *Titford, 1972.*

in leisure boating on the system, though possibly not all of the participants would have used that particular adjective. As one correspondent to the BCN Society's *Boundary Post* recalled in 1972, 'What did we find at Tividale just a short distance from our goal? One horsebox, backed into the canal with the words "Gone to fetch crane to lift it out" inscribed thereupon!'

Several books of canal voyages included descriptions of the BCN and a short extract from *Slow Boat Through England* will paint the general picture: 'Factories standing cheek by jowl along the canal side are not such eyesores as the countless basins, now largely dumps or graveyards for rotting narrowboats.' Some of these craft were rescued and restored, bringing work to the few remaining boatyards, some being cut in half and rebuilt as two. The former Fellows, Morton & Clayton butty, *Grange*, built at Ryders Green and registered in Birmingham in 1912, was split into two, the front part retaining the name and the rest renamed *Grange End*.

In an attempt to encourage greater use of the network, various challenges were undertaken, from an attempt on the IWA's Silver Sword in twenty-four hours in 1967 through the BCN Challenge Award Scheme, which encouraged more leisurely exploration of all lengths.

Guidebooks

In the late 1960s, with the increase in leisure boating, British Waterways produced a series of *Inland Cruising Guides*, all beginning 'The British Waterways Board give you a cordial welcome to the ...'. The BCN, being largely Remainder Waterways, where 'The Board is pleased to see users, providing that the boat has their current licence', was not included. To fill the gap, a slim guide, *The BCN*, was produced in July 1969 by K.D. Dunham and R.B. Manion and published by the Staffordshire & Worcestershire Canal Society and the local IWA branch, with a foreword by local boatbuilder, joint founder member of the S&WCS and early IWA member, Malcolm Braine. With masterly understatement, Malcolm acknowledged the compiling of the booklet as 'a not inconsiderable feat, when one ponders the complexity' of the system, and went on to conclude that 'there is no other canal system in the world to compare with the BCN'. In 1977, the BCN Society published its own cruising and towpath guide, organizing the network into seven different routes, and four years later *Along the Birmingham Canals: A boating and walking guide* followed. This covered much the same ground geographically and historically, but also included a few poems and songs to 'provide some additional interest'.

The IWA's Birmingham Branch Waterways Subcommittee followed with a comprehensive cruising and walking guide in 1984. Long a favourite among BCN aficionados, some of whom have been known to colour in the canals for easier reference on the crowded pages, the 'Blue Book' is a notable piece of work. It follows the BW Guide layout of showing the canals as straight lines, which rather spoils the geography, but for the historian the sheer amount of detail, down to the locations of such items as boundary posts, bridge fire doors and stop-plank racks, was its chief attraction, while the traveller appreciated the wealth of information about pubs, letter boxes, bus routes and public conveniences. The 'Blue Book' was a cornucopia, in the days before easy internet access to old maps, showing the locations of disused basins and branches, former factories and furnaces, as it presented a portrait of a system in transition.

Michael Pearson published an informative and idiosyncratic BCN volume in his *Canal Companion* series in 1989, later incorporating parts of it – the Main Line, Birmingham & Fazeley, Dudley and Wyrley & Essington – into the *Stourport & Black Country Rings Birmingham Canal Navigations* edition. As well as portraying the changing network, these guides reflect changing attitudes towards industrial heritage, from Dunham & Manion's 'Whilst climbing the 21 locks, the canal has already entered a very industrialised area, unfortunately a predominant feature of the whole of the ... Route', to Pearson's barely disguised nostalgia for what had been lost. The last quarter-century has seen an increase in books relating to specific historical aspects of the system, notably those by BCN historian Ray Shill, and pictorial 'then and now' style works illustrating the vast changes occurring on the BCN.

The BCN Society

In 1967, Transport Minister Barbara Castle, in her own words 'recorded a victory over the Treasury which had reluctantly agreed to keep open for pleasure cruising some 1,400 miles of non-commercial waterways which, without a subsidy, would have had to close'. The resultant White Paper, *British Waterways: Recreation and Amenity*, also held out the hope of Government assistance for schemes by voluntary bodies to restore disused canals. Continuing uncertainty, however, and particular concern about the future of the Remainder Waterways, led to the formation of the BCN Society, which held its first General Meeting in November 1968 and set about organizing work parties and boat rallies.

The IWA National Rally was held in Birmingham in July 1969 to commemorate the 200th anniversary of the canal and in the same year the Board announced the establishment of a working party to investigate the Remainder sections of the BCN. Its thirteen members, including representatives of local waterways societies and boat clubs, published their report early in 1971. Of the 80 miles (130km) of Remainder Waterway, 66 miles (106km) were suggested as having a valuable future, mostly being then still navigable. No extra expenditure, above and beyond routine maintenance, would be required.

The Titford Canal was reopened in 1974 following two years of BCN Society-led voluntary work greatly supported by the County Borough of Warley. At the same time, work was continuing on clearing other stretches, with the result that in February 1975 Winson Green Loop was declared almost fully navigable for the first time in fifteen years. A BCN Society work party had removed 10 tons of prams, bicycles, pushchairs, washing machines and a 2ft high metal Dr Barnardo's collecting box in one day. As ever, the rubbish reflected the times and a Society spokesman noted that 'we always know when an area has been converted to natural

IWA 1969 Rally.

Horseley Fields Junction.

gas or people have bought colour television sets by the amount of old gas cookers and TVs we find in the canal'.

In 1983, the Society began to erect signposts at all the major junctions and had installed the majority within a decade. One or two have succumbed to tatters; the last was put in at Horseley Fields in 2004, but over two dozen remain, guiding boaters and an increasing number of walkers and cyclists. A work boat, *Phoenix*, was built, courtesy of a Heritage Lottery grant, in 1998, and in 2002 the Titford Pumphouse was reopened as the BCN Society's headquarters following refurbishment. The BCNS continues to organize work parties, clean-ups, campaign cruises and boat gatherings and promotes greater use of the network through Explorer Cruises and an annual 24-Hour Challenge, when boaters are encouraged to explore more remote stretches over a weekend.

Regeneration: Beginnings in Birmingham

In 1968, Barbara Castle approached various councils, including Birmingham, setting out the problems of the cost of maintaining inland waterways and expressing the wish of the Government that a system of real and lasting benefit for the community should be developed. The council agreed to cooperate, with the aim of making use of its canal system for recreation. A preliminary survey, including discussions with British Waterways and the IWA, was to be carried out on their future use and amenity development. Proposals for amenity walks along the canal and the opening up of Gas Street Basin had already been proposed.

A group of 'very substandard cottages' on Kingston Row, including former BCN dwellings, was renovated in 1969 by the city's Housing

Management Department and the Longboat public house was built beside Cambrian Wharf, the remaining stub of the Newhall Branch. It was part of the 'plan to bring life back to this part of the city and at the same time to make use of the city's waterways'. Not surprisingly, a scheme to build blocks of flats behind Cambrian Wharf was heralded in the press as 'part of a bigger plan to create a "Little Venice"'. Released in early 1972, these included making all towpaths between Gas Street and Cambrian Wharf into walkways. The scheme was also rumoured to include a new Register Office with its own private arm 'for carrying boatloads of wedding parties off to the Longboat for receptions'.

Gas Street Basin

The wide reach of canal on the BCN side of Worcester Bar, on the very edge of the town when the Old Wharf was opened, was, by the mid-1960s, an oasis of rare peace and calm in the heart of the city. A journalist described the scene in April 1966: 'A streak of oil stretched across the green water towards a row of moored barges, their dark, rust-flecked hulls reflecting the sombre, derelict mood of the place.' Attempts were being made by resident boat owners to 'tidy the basin, with a slap of whitewash here and there', and George Andrews of the IWA thought it could be an ideal centre for boating, that 'lots of people would like to keep boats in the city ... if the basin was improved'. Its 'improvement' was to prove controversial.

The £8 million recreational amenity development, providing a hotel, restaurant, flats and conference facilities on a site between Gas Street and Bridge Street, was unveiled in February 1972 by British Waterways and agreed in principle by the council. The scheme was supposed to combine the best of the old with the new, with the aim of bringing back life to a large part of the canal, but it came in for much criticism. One correspondent

Gas Street Basin developments, 1986.

to the *Daily Post* in January 1974 stated: 'I have studied proposals for this area and am horrified to find that Gas Street Basin is due to be overrun by multi-storey blocks of offices.' He advised readers to visit the basin, 'for I feel it will soon be too late to appreciate one of the finer parts of our dying city'. Public meetings were held to protest about the development plans, notably by boat owners and residents of the waterway community, who felt that the seclusion of the basin was threatened.

Many of the historic warehouses beside the basin were demolished by the end of the following year, an act that came in for much criticism due to taking away the unique atmosphere of the place. At the beginning of 1976, the Gas Street Basin Preservation Society produced a radio programme, *Locks, Pounds and Paddles*, about their fight to save the basin from the developers. The opening in the spring of 1986 of the James Brindley pub, the first stage of a scheme involving offices and fifty-four canal-side flats, caused more concern, as did plans for a thirty-storey hotel overlooking the basin.

Brindleyplace

A City Centre Canal Walk, linking Gas Street with the Aston Science Park via Farmer's Bridge Locks, was opened in May 1987 and more redevelopment of the former industrial environs of the city centre canals followed. The International Convention Centre, including Symphony Hall, went up between 1984–91 and Brindleyplace, the largest such development in the UK, followed. Built inside and around the Oozells Street loop from 1993 onwards into the 2000s, it covers 17 acres and contains the National Sea Life Centre, offices, public squares, restaurants and the residential Symphony Court. Little, apart from the canal itself, survived from the close-packed industries of a century before; the tube works and rolling mills, brass and iron foundries, glass-cutting works and manufacturers of bedsteads and safes, ivory buttons, pins, engines, hinges, clocks and chandeliers were all swept away, though the 1878 Oozells Street Board School was granted a last-minute reprieve and transformed into the Ikon Gallery, a contemporary arts venue.

Possibly the least-known portrayal of James Brindley – a relief by Birmingham's International Convention Centre.

Apart from the name and a well-hidden relief of James Brindley on the side of ICC Energy Centre, there is little to remind the casual visitor of the engineer's contribution to the area, although, as a poetic correspondent to the *Leeds Intelligencer* had stated a couple of weeks after his death:

There will he shine :- No monumental stone
Need Brindley have, to make his virtues known;
His works proclaim them, and to latest days
Shall faithful history record his praise.

More Redevelopment

The BCN has acted as a focus for redevelopment in locations around the Black Country. Following the 1982 closure of Round Oak Steelworks, opened in 1857 by Lord Ward on the Dudley Canal at Brierley Hill, the site was developed as the Waterfront Business Park, with offices and leisure venues. In 1997, the canal between here and the top lock at the Delph was straightened to gain 6 acres of land for the neighbouring Merry Hill retail park development.

Walsall Town Arm, once busy with basins, a boat dock, brewery and bakery, was, by the end of the 1950s, another boat graveyard and came close to being lost.

Regeneration in the late 1990s saw the provision of a basin and the rebuilding of a wharfinger's cottage and attached warehouse concurrent with the building of a prestigious art gallery and restaurant. More commercial and residential development has since taken place along the arm and around its junction with the main canal at the foot of Walsall Locks. The basin's location, off the more popular sections of the BCN, has led to fewer visiting boats than may have been hoped for. Several incidents of people and cars falling in led to the Canal & River

Walsall Basin, 1992.

Walsall Basin, 2021.

Trust removing 60 tonnes of weed in 2020 and installing a large buoy, emblazoned 'Deep Water', in the basin in 2021.

Wolverhampton's Canalside Quarter has, from the enthusiast's point of view, been largely a story of missed opportunities. It was first proposed in the early 1990s when the stretch of BCN between the top lock and Horseley Fields Junction was the equal of any industrial length on the English canal system, still retaining canal structures from every period of the canal age. Despite reports and articles about the significance of this 'half mile of history', and its designation as a Conservation Area in 1985, its importance has been devalued by demolition and redevelopment. Not only have major structures such as Fellows, Morton & Clayton's former warehouse and the Union Flour Mill been destroyed, but much of the detail that lent interest to the canal scene has also gone. A pair of side bridges, carrying the towpath loftily over the entrances to basins serving the L&NWR's Mill Street Goods Station and a further one into a chemical works, have disappeared, literally flattened when a gas pipeline was laid beneath the towpath. Two were iron-arched and the third was of brick, providing an elegant visual contrast. One fine building has been retained, with Albion Mill converted to flats. Current plans envisage more housing and canoes at Horseley Fields.

While some notable canal-related structures, such as the Smethwick and Titford Pumphouses and stables at Tipton and beside Delph Locks, have been saved, concern is still expressed over other iconic buildings. Tipton Gauging Station and Chillington Wharf, both unique structures, are listed buildings, but have lingered in a moribund state of deterioration for several decades now despite attempts at finding uses for them by both commercial and voluntary groups.

Restoration Schemes

Three schemes are current, located in the north, south and centre of the BCN.

Lichfield & Hatherton Canals Restoration Trust

Having been abandoned in 1954, the thirty locks in 7 miles (11km) Ogley to Huddlesford section of the Wyrley & Essington were mostly drained and filled in during the 1960s and described as 'beyond hope of recovery' in 1971. Four years later, the IWA encouraged members to ensure that canals were noted in the county structure plans then being formulated. Interest in restoration was fostered and a threat to the route by the Birmingham Northern Relief Road (M6 Toll) led to the formation of the Lichfield & Hatherton Canals Restoration Trust

Lichfield & Hatherton Canals Restoration Trust Toll Road Aqueduct, 2018.

in 1988. The Wyrley & Essington stretch was renamed the Lichfield Canal, while the former Staffordshire & Worcestershire Hatherton Branch, along with a planned linking canal, will complete the scheme. The funding and construction of a new aqueduct across the Toll Road in 2003 was a remarkable achievement and work continues along the line of the Lichfield Canal, restoring locks and landscaping, with fundraising continuing for a new tunnel under the railway.

Lapal Canal Trust

Formed in 1990, the Trust aims for the eventual restoration of the 5½-mile (9km) length of the Dudley No.2 Canal between its present terminus at Hawne Basin and Selly Oak, its junction with the Worcester & Birmingham Canal. In 1997, Dudley Council restored part of the western end, an unconnected length running through Leasowes Park in Halesowen.

A feasibility study in 2007 recommended an 'over the top' route following the Woodgate Valley rather than attempting to rebuild Lapal Tunnel. The plan envisages two flights of ten locks, with a back-pumping scheme for water supply, resulting in a continuous canal corridor, bringing benefits to the local community and recreational users as well as boaters. The construction of a major retail park at its eastern end compromised the original route, which has since been diverted and a new winding hole is planned on the Worcester & Birmingham Canal at the junction site, while work continues with vegetation clearance along the line.

Bradley Canal Restoration Society

Abandoned in the early 1960s and subsequently largely infilled, this mile-long (1.6km) link between the Old Main Line by Bradley Workshops and the Walsall Canal at Moorcroft Junction has long been considered as a restoration possibility. As well as re-establishing a direct link between the two historic canals, it will create a new leisure cruising route for boats. The line passes through an essentially urban area with a long industrial history stretching back to John Wilkinson's Bradley Ironworks, although the loss of industry has resulted in most of it now being surrounded by public open space. A feasibility study

Inside Bradley workshops.

BCN BOAT MOVEMENTS, 2019

Rank (of 156)	Location	Lockage
70	Lock 17, Wolverhampton	1,745
73	Birmingham & Fazeley, Curdworth	1,647
93	Lock 2, Farmer's Bridge	1,352
153	Lock 2, Rushall Canal	164

commissioned by the Canal & River Trust and the West Midlands Partnership in 2015 sparked more interest, leading to the setting up of the Bradley Canal Restoration Society in November 2019 with a major aim of engaging the local community. The main obstacle to restoration is a lowered bridge by the Bradley Workshops, as the nine lock chambers of the Bradley flight are still in place, although the upper seven are buried.

The BCN Now

The Canal & River Trust charity succeeded British Waterways in 2012 and the 100 or so miles (160km) of the surviving BCN make up about 18 per cent of its West Midlands network. The Trust records lockage, mainly by telemetry at various places, and in 2019 the busiest location on the whole network, with 8,362 lockages, was at the paired locks 2 & 3 at Hillmorton on the Oxford Canal, followed by 7,711 at New Marton on the Llangollen Canal. On the engineering side, the Canal & River Trust continues to use Bradley Workshops with occasional open days, when visitors can appreciate lock gate building.

Along with maintaining the waterways, a major current part of the Trust's remit is to encourage 'Wellbeing by water'. This is especially relevant in the BCN area and it is estimated that around 51 per cent of Birmingham's population lives

A POINTER TO THE FUTURE? URBAN MOORINGS, WOLVERHAMPTON

Just beyond the former stop lock at Horseley Fields Junction is a little peninsula between the canal and a now truncated basin. It has a long history as a coal and lime wharf and was the site of a boat maintenance yard with slipways built by the L&NWR in 1890. Later, from about 1958–70, it was used by enthusiasts to convert former working boats for leisure use. Subsequently falling into disuse, the dock and stables were renovated by West Midlands County Council in 1982, with the unfulfilled intention of developing craft workshops. The slipway was in use until the early 1990s, but the site declined and dereliction set in. It appeared that another part of BCN history was to be lost.

In 2016, the site was adopted by Urban Moorings CIC, a community group of boaters aiming to develop it through a process of 'Slow Regeneration', allowing moorings to be put in at low cost and 'without having to spend millions of pounds and digging big soulless holes filled with water'. Having received the Canal & River Trust's blessing but with no land approach yet agreed, arrival on site was by boat, with access being gained by gangplanks and loppers. A jungle of buddleia and rank vegetation, plus a further one of method statements and risk assessments, had to be cleared before approval to build a walkway around the site for mooring access could be secured and the area cleared of the accumulated detritus of decades. This has now largely been achieved and much of the dumped material recycled, vegetables and grass planted, buildings constructed and pathways created.

Future aims include development as an eco-zero waste site, putting an emphasis on reusing waste in imaginative and inventive ways, to show that it is possible to reclaim once-polluted and derelict sites with little commercial potential and regenerate them as community and creative sites to complement the surroundings and to provide a space for micro-businesses to operate on a flexible basis and to share ideas.

Urban Moorings, 2021.

within walking distance of their local canal. The Revolution Walk, a 4½-mile (7km) route along towpaths between The Roundhouse in Birmingham and Chance Glass Works in Smethwick, was acknowledged with a Green Flag Award for environmental standards in 2020.

In such a built-up area, towpaths have long been used as cycle routes and, with the decline in canal traffic and the authority's ability to regulate it, cycling increased and is now encouraged. Legally, cyclists were obliged to obtain a licence to use British Waterways towpaths, a request largely ignored, and the obligation was relaxed after the Canal & River Trust succeeded British Waterways. Lengths of towpath, including over 31 miles (50km) in Birmingham and along the New Main Line, have been upgraded and surfaced.

A 4-mile (6km) length of the Wyrley & Essington at Wednesfield achieved Local Nature Reserve status in 2018 and otters have been recorded there as well as in other locations around the BCN. A current initiative, the Great Canal Orchard, has stretched out along the Main Line, reaching Aldersley in 2021, propagating and planting rare local species as well as modern varieties of fruit trees in various locations.

Around the turn of the Millennium and to mark the reopening of the Titford Pumphouse, British Waterways asked the question on the poster below.

After a quarter-millennium, from initiation, through growth, decline and the acceptance of a very different role from that first envisaged, the Birmingham Canal Navigations, through innovation, engineering achievement and location at the heart of the canal network, remains a most worthy contender.

One of the books that sparked my interest in the Birmingham Canal Navigations was Ronald Russell's *Lost Canals of England and Wales*. Thankfully, with the Ridgacre Branch exception, no more of the system has been lost since that book's publication half a century ago. A sentence from it is as relevant now as it was then: 'The more one knows of the BCN, the more one wants to know.'

British Waterways question.

Bibliography and References

Allen, J.S., *A History of Horseley, Tipton* (Landmark, 1997)

Barker, P. et al., *The Cannock Chase Coalfield and its Mines* (Cannock Chase Mining Historical Soc., 2005)

Beavon, J.R.G., *Along the Birmingham Canals: A boating and walking guide* (Tetradon Publications, 1981)

Beete Jukes, J., *Memoirs of the Geological Survey of Great Britain: The South Staffordshire Coalfield* (Longman, Green, Longman and Roberts, 1859)

Boughey, Joseph & Hadfield, Charles, *British Canals: The Standard History* (Tempus, 2008)

Broadbridge, S.R., *The Birmingham Canal Navigations, Volume 1, 1768–1846* (David & Charles, 1974)

Burton, Anthony, *Back Door Britain* (André Deutsch, 1977), republished as *Around Britain by Canal* (Pen & Sword 2018)

Castle, Barbara, *The Castle Diaries, 1964–1970* (Weidenfeld & Nicolson, 1984)

Chapman, Nigel A., *A History of the Sandwell Park Collieries* (Heartland Press, 1997)

Christiansen, Rex, *The West Midlands, Vol. 7 of A Regional History of the Railways of Great Britain* (David & Charles, 1973)

Codling, Alan, *Birmingham Canal Navigations: A Cruising and Walking Guide* (The Waterways Sub-Committee, Birmingham Branch, IWA, 1984)

Dilworth, D., *The Tame Mills of Staffordshire* (Phillimore, 1976)

Doerflinger, F., *Slow Boat Through England* (Tandem, 1970)

Faulkner, Alan H., *Claytons of Oldbury* (Robert Wilson, 1978)

Foxon, Tom, *Number One!* (J.M. Pearson & Son, 1991)

Foxon, Tom, *The Industrial Canal, Volume 2, The Railway Interchange Trade* (Heartland Press, 1998)

Hadfield, Charles, *The Canals of the East Midlands* (second edition) (David & Charles, 1970)

Hadfield, Charles, *The Canals of the West Midlands* (third edition) (David & Charles, 1985)

Hadfield, Charles (editor), *Canal Enthusiasts' Handbook 1970–71* (David & Charles, 1970)

Hopkins, Eric, *The Rise of the Manufacturing Town, Birmingham and the Industrial Revolution* (revised) (Sutton, 1998)

Hutton, William, *History of Birmingham* (1783)

Lewis, Christopher, *The Canal Pioneers* (The History Press, 2011)

Lewis, R.A., *Staffordshire Roads 1700–1840* (Staffordshire County Council Education Department Local History Source Book, 1975)

Owen, David, *Exploring England by Canal* (David & Charles, 1986)

Raven, Jon, *The Urban and Industrial Songs of the Black Country and Birmingham* (Broadside, 1977)

Raybould, T.J., *The Economic Emergence of the Black Country* (David & Charles, 1973)

Rolt, L.T.C., *Landscape with Canals* (Alan Sutton, 1984)

Russell, Ronald, *Lost Canals of England and Wales* (David & Charles, 1971)

Shill, Ray, *A Gas Street Trail* (Heartland Press, 1994)

Shill, Ray, *The Industrial Canal, Vol. 1, The Coal Trade* (Heartland Press, 1996)

Shill, Ray, *The Wyrley & Essington Canal: A study of its construction, development and trade* (The BCN Society)

Smith, Jane, *Accidents: Nineteenth Century Accidents in Wolverhampton* (Share Our Past Ltd, 2015)

Smyth, W.W., *A Rudimentary Treatise on Coal and Coal Mining* (Lockwood & Co., 1873)

Squires, Roger W., *Canals Revived* (Moonraker Press, 1979)

Uglow, Jenny, *The Lunar Men* (Faber & Faber, 2002)

Upton, Chris, *A History of Birmingham* (Phillimore, 1993)

Whyman, Susan E., *The Useful Knowledge of William Hutton* (Oxford University Press, 2018)

Other Sources Used

Extensive use has been made of BCN records held by the BCN Society and at the National Archives. References to specific items are not included in the text, but if any reader wishes to follow up a particular trail, the author would be happy to supply the relevant source.

BCN atmosphere.
MARIA NICHOLSON

Index

accounts 144
Aickman, Robert 154, 157–8
air raid 135–6
Albion 46
Aldersley 15, 22, 24, 33, 138, 152, 171
Allen, Les 104, 145, 155, 159
Andrews, George 164
Anglesey Basin 77–8
Anson Branch canal 46, 50, 65, 148
Aris's Gazette 17, 35, 41, 76, 99, 105
Ashted 115
Aston 29, 53, 79, 95, 165
Atlee, Clement 144
Autherley 15, 22, 24, 49, 91, 114

Barnett, Samuel 131–3
basins 82, 143
Bee 65
Bentley Branch canal 49–50, 148
Bentley, William 14, 16, 19, 59, 90, 125
Bilston 13, 19, 22, 66, 92, 149, 155
Birchills 103
Birmingham 7, 10–11, 12–15, 18–19, 26–8, 36, 42, 44, 48, 50, 74, 76, 82 84–5, 90, 92, 94, 99, 102, 106–7, 112–3, 116–7, 120, 134–5, 138, 144, 157, 163, 170–1
 & Fazeley Canal 27–8, 32, 40, 93, 95, 152
 & Liverpool Junction Canal 113–4
 Boat Company 105
 Canal Navigations Society 161–3
 Chronicle 112, 131, 150
 Daily Post 107, 132, 149, 156–7
 Gazette 12, 112, 135
 Heath 97, 99, 105
 Journal 44
 Mail 142
Black Country 7–8, 10, 12, 53, 58, 76, 78–9, 81, 102, 120, 129, 130, 135, 147, 154–5, 166
Blackbrook 56–7, 140
Blakeley Hall 142
Bloomfield 42, 46–7, 154
Boatmen's Rests 106–7
boiler 67, 70, 101–2
Bough, James 29–31, 40–1, 82, 92–3
Boulton & Watt 31, 67, 69, 71

Boulton, Matthew 8, 10, 12, 16, 42, 59, 66, 82
Brades 42
Bradley 42–3, 128, 148, 157
 Canal Restoration Society 168
 Workshops 168–9
Braine, Malcolm 148, 161
breaches 131–3
Brewin, Thomas 57, 118, 139
Brickiln Piece 18, 20–2, 75–6
bricks 16–17, 22, 23, 29, 32, 88, 130
Bridgewater, Duke of 9, 99, 112
 Canal 117
Brierley Hill 166
Brindley, James 13, 15–19, 24, 59, 61, 66, 89–90, 111, 125, 148, 165–6
Brindleyplace 12, 165
British Transport Commission 145, 157
British Waterways 96, 157–8, 161, 164, 170–1
 Board 148, 152
Broadwaters 27, 29, 40, 70
Brookes, John 90–1, 130–1
Brownhills 64
Bull, Samuel 29–31, 41, 61, 66, 70, 92–3, 125
Bumblehole 54, 57

Cadbury, George 63
 Paul 155
Cambrian Wharf 164
Canal & River Trust 64, 166, 169
Canal Mania 37
Cannock 108, 129, 141, 155, 153
 Chase 77
 Extension canal 7, 57, 77, 130, 147
Castle, Barbara 162–3
Castle Mill 33, 35
Catchems Corner 102
Central Electricity Generating Board 81, 145–6
Churchbridge 58, 148
Clayton, Thomas 83, 109, 151, 154
Clowes, Josiah 35
coal 11–13, 15, 17, 19, 21, 26–7, 32–3, 36, 38, 48, 54, 71, 73–82, 86, 88, 129–130, 142
 Thick 8, 32, 71, 76–8, 129
Coleshill 27, 30

Colmore, Charles 18, 20
Commissioners 66
Committee 14, 16, 18–19, 24, 29–30, 40–2, 55–6, 59, 66, 74, 82, 90, 100–1, 105, 111–2, 117, 124–5, 130–1
Coneygre 66
Conurbation 63, 154
Coseley 42
 Tunnel 46–7, 154
cottages 24, 94–7
Coventry Canal 10, 22, 26, 32, 38, 43, 116
Curdworth 28, 32

Dadford, Thomas
 Junior 33
 Senior 30, 32–3
Daimler House 126, 142
Danks Branch 52
Dartmouth, Lord 14, 23, 59, 74, 78, 112
Daw End Branch 52
day boat 101
Deep Cutting 20
Deepfields 42, 46–7, 128, 131, 136, 154
deficit 138
Delph 166
 Locks 56–7, 108
derelict land 155
Digbeth 27–9, 120
Distance Tables 104
dividend 118, 138
Docks & Inland Waterways Executive 145
dredger 99–100
Dudley 9–10, 12, 32, 84, 92, 113, 118, 131, 138, 155
 Canal 33–4, 81, 94, 116, 118, 166
 Number 1 33–5
 Number 2 36–7, 57, 157, 147
 Trust 7
 Castle 85
 Lord 32–3, 54, 70
 Port 54–5, 71, 84, 131
 Tunnel 10, 53, 128, 157–9
Dunkirk 137
Dunlop 85–6

Electra 159
Elements, T&S 127
Engine 41

174

INDEX

Branch 67
fire 16, 66
Euphrates 84, 101
Essington 37, 141

Factory Bridge 84
   Locks 46, 85, 108
Farmers Bridge 29, 50, 79, 105, 143
Fazeley 10, 26–9, 31, 50, 112, 115
feeder 60, 62, 65
Fellows, Morton & Clayton 7, 161, 167
First World War 126, 134–5, 141
fishing 61–2
fog 129
Fownes & Aston 74–5, 130–1
Freeth, John (Junior) 89, 114
Freeth, John (Senior) 11–12, 48–9, 54
Friday Street 18, 73
frost 125
Future of the Waterways, The 159

Galton, Samuel 13, 34,
   Bridge 45–6, 136
   Tertius 114
   Valley 46, 69
Garbett, Samuel 13, 19, 26
garden land 95
gauging 97–98
gas 55
   works 81
Gas Street 81, 154, 163–5
General Assembly 15, 17, 18–19, 24, 29, 40, 75, 89, 124, 144
General Strike 143
Golds Hill 86–7, 108
Gornal 22, 92
Gosty (Gorsty) Hill 36, 128, 138, 142
Gower Branch 48
   Lord 14
Great Bridge 107
guidebooks 161

Halesowen 157
Hamstead Colliery 78
Harecastle Tunnel 43
Hawne Basin 128–9, 147 168
Hay Head 53
Haywood 12
Hednesford 7, 58, 77, 79, 106–7
Henshaw, T.A. 90, 143
Hilton Main Colliery 78, 81
Hingley, Messrs N. & Sons 142
Holloway, George 14, 89, 90, 99
Home Guard 135
horse 44, 92–3, 103, 107–9, 151
Horseley Company 46
   bridges 57
   Fields 37–8, 167

Houghton, John 35, 38, 59, 75, 89, 93, 125–6
House of Commons 18
houses *see* cottages
Huddlesford 30, 38, 64, 167, 141
Hutton, William 13, 27, 107

ice boats 125–8
Inland Waterways Association (IWA) 64, 139, 147, 154, 161–2
   Executive 157
interchange basin 120–3
Institution of Civil Engineers 43, 54
Island Line 46, 48
iron 7–9
   stone 88
   trade 28, 71

Jebb, George Robert 58, 65, 70, 72, 88, 108, 131–4, 138–40, 144
Joey boat 101–2
Jubilee Colliery 78, 145
Judge, Jack 62

Keay 146
Kettle, John 15, 19
King, William (Bill) 157

Lapal Canal Trust 168
   Tunnel 36, 139, 157
Leader Williams, Sir Edward 133
Lee, Thomas 66,
   Bridge 44, 105
   Thomas Eyre 112, 114
Leicester Navigation 65
Lichfield 22, 26, 30, 98
   & Hatherton Canals Restoration Trust 167
limestone 33–5, 38–9, 80, 88
Loch, James 112–3, 115
locks 10, 11, 16, 41–2, 125, 127
London 15, 27, 116, 141, 157
Lord Hays Branch 111, 141
Lord Ward's Canal 34

M5 45, 64
Manchester 9
   Ship Canal 144
manure 88
Matty, Alfred 128, 151, 157
Maxwell, C.E. 72, 98
Meredith, John 14–15, 31, 67, 69, 74, 89, 124–5
Minworth 31–2
mills 59, 65–6
Moat Colliery 71
moles 93
Monk, Thomas 84–5, 101

Moxley 152
Murchison, Sir Roderick 78, 85

nationalization 123, 144
Napoleonic Wars 42
Netherton 138
   Tunnel 53–7, 152
New Hall Branch 164, 143
   Ring 18, 20–2
New Main Line canal 66, 131, 136–7, 152, 154, 171,
New Street Station 135
Newcomen, Thomas 66
Nicholls, Sir G. 55
Norman Chamberlain 155
Norton Bog 64

Ocker Hill 67, 69–71, 100–1, 108, 148–9
Octagon 94
Ogley 167
   Locks 127, 141
Oldbury 13, 19, 42, 55, 59, 66, 92, 131, 149, 151, 154–5
Old Hill 55, 142
Old Main Line 62, 69, 72, 78, 131–2, 151, 153–4
Old Turn 135
Old Wharf 135, 143, 164
Oxford 27
   Canal 116

Paradise Street 21, 75, 82, 142
Park Head 95, 158
Parliament 33, 54, 130
   Act of 14–15, 18, 23–4, 32, 42, 59, 90, 93, 117
passengers 84–6
Pearsehouse, Albert H. 90, 143
Pelsall 58, 128
Perry Barr 51–2
Pinkerton, George 32
   John 29–30, 32, 34–5
Portal, The 159
power station 79
   Birchills 80–1, 145
   Ocker Hill 80, 145
   Wolverhampton 79–80, 145
Pratt, Edwin A. 138–9
Proprietors 14–15, 18–19, 82, 105, 113, 133, 142, 144
puddle 133, 138
pumphouses 167
pumping engines
   Ocker Hill 69–70
   Smethwick New 69
   Smethwick Old 66–7, 69
   Spon Lane 66–7
Titford 171

INDEX

railways
 Birmingham & Liverpool 76, 112–3, 115
 Birmingham, Dudley & Wolverhampton 113
 Birmingham, Wolverhampton & Dudley 117
 Grand Junction 48, 52, 114, 117–8
 Liverpool & Manchester 112
 London & Birmingham 115–7
 London & North Western 10, 77, 98, 117, 135, 138
 London, Midland & Scottish 122–3, 144
 Midland 122
 Oxford, Worcester & Wolverhampton 118
 Shrewsbury & Birmingham 117, 120–1
 South Staffordshire 65
 Stour Valley 85
Rattlechain Brickworks 131, 151
Remainder Waterways 152, 159, 161–2
reservoirs 18–19, 34–5, 59
 Chasewater (Cannock Chase) 58, 64–5, 72, 77
 Lodge Farm 72
 Rotton Park 44, 62, 72, 135
 Smethwick Great 59–62
 Smethwick Small 60–1
 Sneyd 64–5, 72
 Titford 61–3
Revolution Walk 170
Ridgacre Branch 46, 150, 171
rivers
 Humber 138, 155
 Mersey 138, 155
 Rea 66
 Severn 9, 12, 26, 138
 Stour 8–9, 26, 66
 Tame 8, 26, 27, 34, 44, 52, 64, 66
 Thames 138
 Trent 9, 12, 26–7, 49
 Weaver 12
Rolt, Tom 154
Rowley 54
 Hills 62, 131
Royal Commission on Canals 138–9
Rumer Hill 58
Rushall Canal 50, 52–3, 87, 107, 127, 160
Ryders Green 15, 27–9, 31, 66, 108, 141, 161

Salford Bridge 26, 50, 99
Sandwell Park Colliery 78–9, 145
Saturn 157
Second World War 62, 135, 144
Selene 101
Selly Oak 139, 157, 168
Sheasby, Thomas 31–2
Shipton, James 85
Simcock, Samuel 17, 19–20, 22, 59, 148
Smeaton, John 29, 32, 41, 43, 50, 67, 70, 93
Smethwick 13, 16, 18–19, 40–1, 43–4, 47, 59, 74, 82, 95, 97, 136 154, 170
 Engine 66–7, 69
Sneyd 37, 136, 141
Soho 42
Spon Lane 41, 44, 46
 Engine 66–7
stables 107
Stafford, Marquis of 112, 115
Staffordshire & Worcestershire Canal 13, 19–20, 23–24, 33, 43, 58, 117, 168
 Society 148, 161
Steward Aqueduct 45, 136
Stewarts & Lloyds 103, 142
Stevens, Alan (Caggy) 128, 151
Stourbridge 10, 33–4, 152
subsidence 71, 139–40
summit 17, 40
Superintendent 40, 92–3
Surveyor 30, 89, 92
Swan Inn 13, 17
Swift Packet 85

Tame Valley Canal 50–2, 86, 116, 129, 137, 160
Telford, Thomas 43–6, 54, 61–2, 67, 114–5, 154
 Aqueduct 45
Thomas Ernest 146
Tipton 13, 46, 71, 97–8, 106, 130, 134
Tipton Green & Toll End Communications 42, 148–9
Titford 62, 155, 163
 Canal 46, 48, 72 162
Tividale 18, 55, 71, 149
Toll End 42, 75, 102
 Branch 68
towpath 29, 155, 170–1
Transport Act, 1962 152
Trent & Mersey (Grand Trunk) Canal 11, 27, 30–1, 93

tunnel 16, 42–3
turnpike 9, 43–4, 48, 113
Two Lock Line 56–7, 140

Urban Moorings 170

Vernon, Henry 111

Walker, James R. 49, 52, 54–5
Walsall 22, 26, 37, 42, 53, 93, 106–7, 112, 146–7, 152
 Canal 49, 152
 Town Arm 166
Warwick 26
 & Birmingham Canal 43, 52, 115
 & Napton Canal 116
 Bar 136
watershed 10, 26
Watt, James 8, 10, 11, 29, 67, 69
 Junior 114
Wedgewood, Josiah 11
Wednesbury 7, 9, 11, 17, 26–7, 41, 46, 48, 50, 73, 76, 93, 150
 Oak Loop 48, 148
West Bromwich 82, 92
Whitmores Arm 143
Whittington 28, 31,
Whitworth, Robert 15
Wilkinson, John 8, 67
Wilkinson, Joseph 14
Willet, A.W. 108, 139
Windmill End 54
Wolverhampton 10, 17–18, 26, 40–2, 53, 66, 71, 73, 75, 79, 88, 90–1, 94, 119–122, 131, 137, 138
 Canalside Quarter 167
 Chronicle & Advertiser 55, 84, 118–9, 126
 locks 26, 91–2, 95, 139
Worcester & Birmingham Canal 10, 36, 50, 116, 168,
Worcester Bar 36–7, 48, 81, 116, 152, 164
Worsey, Joseph 102
Wren's Nest 33
Wulfruna Coal 79
Wyrley & Essington Canal 37–9, 48–50, 58, 64, 78, 94, 111–2, 116, 129, 167, 171, 141, 149
Wyrley Bank Branch 65, 141

zeppelin 135